AMERICAN PRISON

THESE ARE UNCORRECTED ADVANCE PROOFS
BOUND FOR YOUR REVIEWING CONVENIENCE

In quoting from this book for reviews or any other
purpose, please refer to the final printed book because
the author may make changes on these proofs before the
book goes to press.

ALSO BY SHANE BAUER

(WITH JOSHUA FATTAL AND SARAH SHOURD)

A Sliver of Light: Three Americans Imprisoned in Iran

AMERICAN PRISON

A REPORTER'S UNDERCOVER JOURNEY

INTO THE BUSINESS OF PUNISHMENT

SHANE BAUER

PENGUIN PRESS

NEW YORK

2018

PENGUIN PRESS
An imprint of Penguin Random House LLC
375 Hudson Street
New York, New York 10014
penguin.com

Copyright © 2018 by Shane Bauer
Penguin supports copyright. Copyright fuels creativity, encourages diverse voices,
promotes free speech, and creates a vibrant culture. Thank you for buying an authorized
edition of this book and for complying with copyright laws by not reproducing, scanning,
or distributing any part of it in any form without permission. You are supporting
writers and allowing Penguin to continue to publish books for every reader.
Portions of this book first appeared in *Mother Jones* July-August 2016 issue.

LIBRARY OF CONGRESS CATALOGING-IN-PUBLICATION DATA
[INSERT CIP DATA]

Printed in the United States of America
1   3   5   7   9   10   8   6   4   2

DESIGNED BY MEIGHAN CAVANAUGH

Some names and identifying characteristics have been changed
to protect the privacy of the individuals involved.

For the prisoners in America

We all want to believe in our inner power, our sense of personal agency, to resist external situational forces of the kinds operating in this Stanford Prison Experiment. . . . For many, that belief of personal power to resist powerful situational and systemic forces is little more than a reassuring illusion of invulnerability.

—*Philip Zimbardo*

You just sell it like you were selling cars, or real estate, or hamburgers.

—*Corrections Corporation of America cofounder Thomas Beasley*

[MAP OF PRISON (2-PG SPREAD) TK]

[MAP OF PRISON (2-PG SPREAD) TK]

AMERICAN PRISON

INTRODUCTION

Have you ever had a riot? I ask a recruiter from the Corrections Corporation of America.

The last riot we had was two years ago, he says over the phone.

Yeah, but that was with the Puerto Ricans! a woman's voice cuts in. She hasn't spoken until this moment. *We got rid of them. Now we just have people from Oklahoma.*

He reads me questions. *There are times that people disagree. When was the last time you disagreed with someone? How did you work it out? A supervisor wants to send you to a seminar on a topic you aren't interested in. How do you react?* He isn't interested in the details of my resume. He doesn't ask about my job history, my current employment with the Foundation for National Progress, publisher of *Mother Jones* magazine, or why someone who writes about criminal justice in California would want to move across the country to work in a prison. It's all in my application: My real name, my personal information, the fact that I was arrested for shoplifting when I was nineteen. Did he Google me? A quick search would have brought up my prison reporting and articles about the two years I spent as a prisoner in Iran. He doesn't ask about many of the things I feared he would, so I don't bring them up.

I am tempted to ask him about the results of the survey I took on CCA's website, testing my instincts about working in a prison. It provided various scenarios, and I was to choose from multiple choices how I would be most likely to respond: "An inmate receives a food tray and eats all the food except the dessert (pudding). The inmate then walks to the food line and asks for a new tray of food because there is hair in the pudding." Would I replace the whole tray, the dessert only, or ignore him? "An inmate tells you that she thinks you don't like her because of her race." Do I tell her she's wrong? Ignore her? Tell her that, in fact, *she* is the one who is racist?

Then there was the section in which, next to dozens of statements, I clicked buttons ranging from "strongly agree" to "strongly disagree":

> "If someone insults you, he/she is asking for a punch in the mouth or worse." Disagree.
> "I am a very productive worker." Strongly agree.
> "I always support the decisions of my boss." Neither agree nor disagree.
> "I have a very strict moral code." Strongly agree.
> "I wouldn't trade my life for anything."

On that last one I clicked "strongly agree," though after I submitted my application to a handful of CCA prisons around the country, I worried that my answer might have made them less likely to hire me.

The man on the phone tells me I would go through four weeks of training. Then I would be expected to work twelve hours a day and sometimes sixteen.

When can you start? he asks.

I tell him I need to think it over.

I take a breath. Am I really going to become a prison guard? Now that it might actually happen, it feels scary and a bit extreme.

I began applying for jobs in private prisons because I wanted to see the inner workings of an industry that holds some 130,000 of our nation's 1.5 million prisoners.* As a journalist, it's nearly impossible to get an unconstrained look inside our penal system. When prisons do let reporters in, it's usually for carefully managed tours and monitored interviews with inmates. Many states don't allow reporters to choose who they want to interview; the prison administration chooses for them. Phone calls are surveilled and letters are opened and read by guards. Inmates who talk freely to a reporter risk retaliation, including solitary confinement. Private prisons are especially secretive. Their records often aren't subject to public access laws; CCA has fought to defeat legislation that would make private prisons subject to the same disclosure rules as its public counterparts. And even if I could get uncensored information from private prison inmates, how would I verify their claims? I keep coming back to this question: Is there any other way to see what really happens inside a private prison?

But now that this is becoming real, there is a competing question: Am I really going *back* to prison? It has only been three years since my own incarceration ended. In 2009 I was working as a freelance reporter in the Middle East, living in Damascus with my partner, Sarah Shourd. When our friend Josh Fattal came to visit, we took a trip to Iraqi Kurdistan, which at that time had a growing tourist industry and was considered safe for Western visitors. During a long hike near a local tourist site, we unknowingly neared the Iranian border. The three of us were arrested and driven across the country to Iran's Evin prison, where we would be interrogated for months while being kept in solitary

---

* This number includes people held in state and federal prisons. It does not include jails, which hold around seven hundred thousand inmates at a given time.

confinement. Josh and I would be celled together after four months, but Sarah would spend more than a year in isolation before being released in 2010. Josh and I would get out after twenty-six months inside.

As I swam in the warm phosphorescent waters of the Gulf of Oman the night of my release, I did not imagine that I would ever look at a prison again. My homecoming was disorienting. In prison I had become accustomed to one or two stimuli at a time: the book I was reading, the sound of footsteps coming down the hallway, the noises Josh was making on the other side of the cell. The free world is infinitely complex, and for a while it all came at me in a jumble. It was difficult for me to filter out what was important from the constant background noise of daily life. I also had to rebuild the mental capacity to make choices. After dreaming of food for two years, I found myself staring at menus, unable to decide what to eat, so I relied on other people to choose for me. I was constantly on edge, tense to the point of breaking. I sometimes had to leave crowded places suddenly. Other times I couldn't handle the oppressive feeling of being in a room alone. I had nightmares nearly every night about being thrown back into prison. I found myself overreacting to people who had any amount of authority, as though they were guards. I felt angry at everything.

American prisons helped me to anchor myself. During my early days of freedom, I heard about a hunger strike taking place throughout prisons in California, where I lived. Inmates were protesting the use of long-term solitary confinement: Nearly 4,000 prisoners were serving indeterminate sentences in "the hole." We have about 80,000 people in solitary confinement in this country, more than anywhere in the world. In California's Pelican Bay state prison alone, more than 500 prisoners had spent at least a decade in the hole. Eighty-nine had been there for at least 20 years. One had been in solitary for 42 years.

As I was coming to terms with what I'd been through during my own two years of captivity, struggling to readjust and overcome post-traumatic stress disorder, I began to correspond with some of the men in solitary located here in the United States. I found that some were vigilant about keeping their minds sharp; others were broken, their letters indecipherable. I began to read through their prison records and learned that many who had been in the hole for years had not committed violent offenses in prison. Some were indeed dangerous gang members, while others were put in solitary because of people they hung out with, for their work as jailhouse lawyers, or because they possessed books on African American history. Seven months after my release from prison, I visited Pelican Bay prison, one of the first institutions built for long-term solitary confinement. There I saw men in eleven-by-seven-foot cells with no windows. I met one man who went twelve years without ever seeing a tree. The four months I'd spent in solitary confinement in Iran was an eternity I will never erase from my psyche, but the abyss of isolation these prisoners lived in helped me to put my own struggle into perspective.

I still intended to go back to the Middle East. I spoke Arabic, and the Arab Spring was devolving into war. But I was never able to turn away from the American prison system; quite the opposite. We are living through a time of mass incarceration with few parallels in world history. The United States imprisons a higher portion of its population than any country in the world. In 2017 we had 2.2 million people in prisons and jails, a 500 percent increase over the last forty years. We now have almost 5 percent of the world's population and nearly a quarter of its prisoners. When we look back in a century, I am convinced that our prison system will be one of the main factors that define the current era.

This book focuses on one private prison during a four-month period. It also examines how the profit motive has shaped America's prison system for the last 250 years. Private prisons do not drive mass incarceration today; they merely profit from it. Who will end up in prison is not determined by the prisons but by police, prosecutors, and judges. The reasons for our overinflated prison system are complex and highly debated, but few scholars deny that racism has been a major factor. For much of America's history, racism, captivity, and profit were intertwined. Slavery, the root of antiblack racism in America, was a for-profit venture. When slavery ended, powerful interests immediately figured out how to continue profiting from the captive bodies of African Americans and other poor people. My research took me inside a private prison, but it also took me to history books, old newspapers, forgotten memoirs, and penitentiary reports stuffed away in state archives. Through the course of my digging, it has become clear that there has never been a time in American history in which companies or governments weren't trying to make money from other people's captivity. I have attempted to weave this larger history into the story of my eyewitness reporting, in the hope that I can adequately convey the scope and stakes of what is surely a national disaster.

Within two weeks of filling out its online application, I get callbacks from Corrections Corporation of America's prisons in Oklahoma, Louisiana, and Colorado, and an immigrant detention center in Arizona. When I call Winn Correctional Center in Winnfield, Louisiana, the lady who answers is chipper and has a smoky southern voice.

I should tell you up front that the job only pays nine dollars an hour, but the prison is in the middle of a national forest. Do you like to hunt and fish?

I like fishing.

Well there is plenty of fishing and people around here like to hunt squirrels. You ever squirrel hunt?

No.

Well I think you'll like Louisiana. I know it's not a lot of money but they

say you can go from a CO [corrections officer] to a warden in just seven years!
The CEO of the company started out as a CO.

When I do an official interview a few days later, they ask me a lot of the same boilerplate questions as the other prisons, and then: "What is your idea of customer service? How does this term relate to providing services to inmates?" I fumble through a nonanswer about the customer always being right, but maybe not in a prison? *Well, we're both looking at each other, and I can tell you right now we think you'd be a good fit,* the recruiter says. So long as I pass the background check, she tells me, I'm hired.

My editors at *Mother Jones* and I talk through hypotheticals. What would I do if my cover was blown? We work out bureaucratic details like making sure I have workers' comp to cover things like getting stabbed on the job. Our lawyers study Louisiana law to make sure I'm not doing anything illegal. My editors leave the assignment open-ended and tell me that if I want to end the project at any point, for any reason, I should do so without hesitation. I will use my real name. I don't need to divulge everything about myself, but I will never lie. If someone asks if I am a journalist, I will say yes.

We deliberate over the legal and ethical issues. For some, undercover journalism is taboo; many newsrooms require that reporters disclose themselves as such under all circumstances. But my project fit the Poynter guidelines for undercover reporting perfectly: The subject was of vital public interest; there were no other means to get the story; I would disclose, in my writing, the nature and reason of any deception; the news organization would not skimp on the funding and time needed to fully pursue the story; and the potential harm prevented by the reporting outweighed the potential harm caused.

Unless otherwise noted, I have changed the names of the people I met at Winn to protect their identities. I was careful to use people's words verbatim as much as possible. Throughout this book, everything between quotation marks was captured by a recording device or copied from documents. Dialogue in italics is based on my notes of those moments when I couldn't use my equipment. In some instances dialogue was rearranged slightly for smoother flow.

Undercover reporting has only fairly recently become such a sensitive topic. Our country has a rich history of it. In 1859 Northern reporters posed as slave buyers attending a Georgia auction, because it was the only way they could get near it. Their reporting was rich in details unknown to most Northerners: the examinations of humans like they were livestock, the twisted pride a slave would sometimes take in demanding a high price, and the unimaginable heartbreak of children being torn from their mothers. In 1887 Nellie Bly famously feigned insanity to get herself involuntarily committed to an insane asylum for women for ten days, an experience she chronicled for Joseph Pulitzer's the *New York World*. Her reporting led New York to increase the budget of the Department of Public Charities and change regulations to better ensure that only the seriously mentally ill were committed. In 1892 *San Francisco Examiner* reporter W. H. Brommage took a job as a sailor to investigate the practice of blackbirding, in which ship captains tricked Pacific Islanders into contracts of indentured servitude on sugar cane plantations in Guatemala. In 1959 John Howard Griffin took a medication that darkened his skin and traveled for six weeks in the Deep South to investigate segregation. In 1977 the *Chicago Sun-Times* bought a bar, staffed it with reporters, and installed hidden cameras to investigate corrupt city inspectors who were willing to overlook anything for twenty bucks. Barbara Ehrenreich took low-wage jobs as a waitress, a Walmart clerk, and a cleaning woman to bring attention to the struggles of the working poor. And Ted Conover, whose book was one of the inspirations for my project, worked for a year as a prison guard in New York's Sing Sing prison in the late 1990s.

Why are these types of investigations so rare today? A big reason is litigation. As *Mother Jones* editor in chief Clara Jeffery writes:

> When ABC News busted Food Lion for repackaging spoiled meat for sale back in 1992, a jury bought the company's line that the real offense had been the falsification of employment applications and the reporters' failure to fulfill their assigned duties— i.e., *repackaging spoiled meat!* The $5.5 million damage award was eventually knocked down to just two dollars, but it put a chill on this kind of muckraking for a generation, and during that time, corporate and official entities built an ever-tighter web of legal protections. Nondisclosure agreements—once mainly the provenance of people who work on Apple product launches and Beyoncé videos—are now seeping into jobs of all stripes, where they commingle with various other "non-disparagement" clauses and "employer protection statutes." Somewhere along the way, employers' legitimate interest in protecting hard-won trade secrets has turned into an all-purpose tool for shutting down public scrutiny—even when the organizations involved are more powerful than agencies of government.

I have a number of job offers from CCA prisons. Ultimately I choose Winn. Not only does Louisiana have the highest incarceration rate in the world—roughly five times that of China—but Winn is the oldest privately operated medium-security prison in the country.

I call Winn's HR director and tell her I'll take the job.

Well, poop can stick! she says.

I pass the background check within twenty-four hours.

| 1 |

Two weeks after accepting the job, in November 2014, having grown a goatee, pulled the plugs from my earlobes, and bought a beat up Dodge Ram pickup, I pull into Winnfield, a town of approximately 4,600 people three hours north of Baton Rouge. If you happened to drive through it, it's the kind of place you'd only remember because some lonesome image stuck in your mind: a street of collapsed wooden houses, empty except for a tethered dog and a gaunt white woman carrying a laundry basket on her hip; the former Mexican restaurant that serves daiquiris in Styrofoam cups to drivers as they come home from work; a stack of local newspapers with headlines about a Civil War general; a black lady picking pennies up off of the pavement outside the gas station. About 38 percent of households here live below the poverty line; the median household income is $25,000. Residents are proud of the fact that three governors came from Winnfield before 1940, including agrarian populist Huey Long. They are less proud that the last sheriff was locked up for dealing meth.

Winn Correctional Center is thirteen miles from town, set in the middle of the Kisatchie National Forest, a more than six hundred thousand-acre expanse of southern yellow pines crosshatched with dirt roads. As I drive through the thick forest on December 1, 2014, the prison emerges from the fog—a dull expanse of bland cement buildings and corrugated metal sheds. One could mistake it for an oddly placed factory were it not so well branded. On the side of the road is the kind of large sign one finds in suburban business parks, displaying CCA's corporate logo, with the negative space of the letter A shaped like the head of a screeching bald eagle.

At the entrance, a guard who looks about sixty, with a gun on her hip, asks me to turn off my truck, open the doors, and step out. A tall, stern-faced white man leads a German shepherd into the cab. My heart hammers. There is camera equipment lying on the seat. I tell the woman I am a new cadet, here to begin my four weeks of training. She directs me to a building just outside the prison fence.

Have a good one, baby, she says as I pull through the gate. I exhale.

I park and sit in my truck. In the front seat of a nearby car, a guard checks her makeup in her visor mirror. A family sits in a four-door sedan, probably waiting to visit a loved one, legs dangling idly out of open doors. In front of me two tall chain-link fences surround the prison, razor wire spooled out along the top. A cat walks slowly across a large, empty expanse of pavement inside. A metallic church steeple pokes above the buildings. The pine forest surrounds the compound, thick and tall.

I get out and walk across the lot, my mind focused on the guard towers, where I imagine officers are watching me. The prison's HR director told me last week that Lane Blair, one of the company's managing directors, had called to ask about me. She said it was very unusual that corporate would take an interest in a particular cadet. Since then, I have been certain that the company's higher-ups know who I am. When I enter the classroom, no one is there. The longer I sit, the more I am convinced it is a trap. What will happen if they come for me?

Another cadet enters, sits next to me, and introduces himself. He's nineteen years old, black, and just out of high school. His name is Reynolds.

You nervous? he asks.

A little, I say. *You?*

Nah, I been around, he says. *I seen killin'. My uncle killed three people. My brother been in jail and my cousin. I ain't nervous.* He says he just needs a job for a while until he begins college in a few months. He has a baby to feed. He also wants to put speakers in his new truck. They told him he could work on his days off, so he'll probably come in every day. *That will be a fat paycheck,* he says. He puts his head down and falls asleep.

Four more students trickle in, and then the HR director. She scolds Reynolds for napping, and he perks up when she tells us that if we recruit a friend to work here, we'll get five hundred bucks. She gives us a random assortment of other tips: Don't eat the food given to inmates; don't have sex with the inmates or you could be fined $10,000 or get sentenced to "ten years at hard labor"; try not to get sick, because we don't get paid sick time. If we have friends or relatives incarcerated here, we need to report it. She hands out magnets to put on our fridges with a hotline to call in case we become suicidal or begin fighting with our families. We get three counseling sessions for free.

I studiously jot down notes as the HR director fires up a video of the company's CEO, who tells us in a corporate-promotional tone what a great opportunity it is to be a corrections officer at CCA. He is our shining light, an example of a man who climbed all the way up the ladder. (In 2017 he will make $4 million a year, twenty times the salary of the director of the Federal Bureau of Prisons.) *You may be brand-new to CCA, but we need you,* he says. *We need your enthusiasm. We need your bright ideas. During the academy, I felt camaraderie. I felt a little anxiety too. That is completely normal. The other thing I felt was tremendous excitement.*

I look around the room. Not one person—not the high school graduate, not the former Walmart manager, not the nurse, not the single mom who came back after eleven years of McDonald's and a stint in the military—betrays anything resembling excitement.

I don't think this is for me, a post office worker says.

When the video stops, a thirtysomething black woman with long eyelashes and perfectly manicured fingernails stands in the front of the room. She tells us she is the head of training. Her name is Miss Blanchard. Do we know who was talking in the video? she asks.

The CEO, I say.

What was his name? she asks.

I don't know.

She looks at me like an elementary school student who wasn't paying attention. *Y'all are going to have to know this for the quiz at the end of the class.*

Reynolds jolts his head up. *There's gonna be a quiz?*

His name is Damon Hininger, she says. *There are also three founders. There is Thomas Beasley and T. Don Hutto. They are still with us. Then there is Dr. Crants.* She slips in another VHS tape.

In the video, Hutto and Beasley tell their company's origin story. In 1983, they recount, they won "the first contract ever to design, build, finance, and operate a secure correctional facility in the world." The Immigration and Naturalization Service gave them just ninety days to do it. Hutto is frail, with a shiny white head and oversize glasses, and he smiles slightly with his hands folded in front of him. When he speaks, he gives the impression of a warm-faced grandfather who likes to repeat the "lost my thumb" trick to children. He recalls the story of obtaining their first prison contract like an old man giving a blow-by-blow accounting of his winning high school touchdown. Rushed for time, he and Beasley convinced the owner of a motel in Houston to lease it to them, eventually hiring "all his family" as staff to seal the deal. They then quickly surrounded the motel with a twelve-foot fence topped with coiled barbed wire. They left up the Day Rates Available sign. "We opened the facility on Super Bowl Sunday the end of that January," Hutto recalls. "So about ten o'clock that night we start receiving inmates. I actually took their pictures and fingerprinted them. Several other people walked them to their 'rooms,' if you will, and we got our first day's pay for eighty-seven undocumented aliens." Both men chuckle.

For Beasley, the notion of running a prison as a moneymaking enterprise was new and innovative. But for Hutto, I would discover, the idea of making money from prisoners was as old as the idea of forcing black men to pick cotton.

A white man on horseback, holding a rifle, looked out over an expanse of cotton that stretched beyond the horizon. Four packs of bloodhounds lay on the edge of the field. One dog had gold caps on two of his teeth, a mark of distinction for tracking a runaway for days and bringing him back to the plantation. Black men were lined up in squads, hunched over as they pick. The white man couldn't hear what they were singing, but he'd heard the songs before. Sometimes, as they worked, a man would sing out, "Old Master don't you whip me, I'll give you half a dollar." A group of men reply in unison, "Johnny, won't you ramble, Johnny, won't you ramble."

Old Master and old Mistress is sitting' in the parlor
Johnny, won't you ramble, Johnny, won't you ramble
Well a-figurin' out a plan to work a man harder
Johnny, won't you ramble, Johnny, won't you ramble
Old Marster told Mistress, they sittin' in the parlor
Johnny, won't you ramble, Johnny, won't you ramble

Old Marster told old Mistress to take the half a dollar
Johnny, won't you ramble, Johnny, won't you ramble
"Well I don't want his dollar, I'd rather hear him holler"
Johnny, won't you ramble, Johnny, won't you ramble

One of the men, Albert Race Sample, was picking cotton for the first time. Throughout the course of his life, he'd shined shoes, worked the circus, shot craps, and cleaned brothel rooms after prostitutes, but he had never worked in a field. His only connection to cotton was that his white father, who used to pay his black mother for sex, was a cotton broker. Sample lined up in a row with the other men in his squad, picking the bolls one by one and dropping them into the fourteen-foot sacks they dragged along. The white "bosses" assigned the fastest pickers to head each squad, making everyone else struggle to keep up. By the time Sample picked the cotton from two stalks, the rest of the row was twenty feet ahead of him. One of the bosses, known as Deadeye, walked his horse over to Sample and scrutinized his every move.

Sample grew up in his mother's brothel. As a boy, he served bootleg liquor to the men who gambled there and had sex in his bed. He would practice his dice techniques on the floor, learning how to set them in his hand and throw them in a way that would make them land just how he wanted. His mom liked to play too. Once, in the middle of a game, she told him to fetch her a roll of nickels. When he told her he lost it, she slapped him in the mouth, knocking a tooth loose, and went back to her game. Sample caught a train out of town and survived on tins of sardines, food he stole from restaurants, and picking pockets at racetracks.

Picking cotton, like picking pockets, is a skill that takes time to master. Grab too much and fingers get pricked on the boll's dried base. Grab too little and only a few strands come off. The faster Sample tried to pick, the more he dropped. The more he dropped, the more time he wasted trying to get the dirt, leaves, and stems out before putting it in his sack. "Nigger, you better go feedin' that bag and movin' them shit scratchers like you aim to do somethin'!" Deadeye shouted.

Sample's back hurt.

Eventually the bosses ordered the men to bring their sacks to the scales. The head of the squad had picked 230 pounds. One man had only picked 190 pounds, and Deadeye shouted at him. When Sample put his sack on the scale, one of the bosses, Captain Smooth, looked at Sample like he'd spit in his face. "Forty pounds!" Captain Smooth shouted. "Can you believe it? Forty fuckin' pounds of cotton!" Deadeye got a wild look in his face. "Cap'n, I'm willing to forfeit a whole month's wages if you just look the other way for five seconds so's I can throw this worthless sonofabitch away." He pointed his double-barrel shotgun, hands trembling, at Sample and laid the hammers back. Those waiting to weigh their cotton scampered away.

"Naw Boss," Captain Smooth said. "I don't believe this bastard's even worth the price of a good load of buckshot. Besides, you might splatter nigger shit all over my boots and mess up my shine." Boss Deadeye lowered his shotgun. "Where you from nigger! I suppose you one'a them city niggers that rather steal than work. Where'd you say you come from?" When Sample attempted to answer, Deadeye shouted at him. "Dry up that fuckin' ol' mouth when I'm talkin' to you!"

As punishment for his impertinence and unproductiveness, Sample would not be allowed to eat lunch or drink water for the rest of the work day. "As for you nigger, you better git your goat-smelling ass back out longer and go to picking that Godamn cotton!"

The year was 1956, nearly a century since slavery had been abolished. Sample had been convicted of robbery by assault and sentenced to thirty years in prison. In Texas, all the black convicts, and some white convicts, were forced into unpaid plantation labor, mostly in cotton fields. From the time Sample arrived and into the 1960s, sales from the plantation prisons brought the state an average of $1.7 million per year ($13 million in 2018 dollars). Nationwide, it cost states $3.50 per day to keep an inmate in prison. But in Texas it only cost about $1.50.

Like prison systems throughout the South, Texas's grew directly out of slavery. After the Civil War the state's economy was in disarray, and cotton and sugar planters suddenly found themselves without hands they could force to work. Fortunately for them, the Thirteenth Amendment, which abolished slavery, left a loophole. It said that "neither slavery nor involuntary servitude" shall exist in the United States "except as punishment for a crime." As long as black men were convicted of crimes, Texas could lease all of its prisoners to private cotton and sugar plantations and companies running lumber camps, coal mines, and building railroads. It did this for five decades after the abolition of slavery, but the state eventually became jealous of the revenue private companies and planters were earning from its prisoners. So the state bought thirteen plantations of its own. In 1913 it began running them as prisons.

Forced labor was undeniably productive. An enslaved person in an antebellum cotton field picked around 75 percent more cotton per hour than a free farmer. Similarly, Texas prison farms into the 1960s produced a higher yield than farms worked by free laborers in the surrounding area. The reason is simple: People work harder when driven by torture. Texas allowed whipping in its prisons until 1941. Other states banned it much later. Arkansas prisons used the lash until 1967. But even after the whip, prisons found other ways to make inmates work harder. The morning after Sample's first day of picking in 1956, the guards sent him, along with eight other men, to a four-by-eight-foot concrete and steel chamber to punish them for not making quota. The room was called "the pisser" and there was no light or water inside. A hole the size of a fifty-cent piece in the center of the floor served as the lavatory. The men's panting breaths depleted the oxygen in the rancid air. "The nine of us writhed and twisted for space like maggots in a cesspool," Sample recalled in his memoir. If someone took up too much space, a fight could break out. They stayed in the pisser all night, each taking turns lying down as the rest stood or squatted. In the morning they were brought straight out to the cotton fields.

Sample went back and forth between the fields and the pisser as the season wore on. When his cotton bags finally started to weigh in at one hundred pounds, they gave him a different punishment: the cuffs. The first time he was subjected to this, a guard told him to get on the floor. He put a cuff link around Sample's right wrist, closed it as tight as he could, and then stomped it tighter with his foot. He then looped the cuffs through some prison bars above Sample's head and fastened them onto his left wrist. He was left hanging with his toes barely touching the floor. Other men hung alongside him; after an hour or so some of them began to groan. Pains shot through Sample's arms and he bit his lip to keep from crying out. Inmates filed past the hanging men on their way to the mess hall, each avoiding looking in the direction of the ones being tortured. Eventually the lights were dimmed and the night-time hours crept by. Around six hours in, one of the hanging men began violently jerking and twisting until he was facing the bars. He used his feet to push against them, straining to loosen himself from the cuffs. When it didn't work, he bit into his wrists, gnawing at them like an animal in a steel trap. Another inmate called for a guard, who splashed the frantic man with water until he stopped. In the morning they were uncuffed and sent back to work.

As the season progressed, Sample became skinnier and skinnier. The bosses regularly denied him meals as punishment for substandard picking. But after a dozen more trips to the pisser and several more rounds with the cuffs, his picking skills improved considerably. As one guard told him, "those miss meal cramps" have a phenomenal effect on the development of cotton picking speed.

. . .

It was in this world that CCA cofounder Terrell Don Hutto learned how to run a prison. In 1967 Hutto became warden of the Ramsey plantation, which was just down the road from where Sample had been incarcerated. Before running prisons, Hutto had been a pastor, studied history, spent two years in the US Army, and did graduate work in education at the American University in Washington, DC. There was little that distinguished the Ramsey plantation from the one Sample had been imprisoned on. Aside from the banning of the whip, the modes of punishment and labor were the same when Hutto began as they'd been when the state opened its plantation prisons in 1913. The main difference between Hutto's plantation and Sample's was scale: Ramsey was as large as Manhattan, twice the size of Sample's plantation, and it had fifteen thousand inmates working its fields. At Ramsey, Hutto learned how to think about prison as a moneymaking venture. Corners could always be cut to service the bottom line. Much in the way that slaveholders had selected certain slaves to manage and punish the rest of their chattel, Hutto learned the Texas policy of empowering certain inmates to manage and punish other prisoners. These inmates ran the prison's living quarters with brutal force, sometimes wielding knives to keep other inmates under control. By using them, Hutto could save money that would otherwise be spent on guard wages.

Hutto and his family settled into their plantation home in 1967. "All You Need Is Love," by the Beatles was a new hit, and the Huttos might have listened to it in their living room while their "houseboy" cooked and served them. The houseboys were prisoners, almost always black; they made their beds, cleaned, and babysat their children. Personnel at the Texas Department of Corrections considered the provision of convict servants to be an indispensable perk that guaranteed it could "attract the type of men who could do the job."

The regulations of houseboys echoed the fears of slaveholders toward their house slaves. Policy prohibited Hutto's wife from conversing with houseboys or being overly "familiar" with them. Houseboys were prohibited from washing her underwear. Joking with houseboys was banned, as was allowing them to sit with the family to listen to the radio or watch television for fear it would lead to impertinence. Hutto would live as the master of this and other plantations for a decade, distinguishing himself by making some of them more profitable than they'd been before he took charge. A handful of years later, after leaving the plantations, he would open the latest chapter of a story that goes back to the foundation of this country, wherein white people continue to reinvent ways to cash in on captive human beings. He would create CCA.

| 3 |

On my second day, I wake up at six a.m. in my cottage on Sibley Lake near the edge of Natchitoches, a town of eighteen thousand located about a forty-minute drive from Winnfield, Louisiana. I decided to live here to minimize my chances of running into off-duty guards. As I eat breakfast, I watch a soft drizzle on the water outside of my kitchen window. I feel a shaky, electric nervousness as I put a pen that doubles as an audio recorder into my shirt pocket. I pour coffee into a stainless steel thermos that has a small hidden camera built into its lid. I don't know what will happen if these items are found, but I think the risk is worth it: I don't want to rely on the fickleness of memory.

On my way to work, steam begins pouring out of the hood of my truck and the engine sputters and fails. I feel immediately anxious about being late—tardiness, we were told, is the same as stealing from the company. Will I be disciplined? I stand in the rain with my thumb out. Trucks pass, a couple of sheriff's cars go by, and I become wet. Eventually a pickup pulls over and I get in the back seat. The driver tells me he is a logger. The teenager in the passenger seat sticks some dip into his front lip. I tell them I'm headed to Winn for my second day of work.

"I know several people in there," the driver says. "There's too many in there for the wrong reasons and too many out who should be in there." Suddenly he's distracted by something on the side of the road. He reaches across the teenager to point out the passenger window. "Them nigger geese or geese?!" he asks.

"I think them are geese," the teenager says and spits into a plastic cup.

The man leans back against his seat. "What you make there?" he asks me.

"Nine bucks an hour," I say. "It's not much."

"Sometimes I wish I was making nine dollars an hour," he says. He says he had a cousin who worked at Winn but only lasted a month. "They always quittin' there." He lets me out at the front gate.

When I slip into class, I'm relieved there is no instructor in the room. The students are watching a video about the use of force. "There's forty of them to one of us," a man on the TV says. "I don't like those odds. It didn't work in the Alamo. It ain't going to work here." When the video finishes, a middle-aged black instructor enters the classroom, his black fatigues tucked into his shiny black boots. His name is Mr. Tucker and he's the head of the prison's Special Operations Response Team, or SORT, the prison's SWAT-like tactical unit. My pen recorder, sitting innocuously on the table, is running. The tiny lens at the top of the thermos is pointed at him.

"If an inmate was to spit in your face, what do you do?" he asks, standing tall, his face deadpan. Some cadets say they would write him up. One woman who has worked here for thirteen years and is doing her annual retraining, says, "I'd want to hit him. Depending on where the camera is, he might would get hit."

Mr. Tucker pauses and looks around to see if anyone else has a response. "If your personality if someone spit on you is to knock the fuck out of him, you gonna knock the fuck out of him," he says, pacing slowly. "If a' inmate hit me, I'm go' hit his ass right back. I don't care if the camera's rolling. If a' inmate spit on me, he's gonna have a very bad day." Mr. Tucker says we should call for backup in any confrontation. "If a midget spit on you, guess what? You still supposed to call for backup. You don't supposed to ever get in a one-on-one encounter with anybody. Period. Whether you can take him or not. Hell, if you got a problem with a midget, call me. I'll help you. Me and you can whoop the hell out of him." But if we are going to hit an inmate, we should make sure to do it before he's cuffed, he tells us, because once the cuffs are on, the window to "retaliate" is closed. "But if you see me doin' it, mind your own business."

Above all, we must maintain a united front. "If you are an officer and you do something one hundred percent wrong, I'm going to take your side right on the spot."

Mr. Tucker asks what we should do if we see two inmates stabbing each other.

"I'd probably call somebody," a cadet offers.

"I'd sit there and holler stop," says a veteran guard.

Smith points at her. "Damn right. That's it. If they don't pay attention to you, hey, there ain't nothing else you can do."

He cups his hands around his mouth. "Stop fighting," he says to some invisible prisoners. "I said stop fighting." His voice is nonchalant. "Y'all ain't go' stop, huh?" He makes like he's backing out of a door and slams it shut. "Leave your ass in there!" He turns to face us. "Somebody's go' win. Somebody's go' lose. Hell, they both might lose, but hey, did you do your job? Hell yeah!" The classroom erupts in laughter. We *could* try to break up a fight if we wanted to, he says, but he wouldn't recommend it. "We are not going to pay you that much," he says emphatically. "The next raise you get is not going to be much more than the one you got last time. The only thing that's important to us is that we go home at the end of the day. Period. So if them fools want to cut each other, well, happy cutting."

I raise my hand. Why wouldn't we use pepper spray if people are stabbing each other? I ask. "You think we are going to give you pepper spray?" he says. We won't have pepper spray. We won't have nightsticks. All we will have are radios.

During break I go to the kitchen where I meet some cadets in a class ahead of us. "This your first week?" one asks me. "Have fun!" The cadets with him laugh. He says that during his first week, all he did was strip-search inmates. "All I know is I got sick of seeing two things: nuts and butts."

After break Mr. Tucker walks over to the exit door next to me and opens it slightly. He tells me to imagine that four inmates were holding us all as hostages and that, while they were across the room, I noticed the door was cracked. "Would you run out that door and leave us in there?"

I chuckle nervously.

"Haha my ass. Answer the question."

"Nah, I wouldn't," I say. "I just wouldn't want to leave everyone. They might punish them for me running out."

"You got kids?"

"No."

"Other family members? Brothers? Sisters? You wouldn't think about that? You are *not* my brother. I don't even know you. I'll leave y'all *so* quick. If I left, I know y'all go' get y'all's butt whooped but, oh well! I know whose butts not gonna get whooped—mine!"

He teaches us what to do if we are ever held hostage. First we should stay calm and be cooperative. "Whatever problem they have with y'all, I'm gonna have that problem with y'all too. Hey, if they gettin' a tattoo, guess what? Mr. Tucker gettin' 'fuck the police' right across my chest." We should make eye contact with our captors, because once a human bond is established, they will be less likely to hurt us. We should be vigilant, however, against Stockholm Syndrome. "You could get into a certain situation where they start looking human to you, and then you don't want the police to come in and do anything to 'em. All them people together in a stressful situation, even if for different reasons, will develop a common bond."

But we don't need to worry about it too much, Mr. Tucker continues. He sets a grenade launcher and tear gas canisters on the table. "On any given day, they can take this facility. At chow time there are eight hundred inmates and just two COs. But with just this class, we could take it back." He passes out sheets of paper for us to sign, stating that we volunteer to be teargassed. If we do not sign, he says, our training is over, which means our jobs end right here.* "Anybody have asthma?" Mr. Tucker asks. No one raises their hand. "Two people had asthma in the last class and I said, 'Okay, well, I'ma spray 'em anyway.' Can we spray an inmate with asthma? The answer is yes."

He takes us out onto the mowed lawn and tells us to stand in a row with our arms linked. He tests the wind with a finger and then drops a tear gas cartridge. The gas slowly rises, opaque and well defined like clouds below an airplane. As it washes over us, the object is to avoid panicking, staying in the same place until the gas dissipates. My throat is suddenly on fire and my eyes seal shut. I try desperately to breathe, but I can only choke. "Do not run!" I hear Mr. Tucker shout at a cadet who is stumbling off blindly. I double over involuntarily. I want to throw up. I hear a woman crying and Reynolds gagging. My upper lip is thick with snot. When our breath begins coming back, the two women linked to me hug each other. I want to hug them too. The three of us laugh a little as tears pour down our cheeks.

---

* When I later ask CCA if its staff members are required to be exposed to tear gas, spokesman Steven Owen says no.

. . .

Another of our teachers is Kenny, a fortysomething, chubby faced white officer. He wears a baseball cap low over his eyes, the bill curled down tightly at the sides. His button up shirt is always tucked in and his waistline is as thick as his accent. Kenny's been working here for twelve years, and he views inmates as "customers." He says CCA is "a good place to be. Working here we know what we dealin' wit'. No offense to anybody who worked at Walmart but if you work at Walmart, you don't know what's coming in them front doors. Someone could be packing weapons and knives. You're more safe in here than you are out there in the world. I'll tell you that much."

He lectures us on CCA's principle of cost effectiveness, which requires us to "provide honest and fair, competitive pricing to our partner and deliver value to our shareholders." Part of being cost effective is not getting sued too often. "The Department of Corrections gives us a certain amount of money to run this facility," he says. "They set a portion of money back for lawsuits, but if we go over budget, it's just like any other job. We got sixtysomething-plus facilities. If they not making no money at Winn Correctional Center, guess what? We not go' be employed." Being cost effective means it's also our duty to prevent inmates from wasting paper forms and washing their clothes in the sinks between laundry days. When the company is hurt, we all hurt. "There ain't no I in team."

Kenny is detached and cool. He says he used to have a temper but he's learned to control it. He releases tension by fishing on the weekends and by saying a prayer every morning on his drive to work. He used to play in a rock band at nightclubs; now he only plays the drums for Jesus. He doesn't use curse words or shout anymore. He doesn't sit in bed at night with the lamp on, writing disciplinary reports while his wife sleeps like he did years ago. If an inmate gives him a smart mouth or doesn't keep a tidy bed, he'll quietly throw him in a segregation cell to set an example. There are rules and they are meant to be followed. This goes both ways: When he has any say, he makes sure inmates get what they are entitled to. He prides himself on his fairness. "All them inmates ain't bad," he reminds us. Everyone deserves a chance at redemption.

Still, we must never let prisoners forget their place. "When you a' inmate and you talk too much and you think you free, it's time for you to go," he says. "You got some of these guys, they smart. They real educated. I know one and I be talkin' to him and he smarter than me. Now he might have more book sense, but he ain't got more common sense. He go' talk to me at a' inmate level, not at no staff level. You got to put 'em in check sometimes. He'll sit there and argue. That's a defiance charge. No matter how smart they are or what kind of degree they got or who they work for, a' inmate is a' inmate.

"This job you got to come in mentally prepared," Kenny says. "It's more mental than it is physical." He writes the word "manipulation" on the board. "They don't call 'em cons for no reason." To gain psychological control over officers, Kenny says, the first thing inmates do is build a relationship. He points at the camo hat I'm wearing. "If I'm a' inmate, that's what I'ma be lookin' at. 'Oh you like to hunt? You sit up in that box stand?' That's just how they work. And us not knowing, we just say, 'Yeah man. I like to hunt.' They tryin' to get you comfortable. They gonna be 'yes sir' and 'no sir' and work hard and all that kinda stuff. They just tryin' to feel you out. Don't overcommunicate wit' 'em. Just leave that alone." Some will manipulate us by offering help, like pushing a mop bucket or carrying a bag. "Don't let them inmates get that close to you." We should also watch out for prisoners complimenting us on our professionalism and complaining about other officers. "They want to get you away from the team." Even snitching on other inmates is a sign that a prisoner could be buttering us up for something more devious. Is there anything an inmate can do that he does not consider an attempt to get in our heads?

Many of us, both men and women, will be tempted by sex, he says. "I don't care if you married. We got some folks come in here with relationships on the outside and it just blows my mind how these inmates get in that ear and they wind up falling victim to being involved wit' a' inmate. At one point or another, you go' be challenged. Someone's go' come up to you with a letter or they gonna tell you how you look."

There was a female guard who began having trysts with a prisoner in the kitchen, he tells us. Another inmate who worked in the kitchen said, "Well guess what? He gettin' his. I want mine!" She was afraid the second inmate would tell on her, so she began having sex with him too. Then a third inmate said, "Well she's doin' him and doin' him. She should be doin' me too!" So guess what? "She starts doin' him too." After a while "about ten inmates" were having sex with her. "Guess how we found out about it?" Kenny asks, smacking his hands together. "All ten of them inmates go to fightin' each other. That's how it come out in the wash."

He says back when he was a unit manager, there was a female officer he didn't like. Many prisoners didn't like her either, and one in particular was "bound and determined to get this girl fired." One night the woman fell asleep in a chair in her unit, he says. She had also left the inmate's tier door open, so he crept quietly out of the tier, pulled his penis out, and "went to town wit' it" inches from her head. When she woke, she didn't know who it was that "done his thing all over the back of her clothes." Not long afterward, the inmate was released, and he sent a letter to the prison, telling them to look at the surveillance footage from that night. They did. CCA fired the guard for sleeping on the job and for leaving the tier door open, Kenny recalls.

"Ain't nuttin' we could do to him," Kenny says of the inmate. "That's over wit'. He gone home. I laughed, but it was also kind of scary. I don't want nothing bad to happen to nobody." It strikes me that had CCA reported it, it would have been an open and shut sexual assault case. But, he says, "We was lookin' to get her too. He got her for us. It worked out on both ends."*

Kenny makes me nervous. He tells us he sits on the hiring committee. "We don't know what you here for," he says to the class. Then he glances at me. "There might be somebody in this room here hooked up wit' a' inmate," perhaps to sell drugs. He asks me my name, in front of the class, for the third time today. When I tell him, he writes "Bauer" on the board. "My job is to monitor inmates; it's also to monitor staff," he says. "I'm a sneaky junker." He turns and looks me directly in the eyes. "I come up here and tell you I don't know what your name is? I know what your name is. That's just a game I'm playing with you." I feel my face flush and I chuckle nervously. He has to know. "I play games just like they play games. I test my staff to test their loyalty. I report to the warden about what I see. It's a game, but it's also a part of the bid'ness." As I drive home, I tease out the possibilities in my mind about exactly what game Kenny is playing.

One morning as we wait for class to begin, Kenny sits a couple of rows behind me. I can feel him watching me, the only person in class with a notebook, its pages filled with writing. I unscrew the top of my coffee thermos, take a tiny sip of the cold liquid inside, exhale as though satisfied, and screw it back on. When I set it down, I point the pinhole in its lid away from him, afraid that his scrutinizing gaze will detect the tiny camera lens. I slouch.

Miss Blanchard comes out of her office. Through a large window,

----

* CCA says it is unaware of such an incident and that it would have reported the inmate to law enforcement.

it's apparent that her workspace is full of blue dolphins: glass dolphins, dolphin stickers, paintings of frolicking dolphins, porcelain dolphins, metal dolphin figurines. She asks if any of us have been offended by anything Mr. Tucker has said. Was he dropping too many "f-bombs?" One of our classmates quit, she says, because he was too abrasive.

A cadet scoffs. "If you are real Christian-like, you don't need to be here," she admonishes. "This isn't for Holy Roller types."

Mr. Tucker arrives and tells us all to line up against the wall. Fear is necessary in prison, he tells us. "No one in this room is beyond being intimidated. If you not intimidated, then either you one of them or you shouldn't be here." I glance over at Kenny. His face is inscrutable.

Mr. Tucker pulls out a red plastic knife and tells us to choose a partner for some self-defense drills. I need to confront this problem, so I grab a plastic knife and walk straight over to Kenny. As instructed, I swing the knife down with an overhead motion in a slow, unrealistic imitation of an attack. Kenny chops my forearm hard with the edge of his hand, his jaw set, looking me square in the eyes. We hold each other's gaze as we repeat the exercise. My arm bone throbs. When we switch roles, I strike his cutting arm over and over, swing after swing, resisting all temptation to look away from his face. After a while the motions become robotic, his stabbings limp. His eyes cloud and he looks off over my shoulder. I look out the window. The tension dissipates.

During break we go outside and the cadets pull out their cigarettes. Kenny lights up, inhales through his teeth, and walks a few feet out onto the grass, where he watches us from a distance.

The cadet Miss Sterling looks despondent. I've been noticing her getting more frustrated with the way Mr. Tucker teases her in front of the class. She is pretty in a popular-girl-in-high-school sort of way: early twenties, white, petite, and with long, jet-black hair. Mr. Tucker makes fun of her during the self-defense drills. She tells us she hates doing them, especially the choke hold escapes because they bring back memories of her baby's dad. He used to cook meth in the toolshed behind her house and once beat her so badly he dislocated her shoulder and knee. "You know that bone in the back of your neck? He pushed it up into my head," she says.

If he ends up in this prison, an eighteen-year-old cadet assured her, we could "make his life hell." His name is Collinsworth, and his chubby white baby face is hidden behind a brown beard and a wisp of bangs. Before CCA he worked at a Starbucks. He moved to Winnfield from out of state to help out with family, and this was the first job he could get. He can be rambunctious, a symptom of his ADHD. Earlier today Mr. Tucker threatened to kick him out of class after Collinsworth, a little unhinged, jokingly threatened to stab him with the plastic training knife. Collinsworth is the most innocent of the group. He confides in older cadets about whether he is experiencing true love for the first time. He and Reynolds have debated the merits of getting high off "sizzurp"— cough syrup, Sprite, and Jolly Ranchers—versus Xanax with barbiturates. With the random drug tests, marijuana is now out of the question, which is unfortunate, because Collinsworth says smoking weed is like "seeing God."

He, along with Miss Sterling, began a couple of weeks before my class, and he's boasted to me about inmate management tactics he's already learned from more seasoned officers. "You just pit 'em against each other and that's the easiest way to get your job done," he said. "You want to get it to where, if someone gets out of line, another inmate tells him, 'I'm gonna rape you if you try that shit again.' Or something; whatever it takes."

I would kill an inmate if I had to, Collinsworth says, reflecting on our self-defense training. *I wouldn't feel bad about it, not if they were attacking me.*

You got to feel some kinda remorse if you a human being, another cadet says.

I can't see why you'd need to kill anyone, Miss Stirling says.

You might have to, says Collinsworth.

The conversation draws Kenny over to us. *I do what needs to get done,* he says, a thumb hooked into the pocket of his jeans. *I just had a use of force on an inmate who just got out of open heart surgery.** *It's all part of the bid'ness.*

Miss Doucet, a stocky redheaded cadet in her late fifties, thinks that if kids were made to read the Bible in school, we wouldn't need to worry about this stuff because fewer would wind up in prison in the first place. But she also sticks pins in a voodoo doll to mete out vengeance. *I swing both ways,* she says. She's more enthusiastic about the self-defense training than anyone, usually following her blocks with an extra punch to the gut or an elbow to the chin. She says that normally she carries two knives in her car, two in her purse, and one in her pocket. She lives in a camper with her daughter and grandkids. She's hoping to save up for a double-wide trailer.

Miss Doucet worked at the lumber mill in Winnfield for years, but as her asthma got worse, she couldn't swing it anymore. Lifting wood got her heart going and then her breath, which triggered attacks. She's been hospitalized several times this year and says she almost died once. She's worried the stress of working here will have the same effect, and she says they told her if she has an attack, the doctors and nurses at the infirmary can't help her. "They don't even want me to bring this in," she whispers, pulling her inhaler out of her pocket. "I'm not supposed to, but I do. They ain't takin' it away from me." She takes a long drag from her cigarette.

"What if the inmates get ahold of it?" Miss Sterling asks.

---

* CCA says it cannot confirm this incident.

"They gotta find it first! I got it tucked up in my pants." She laughs wheezily.

Miss Doucet and several others from the class ahead of mine go to the front office to get their first paycheck for two weeks of work. When they return, Collinsworth's shoulders are slumping. He says his two-week check was for $577. "They took a hundred twenty-one dollars in taxes."

"Dang. That hurts."

"All my days they say I'm off, I'ma be workin'," one says. "I ain't got no food."

Miss Doucet says they withheld one hundred fourteen dollars from her check.

"They took less for you?!" Collinsworth says.

"I'm *may-ried*!" she says in a singsong voice. "I got a *chi-ild*!"

Paychecks in hand, everyone begins to get excited about drinking. Kenny likes tequila with cinnamon schnapps. Collinsworth prefers beer, and he often gets into fights. To avoid getting drunk, Miss Doucet recommends eating fried chicken beforehand. "I love gettin' drunk," she says. "I like my clear liquor. My vodka. My giiiin. Tutti Fruiti. Jamaican Me Crazy. I can taste one now." Outwardly she is jovial and cocky, but she is already making mental adjustments to her dreams. The double-wide trailer she imagines her and her grandkids spreading out in becomes a single wide. She figures she can get $5,000 for the RV when they move out of it.

| 4 |

Terrell Don Hutto cofounded the Corrections Corporation of America sixteen years after becoming warden of the Ramsey plantation. In the decades after his job in Texas, the national prison population skyrocketed. Faced with an unprecedented influx of inmates, prisons could no longer function primarily as labor camps. Some inmates still worked, and their labor continues to be an essential component of keeping prisons functioning today, but as the inmate population climbed, the portion of those with jobs began to dwindle. Instead, prisons became something closer to human warehouses, in which most inmates served their time in idleness, without work or much opportunity for education. To deal with the growing inmate population, more and more prisons needed to be built. They became a significant economic burden. Between 1980 and 1990, spending on prisons quadrupled as states scrambled to build more.

In 1983 two old college roommates from West Point, Thomas Beasley and Doctor Robert Crants, saw an opportunity. The drug war was heating up, the length of sentences was increasing, prosecutors were pushing for harsher sentences, and states were beginning to mandate that prisoners serve at least 85 percent of their terms. During the ten-year peak of prison construction, some six hundred new prisons were built in the United States. States were spending $1 billion a year to build new prisons, but they couldn't do it fast enough. There was a gap that needed to be filled. Was there money to be made from it? Privatization was in vogue: The Reagan administration had just released a 23,000-page report that made sweeping recommendations for transferring government functions over to private companies.

Beasley and Crants hit upon the idea of privatized prisons while making small talk at a Republican presidential fund-raiser. An executive from the Magic Stove Company said he thought it would be "a heck of a venture for a young man: to solve the prison problem and make a lot of money at the same time." Beasley, who had recently been chairman of the Tennessee Republican Party, had the political connections they wanted. Crants had experience in real estate. All they needed was someone who knew about managing prisons, and ideally one with a record of running them at a profit. Terrell Don Hutto was the perfect candidate. Hutto had used what he learned about running prison plantations in Texas to run the entire Arkansas prison system at a profit. It had been seven years since he had left Arkansas, and he had just spent five years running the prison system in Virginia. Hutto agreed to join, and the three founded the Corrections Corporation of America. Hutto wasn't above blatant conflict of interests when it helped advance his company. Shortly after creating CCA, he became head of the American Correctional Association (ACA), the largest prison association in the country, and used his position to advocate for privatization. Shortly after CCA began opening prisons, it was accredited by the ACA.

After the trio converted a motel into an immigrant detention center in Houston, they built another one from scratch. Their company then assumed management of a juvenile detention facility and an adult prison in Tennessee. Then, when a federal court declared in 1985 that Tennessee's overcrowded prisons violated the Eighth Amendment's ban on cruel and unusual punishment, CCA made an audacious proposal to take over the state's entire prison system. The company offered $100 million for the right to manage all of its facilities as part of a ninety-nine-year lease and said it would spend another $150 million to build new prison buildings and improve existing ones. In return, the state would pay its usual annual operating cost to CCA. Because the company would run the prisons more cheaply, it expected to make at least an 8 percent profit. The bid was unsuccessful, but it planted an idea in the minds of politicians across the country: They could outsource prison management and save money in the process. Privatization also gave states a way to quickly expand their prison systems without taking on new debt. In the perfect marriage of fiscal and tough-on-crime conservatism, the companies would fund and construct new lockups while the courts would keep them full.

To Beasley, the business of private prisons was simple: "You just sell it like you were selling cars or real estate or hamburgers," he later told *Inc.* magazine. They ran their business a lot like a hotel chain, charging the government a daily rate for each inmate. Early investors included Sodexho Marriott and the venture capitalist Jack Massey, who helped build Kentucky Fried Chicken, Wendy's, and the Hospital Corporation of America.

When CCA shares appeared on the NASDAQ stock exchange in 1986, the company was operating two juvenile detention centers and two immigrant detention centers. The company was so confident about the growth of mass incarceration that, in the 1990s, it began building prisons "on spec," without a contract, expecting that states would fill them. In 2017, the company ran more than eighty facilities, from state prisons and jails to residential reentry facilities to federal immigration detention centers. Altogether, CCA houses some eighty thousand inmates at any given time. Its main competitor, the GEO Group, holds a few thousand more. In 2018, private prisons oversee about 8 percent of the country's total prison population.

Whatever taxpayer money CCA receives has to cover the cost of housing, feeding, and rehabilitating inmates. While I work at Winn, CCA receives about $34 per inmate per day. In comparison, the average daily cost per inmate at the state's publicly run prisons is about $52. Some states pay CCA as much as $80 per prisoner per day. During the year I work at Winn, CCA will report $1.8 billion in revenue, making more than $221 million in net income—more than $3,300 for each prisoner in its care. Roughly two-thirds of private prison contracts include "occupancy guarantees" that require states to pay a fee if they cannot provide a certain number of inmates. Under CCA's contract with Louisiana's Department of Corrections, Winn was guaranteed to be 96 percent full.

The main argument in favor of private prisons—that they save taxpayers money—remains controversial. One study estimated that private prisons cost 15 percent less than public ones; another found that public prisons were 14 percent cheaper. After reviewing these competing claims, researchers concluded that the savings "appear minimal." CCA personnel directed me to a 2013 report—funded in part by the company and GEO Group—that claimed private prisons could save states as much as 59 percent more than public prisons without sacrificing quality.

Private prisons "do not save substantially on costs," according to a recent US Department of Justice (DOJ) study. What savings do exist are achieved mostly through "moderate reductions in staffing patterns, fringe benefits, and other labor-related costs," read another DOJ report. Wages and benefits account for 59 percent of CCA's operating expenses. When I begin at Winn, nonranking guards make $9 an hour, no matter how long they've worked there. The starting pay for guards at public state prisons comes out to $12.50 an hour. CCA's spokesman told me that it "set[s] salaries based on the prevailing wages in local markets," adding that "the wages we provided in Winn Parish were competitive for that area."

The cost per prisoner at Winn, adjusted for inflation, dropped nearly 20 percent between the late nineties and 2014. The pressure to squeeze the most out of every penny at Winn seems evident not only in our paychecks but also in the decisions that keep staffing and staff-intensive programming for inmates at the barest of levels. When I asked CCA about the frequent criticism I heard from both staff and inmates about its relentless focus on the bottom line, its spokesman dismissed the assertion as "a cookie-cutter complaint," adding that it would be false to claim that "CCA prioritizes its own economic gain over the safety of its inmates" or "the needs of its customers."

| 5 |

On the eighth day of training, we are pulled out of CPR class and sent inside the compound to Elm unit, one of the five single-story brick buildings where the inmates live. When we enter the main prison grounds, we are told to empty our pockets and remove our shoes and belts. This is standard procedure, but today it is intensely nerve-racking because it's the first time I'm bringing recording equipment inside the main perimeter. Our instructors encouraged us to invest in a wristwatch because when we document rule infractions it is important that we record the time precisely. I bought one that doubles as a tiny camera. Along with my pocket change and employee ID, I send the watch through the X-ray machine. I walk through the metal detector and a CO runs a wand up and down my body and pats down my chest, back, arms, and legs. On the wall, I notice a photocopied picture of a woman who went to jail for smuggling contraband into a prison.

The other cadets and I gather at a barred gate and an officer, looking at us through thick glass, turns a switch that opens it slowly. We pass through, and after the gate closes behind us, another opens ahead. On the other side, the CCA logo is emblazoned on the wall along with the words "Respect" and "Integrity" and a mural of two anchors that are inexplicably floating at sea. Another gate clangs open and our small group steps onto the main outdoor artery of the prison: "the walk."

From above, the walk is T-shaped. It is fenced in with chain-link and covered with corrugated steel. Yellow lines divide the pavement into three lanes. We cadets travel in a cluster up the middle lane from the administration building as prisoners move down their designated side lanes. Every cadet seems nervous except Collinsworth, who is excited about the new guard jackets we were given this morning. He says that if he ever leaves Winn, he'll make up a story about how his jacket broke and he gave it to Goodwill. That way he can keep it forever.

As we move up the walk, I greet inmates as they pass, trying hard to appear loose and unafraid. Some say good morning. Others stop in their tracks or cling to the fence separating the walk from the rec yards, making a point of looking the female cadets up and down. We walk past the squat, dull buildings that house visitation, programming, the infirmary, and a church with a wrought iron gate shaped into the words "Freedom Chapel." Beyond the gate there is a mural of a fighter jet dropping a bomb into a mountain lake, water blasting skyward, and a giant bald eagle soaring overhead, backgrounded by an American flag. At the top of the T we take a left, past the chow hall and the canteen, where inmates can buy snacks, toiletries, tobacco, music players, and batteries.

The five units sit along the top of the walk. Each is shaped like a letter X and connected to the main walk by its own short, covered walk. Every unit is named after a type of tree. Most are general population units, where inmates mingle in dorm-style halls and can leave for programs and chow. Cypress is the high-security segregation unit, the only one where inmates are confined to cells.

In Dogwood, reserved for the best-behaved inmates, prisoners get special privileges like extra TV time, and many work outside the unit in places like the metal shop, the garment factory, or the chow hall. Some "trusties" even get to work in the front office or beyond the fence to wash employees' personal cars. Birch holds most of the elderly, infirm, and mentally ill inmates, though it doesn't offer any special services. Then there are Ash and Elm, which inmates call "the projects." The more troublesome prisoners live here.

We enter Elm and walk onto an open, shiny cement floor. The air is slightly sweet and musty, like the clothes of a heavy smoker. Elm can house up to 352 inmates. At the center is an enclosed octagonal control room called "the key." Inside, a "key officer," invariably a woman, watches the feeds of the unit's twenty-seven-odd surveillance cameras, keeps a log of significant occurrences, and writes passes that give inmates permission to go to locations outside the unit, like to school or the gym. Also in the key is the office of the unit manager, the "mini-warden" of the unit.

The key stands in the middle of "the floor." Branching out from the floor are the four legs of the X; two tiers run down the length of each leg. Separated from the floor by a locked gate, every tier is an open dormitory that houses up to forty-four men, each with his own narrow bed, thin mattress, and metal locker.

Toward the front of each tier, there are two toilets, a trough-style urinal, and two sinks. There are two showers, open except for a three-foot wall separating them from the common area. Nearby are a microwave, a telephone, and a JPay machine, at which inmates pay to download songs onto their portable players and send short, monitored emails for about thirty cents each. Each tier also has a TV room, which fills up every weekday at twelve thirty p.m. for the prison's most popular show, *The Young and the Restless*.

At Winn, staff and inmates alike refer to guards as "free people." Like the prisoners, the majority of the COs at Winn are African American. More than half are women, and many of them are single moms. But in Ash and Elm, the floor officers—who, more than anyone else, must deal with the inmates face to face—are exclusively men. Floor officers are both enforcers and a prisoner's first point of contact if he needs something. It is their job to conduct security checks every thirty minutes, walking up and down each tier to make sure nothing is awry. Three times per twelve-hour shift, all movement in the prison stops and the floor officers count the inmates. There are almost never more than two floor officers per general population unit. That's one per 176 inmates.*

Kenny is waiting for us on one of Elm's tiers with a tall white CO named Christian, who has a leashed German shepherd with him. Christian looks at us impassively, his head permanently cocked to the left, and tells the female cadets to go to the key and the male cadets to line up along the showers and toilets at the front of the tier. We put on latex gloves. The inmates are sitting on their beds. Two ceiling fans turn slowly. The room is filled with fluorescent light. Almost every prisoner is black.

Christian tells the inmates that they are to approach us wearing nothing more than a pair of underwear, a pair of socks, a pair of shower shoes, and a T-shirt. A group of prisoners files into the shower area. A man, his body full of tattoos, gets into the shower in front of me, pulls his shirt and shorts off, and hands them to me. I feel them around in my hands. "Do a one-finger lift, turn around, bend down, and cough," Christian says from behind me. In one fluid motion the man lifts his penis up, opens his mouth and lifts his tongue, spins around with his ass facing me, squats down, and coughs. He hands me his sandals and lifts his feet so I can see his soles. I hand him his clothes back and he puts his shorts on, walks past me, and nods respectfully.

Like a human assembly line, the inmates file out and enter the TV room and new ones file in. "Beyend, squawt, cough," Christian drawls.

---

* CCA later tells me that the Louisiana DOC considered the "staffing pattern" at Winn "appropriate."

He tells one inmate to open his hand. The inmate uncurls his finger and reveals a SIM card. Christian takes it but otherwise does nothing.

Eventually the TV room is full of prisoners. A guard looks at them, all squeezed in together, and smiles. "Tear 'em up!" he says gesturing down the tier. We walk down, each of us stopping at a bed. The women join us. *Shake down number eight real good*, Christian says. *Just because he pissed me off.* He tells us to search everything. I follow Collinsworth's lead, opening the bottles of toothpaste and lotion and deodorant I find in inmates' lockers. Inside a container of Vaseline, I find a one-hitter pipe made out of a pen. I ask Christian what to do with it. He takes it from me, mutters *eh*, and tosses it on the floor. I go through the mattress, pillow, dirty socks, and underwear. I flip though photos of kids and photos of women posing seductively. I move on to the next bed and locker: ramen, chips, dentures, hygiene products, peanut butter, cocoa powder, cookies, candy, salt, moldy bread, a dirty coffee cup. I find the draft of a novel, Hoodlum Child, dedicated to "all the hustlers, bastards, strugglers, and hoodlum childs who are chasing their dreams."

The entire time I do this, I remember the times I came back to my cell in Iran after my daily allotment of fresh air, finding it ransacked. It was like coming home after a robbery. Even on the occasions when I didn't find letters or books missing, I felt completely violated. As I go through these lockers, I try to show a basic level of respect, carefully putting each object back where I found it.

Kenny notices me doing this and tells me to pull everything out of the lockers and leave it on the beds. I look down the tier and see mattresses on the floor and papers and food dumped across beds. The middle of the floor is strewn with contraband: USB cables refashioned as phone chargers, tubs of butter, slices of cheese, and pills. I find some hamburger patties. Collinsworth tells me to throw them on the floor—they were stolen from the kitchen. He's done a few shakedowns already and he loves them. He brags incessantly about how he is going to find a "gold ring"—a cell phone. Shakedowns are like treasure hunts.

Christian pulls a bag of Styrofoam cups out of a locker and stomps on them. "We don't sell those in the canteen," he says. I find a bag of bread and cafeteria cheese, check to see if anyone is looking, and rather than toss them, stash them in the back of the locker.

Inmates are glued up against the TV-room window, watching Miss Sterling pick through their stuff. She's still in training, but she already has a nickname that's taken throughout the prison: Snow White. The attention makes her uncomfortable; she thinks inmates are gross. Earlier this week she said she would refuse to give an inmate CPR and won't try the cafeteria food because she doesn't want to "eat AIDS." The more she is around prisoners, though, the more I notice her grapple with an inner conflict. "I don't want to treat everyone like he's a criminal because I've done things myself," she says.

She finds a bag of Tylenol in an inmate's locker and a guard tells her to throw it out. Miss Sterling hesitates. Why throw out someone's Tylenol?

"Now let me stop you right there," the female CO says. "Because you know what they do with that? They crush it up. They snort it. They burn it. They put it in a little pipe."

"Tylenol?" I say incredulously.

An inmate steps out of the TV room to get a better look at Miss Sterling, and she yells at him to go back in. He does.

Thank you, she says.

Did she just say thank you? Christian asks. A bunch of COs scoff.

Don't ever say thank you, the female CO says. *That takes the power away from it.*

Christian climbs up on a chair and pries open a ceiling fan. He reaches in, pulls out a big shank, and drops it on the floor. Afterward he unlocks the back door of the tier and leaves. The other guards drop what they are doing and follow. Out behind the unit, where no supervisors or inmates are around, Christian pulls a bag out of his pocket that he found in an inmate's mouth. We gather around as he picks the knot open. "There are some pills, my guess is Xanax," he says.

The female CO reaches for it and he yanks it away—"Let me get my Xanax!" he squeals.

"Man, I don't want to take your pills!" the CO says.

He pulls a little bag out from the bigger bag and smells it. "Ah, that's the real fucking thing." He passes it around and a few of us smell it. It smells like shake weed.

Christian holds the pills up again. "Xanax anybody?"

Our training becomes less and less eventful. Some days there are no more than two hours of classes, and then we have to sit and run the clock to four fifteen p.m. We are not allowed to have phones or outside reading material, so passing the time is challenging. By turns, we each tuck our heads into the crooks of our arms on the table like high school students in detention. We pace the room and the grass outside. The younger cadets eat candy and doodle in cutesy lettering on the board. A heavyset black cadet named Willis works on a "713 Monstas" sketch on his notebook cover. One day he tells us he served seven and a half years in the Texas State Penitentiary.

"What you did, beat up a cop or something?" Reynolds asks. Willis won't say. The other cadets become uncomfortable.*

One of the students breaks the awkward silence by saying she had a friend who worked in a Texas prison. Her job was to go in and make sure all of the computers and electrical equipment were shut down

---

* CCA hires former felons that it deems not to be a security risk; it says background checks for all Winn's guards were also reviewed by the Louisiana DOC.

before someone was executed by electric chair, and then to reboot them when it was over.

I try mostly to stay quiet, but when I slip into describing a backpacking trip I recently took in California, a cadet throws her arms in the air and shouts, *Why are you here?!* I am careful to never lie, instead backing out with generalities like *I came here for work* or *You never know where life will take you*, and no one pries further. Few of my fellow cadets have traveled farther than nearby Oklahoma; they compare towns by debating the size and quality of their Walmarts. I stand out in other ways too. Miss Sterling regularly teases me for how healthy I am because I sometimes eat an apple as a snack and put tomatoes on my sandwiches. The rest of the cadets lunch on pizza pockets or chips and dip.

Miss Blanchard apologizes for our instructors not showing up. She says it's become more and more difficult to keep staff over the years and oftentimes the instructors can't get away because there is no one to fill their positions. Even with Winnfield as poor as it is, not enough people are willing to work here for nine dollars an hour. "People say a lot of negative things about CCA," Miss Blanchard says. "That we'll hire anybody. That we are scraping the bottom of the barrel. Which is not really true, but if you come here and you breathing and you got a valid driver's license and you willing to work, then we're willing to hire you." She looks at us sternly. "You go' realize you ain't getting paid enough for what you putting up with back there," she tells us. "Nine dollars is not a lot of money. You can go get that at McDonald's. For nine dollars, all we really attract is a person who doesn't have responsibilities, doesn't have a lot of bills to pay. If I'm a man trying to support my family on nine dollars an hour, you can't. You gotta pay for gas!" I wonder if she realizes that, from among our whole class, only Collinsworth and I don't have kids.

She warns us that prisoners are going to remind us every day of how little we make. "And then your eyes open up to it. Your *mind* opens up to it. Then they start to ask you to do things for them because they have more money than what you makin' in a day. And that's appealing to a lot of people."

By late morning our instructors haven't shown, so Miss Blanchard tells us we can go to the gym to watch inmates graduate from trade class, where they learn skills like carpentry and plumbing. Prisoners and their families are milling around the basketball court with plates of cake and cups of fruit punch. An inmate offers a piece of red velvet to Miss Sterling. People are smiling, laughing. "When you see an inmate with a smile like that it's worth something," the Winn coach says to a prisoner who is standing with his parents. I feel surprisingly at ease wandering among prisoners in my uniform. "Keep your head up," an older black man in a wheelchair says to me. His legs are stumps. "Always know who you is. I'm not talking about coming out of the suit, I'm talking about being in the suit. Everything gonna be all right." He tells me his name is Robert Scott* and he's been here for twelve years. "I was walking when I got here," he tells me. "Had all my fingers." I notice he is wearing fingerless gloves with nothing poking out of them. "They took my legs in January and my fingers in June. Gangrene don't play. I kept going to the infirmary saying, 'My feet hurt. My feet hurt.' They said, 'Ain't nothin' wrong wicha. I don't *see* nothin' wrong wicha.' They didn't believe me, or they talk bad to me—'I can't believe you comin' up here!'"

He tells me he is suing CCA for neglect, claiming that inmates are denied medical care because the company operates the prison "on a skeleton crew for profitable gain." His medical records show that in the space of four months, he made at least nine requests to see a doctor. He complained of sore spots on his feet, swelling, oozing pus, and pain so severe he couldn't sleep. When he visited the infirmary, medical staff

---

* Robert Scott has allowed me to use his real name.

offered him sole pads, corn removal strips, and Motrin. He says he once showed his swollen foot, dripping with pus, to the warden. On one of these occasions, Scott alleges in his lawsuit, a nurse told him, "Ain't nothing wrong with you. If you make another medical emergency you will receive a disciplinary write-up for malingering." He filed a written request to be taken to a hospital for a second opinion, but it was denied.

Eventually numbness spread to his hands, but the infirmary refused to treat him. At night he sat upright in his chair, trying to ease the pain but getting little sleep. One day he collapsed in exhaustion, banging his head on the concrete floor. He was sent to the infirmary and was returned to his unit without seeing a doctor. His fingertips and toes turned black and wept pus. Inmates began to fear his condition was contagious. When Scott's sleeplessness kept another inmate awake, the inmate threatened to kill him if he was not moved to another tier. A resulting altercation drew the attention of staff, and they finally sent him to the local hospital.

"But when I got my legs cut off they didn't come back and say, 'Robert, I'm sorry.' I done taked my lickin'. Part of being locked up."*

Eventually the coach announces over the PA system that time is up, and the families all file out the side entrance of the gym. A couple of minutes after the last ones leave, the coach shouts, "All inmates on the bleachers!" The mood shifts instantly; curses rise from the crowd of two hundred prisoners. For the first time I realize there are no guards in the building besides us cadets. We all stand near the gym entrance, looking out over the crowd of prisoners. Collinsworth sees one smoking. "I'm going to tell him to put it out," he says and walks across the gym by himself.

"What the fuck is he doing walking in the middle of them?" Willis

---

* CCA eventually settled the case.

says. "They 'bout to smash him over there." Collinsworth pushes into the crowd.

"Security, he's going to need some backup," an inmate calls to us. He sounds sarcastic, but I'm not sure. "Security!" someone else shouts.

"Shit, he probably do need backup," Willis says and begins walking over. His large frame makes his appearance far more intimidating than Collinsworth's. Reynolds and I follow him and we bring Collinsworth back. "If you gonna be the boss man you can't half-ass it," Willis says to Collinsworth. "They'll smash you." Having been a prisoner himself, he's become our main authority on prison life.

"I wasn't even worrying!" Collinsworth says defensively.

Prisoners continue to mill around. Collinsworth suggests that we order everyone to get on the bleachers.

"Nah man," Willis says looking across the gym. "There's only seven of us. We can't take on all of them motherfuckers right there."

Eventually they sit down and the gym grows silent. They stare us down from across the room. The tension ratchets up until an inmate lets out a bloodcurdling scream. The other prisoners laugh.

The coach orders them to form a line in front of us. He will call them to the bathroom one by one to be strip-searched before going back to their units. I brace myself as the inmates stride toward us. Several gather around me and Collinsworth and ask about our watches. Some get up close to mine, looking directly into the camera. One, wearing a cocked gray beanie, asks to buy them. I refuse outright. Collinsworth dithers. "How old you is?" the inmate asks him.

"You never know," Collinsworth says.

"Man, all these fake-ass signals. The best thing you could do is get to know people in the place."

"I understand it's your home," Collinsworth says. "But I'm at work right now."

"It's your home for twelve hours a day! You trippin'. You 'bout to do half my time with me. You straight with that?"

"It's probably true."

"It ain't no probably true. If you go' be at this bitch, you go' do twelve hours a day."

He tells Collinsworth not to bother writing people up for small infractions: "They not payin' you enough for that." Seeming torn between whether to impress me or the inmate, Collinsworth says he will only write up serious offenses, like hiding drugs.

"Drugs?! Don't worry 'bout the drugs." The inmate says he was caught recently with two ounces of "mojo," or synthetic marijuana, which is the drug of choice at Winn, in part because it can't be detected in drug tests. The inmate says the guards turn a blind eye to it. They "ain't trippin' on that shit," he says. "I'm telling you, it ain't that type of camp. You can't come and change things by yourself. You might as well go with the flow. Get this free-ass, easy-ass money and go home." There is a pause. "This job, you'll see. It got benefits."

"Oh, yeah, I got some benefits already," Collinsworth says, "like health insurance."

"I'm not talking about no health insurance. I'm talking about some more money!"

"I'm just here to do my job and take care of my family," Collinsworth says. "I'm not gonna bring stuff in 'cuz even if I don't get caught, there's always the chance that I will."

"Nah. Ain't no chance. I ain't never heard of nobody movin' good and low key gettin' caught. Nah. I know a dude still rolling. He been doin' it six years." He looks at Collinsworth. "Easy."

An inmate picks the podium up over his head and runs with it across the gym. Another throws his graduation certificate dramatically into the trash. The coach shouts, exasperated, as prisoners continue to scramble around. "I can't breathe!" one shouts.

"You see this chaos," the inmate in the beanie says to Collinsworth. "If you'd been to other camps, you'd see the order they got. Ain't no order here. Inmates run this bitch, son."

A week later Mr. Tucker tells us to come in early to do shakedowns. The sky is barely lit as I stand on the walk at six thirty a.m. with the other cadets. Collinsworth tells us another prisoner offered to buy his watch. He said he'd sell it for $600. The inmate declined.

"Don't sell it to him anyway," Miss Sterling admonishes. "You might get six hundred dollars, but if they find out, you ain't go' get no more paychecks."

"Nah, I wouldn't actually do it. I just said six hundred dollars because I know they don't got six hundred dollars to give me."

"Shit," Willis says. "Dudes was showing me pictures. They got money in here. One dude in here, don't say nothin', but he got like six to eight thousand dollars. They got it on cards. Little money cards and shit."

Collinsworth jumps up and down. "Dude, I'ma find me one of them damn cards! Hell yeah. And I will *not* report it."

Officially, inmates are only allowed to keep money in special prison-operated accounts that can be used at the canteen. Into these accounts the prisoners with jobs receive their wages, which may be as little as two cents an hour for a dishwasher and as much as twenty cents an hour for a sewing machine operator at Winn's garment factory. Their families can also deposit money in the accounts.

The prepaid cash cards Willis is referring to are called Green Dots, and they are the currency of the illicit prison economy. Connections on the outside buy them online and then pass on the account numbers to prisoners in encoded messages through the mail or during visits. Inmates with contraband cell phones can do all these transactions themselves, buying the cards and handing out strips of paper as payments for drugs or phones or whatever else.

Miss Sterling divulges that an inmate gave her the digits to a money card as a Christmas gift. "I'm like, damn! I need a new MK watch. I need a new purse. I need some new jeans."

"There was this one dude in Dogwood," she continues. "He came up to the bars and showed me a stack of hundred dollar bills folded up, and it was like this—" She makes like she's holding a wad of cash four inches thick. "And I was like, 'I'm not go' say anything.'"

"Dude! I'ma shake him the fuck down!" Collinsworth says. "I don't care if he's cool."

"He had a phone," Miss Sterling says, "and he's like, 'I don't have the time of day to hide it. I just keep it in the open. I really don't give a fuck.'"

Mr. Tucker tells us to follow him. We shake down tiers all morning. By the time we finish at eleven, everyone is exhausted.

"I'm not mad we had to do shakedowns. I'm just mad we didn't find anything," Collinsworth says.

Christian, who joined us today without his German shepherd, pulls a piece of paper out of his pocket, reading off a string of numbers in a show-offy way. "A Green Dot," he says. Christian hands the slip of paper to one of the cadets, a middle-aged white woman. "You can have this one," he says. "I have plenty already." She smiles coyly.

| 6 |

Our modern private prison system began in the 1980s, but commercial interests have been guiding penal practices since before the American Revolution. During colonial times, Britain used America as a dumping ground for its convicts. In 1718 Britain passed the Transportation Act, providing that people convicted of burglary, robbery, perjury, forgery, and theft could, at the court's discretion, be "transported to America for at least seven years," rather than be hanged. Crimes as minor as poaching fish or stealing a silver spoon were punishable by death, so convicts frequently begged for the mercy of being exiled to America. The convicts were chained below ship decks and brought across the sea by merchant entrepreneurs, many of whom were experienced in the African slave trade. Just a few companies dominated the business, and they charged British authorities up to five pounds for the transport of each convict. But the fee was not enough to entice merchants to cross the Atlantic, so Parliament granted contractors "property and interest in the service" of felons for the duration of their banishment. As soon as the convicts entered the control of the contractors, British authorities relinquished responsibility for their welfare. Once they reached America, the merchants auctioned their human cargo into involuntary servitude under private masters, usually to work on tobacco plantations. Planters often preferred convicts to slaves: They were cheaper, and because they served limited terms, they didn't have to be supported in old age.

Part of Britain's interest in convict servitude, as stated in the preamble of the Transportation Act, was the "great want of servants" in the colonies "who might be the means of improving the colonial plantations and making them more useful to his majesty." It was a relatively easy labor system to regulate: The government could increase or decrease the number of pardons, depending on the need for labor in the colonies. Next to African slaves, felons constituted the largest body of immigrants ever forced to go to America. Between 1718 and 1775, more than two-thirds of convicted felons were transported from Britain to America, some fifty thousand in total. Approximately one quarter of all British immigrants to America in the eighteenth century were convicts.

The American Revolution ended convict servitude, and shortly afterward, reformers set out to end the barbarous types of punishment imposed by the British, especially their zealous use of the death penalty. Thomas Jefferson had suggested that the death penalty should be abolished for all offenses except treason and murder, and replaced with penal slavery. Unlike in pre-Revolution times, this "slavery" would be administered by the states rather than by private plantation owners. Early penal reformers believed that forced labor was common sense. Theft constituted some 90 percent of crimes committed by men, and most penal reformers were Protestant elites who believed that crime was caused not by poverty but by a lack of a work ethic. Rehabilitation, by their logic, was brought about by hard work and discipline.

Ten years after the end of the Revolution, Pennsylvania became the first state to implement Jefferson's ideas, replacing the death penalty for lesser felonies with "continuous hard labor, publicly and disgracefully imposed." Anyone not sentenced to be hanged was put to servitude as "wheelbarrowmen" on the state's roads, highways, forts, and mines. Lawmakers reasoned that the public would benefit from the convicts' labor and that the sight of them would deter others from crime. But this first experiment in republican punishment was widely unpopular. The public laborers often were drunk and rowdy and many escaped. In one incident in Philadelphia during the federal constitutional convention, a group of wheelbarrowmen descended on the carriage of Alexander Hamilton and his wife and tried to rob them.

Particularly distressing to early republicans was the perception that forced public labor threatened American capitalism. Philadelphian essayist and signatory to the Declaration of Independence Benjamin Rush argued that "employing criminals in public labour will render labour of every kind disreputable." Similar to how "white men decline labor" in slaveholding states because they associate it with "Negro slaves," free citizens who witnessed the toil of criminals might come to see labor itself as degrading. The problem, he wrote, was not forced labor itself, but its *publicness*. He proposed the creation of a "house of repentance" in which convicts could reflect on their crimes while continuing to be "profitable to the state" out of public view.

In 1795 Pennsylvania renovated its old Walnut Street Jail, building several workshops and dorms for inmates to sleep in, as well as solitary cells for inmates who were difficult to control. In doing so, it created a new type of institution—the penitentiary—which would differ from the jails that have existed since the beginning of civilization. Unlike penitentiaries, jails were intended to hold people only until they could be judged and physically or monetarily punished. They rarely detained people long term. Now, rather than sentence people to hanging, branding, the whipping post, or the pillory, judges could issue varying sentences of imprisonment and the severity of punishment could be more appropriately tailored to the crime. The penitentiary was invented as a means of penal reform.

As a penitentiary, Walnut Street aimed to turn a profit, though it was ultimately unsuccessful. The prison contracted with local business-men who paid a set price for products made by inmates. Penitentiary agents purchased the raw materials themselves and oversaw inmates who would weave, spin, tailor, chip logwood, saw stone, and make nails and shoes. Counties had an incentive to ship convicts to Walnut Street; the law stipulated that any profits earned from convict labor would be evenly divided among the counties that sent them.

By 1800, ten other states, inspired by Walnut Street, built peniten-tiaries of their own. But many citizens were skeptical of this new mode of punishment. At a moment when indentured servitude was in decline and slavery was being phased out across the Northeast, some feared that the penitentiary would become a new means for a tyrannical state to funnel people into forced labor. Was the Revolution not fought to rid America of servitude, at least for white men? Convicts resisted. When in 1797 Pennsylvania expanded Walnut Street's factory, inmates burned the new buildings down. In other states they sabotaged machin-ery, staged slowdowns, went on strike, and torched wings of the insti-tutions.

Just a couple of decades after the birth of the penitentiary, critics were arguing that they were a failed experiment. They were not gener-ating the revenue that Rush promised. At the same time, lawmakers and the press became convinced that a wave of murder, rape, forgery, and theft was sweeping the country and that the penitentiaries were to blame. They believed that by gathering criminals in one place, peniten-tiaries were teaching the "science of robbery" rather than reforming people. Lawmakers in several states debated abolishing them altogether. In New York, lawmakers proposed demolishing the penitentiaries and

putting convicts to work building roads on the western frontier. Cal-
vinists called for a return to biblical punishments of banishment, execu-
tion, and public chastisement.

Part of what saved the penitentiary system was the phasing out of
slavery in the Northeast. Whites feared large numbers of free black
men and the penitentiary offered a way to enforce compliance and obe-
dience of free African Americans. As a model of forced labor, it was
more efficient than slavery, and unlike slavery, prison labor directly
benefited the state. Arguments for the abolishment of slavery and the
erection of penitentiaries sometimes went hand in hand. In 1817 a New
York banker named Thomas Eddy helped to convince the legislature to
gradually emancipate the state's slaves. Eddy also convinced it to fund a
new penitentiary at Auburn, complete with a factory. Fifteen years after
slavery was abolished, one in five New York prisoners would be black,
their representation behind bars nearly ten times greater than it was in
the population at large.

New York, like other states, struggled to fund its penitentiary. As a
remedy, Auburn sought to lease convict labor to private interests in
1825. Contractors were reluctant: Penitentiaries had become notorious
for their riots and sabotage. Just a few years earlier, prisoners at Auburn
rioted and struck in the workshops, destroyed tools, and allegedly set
the prison on fire. After contractors balked, Auburn's inspectors recommended a thorough overhaul of prison discipline. To prevent collec-
tive action, the penitentiary enforced a strict code of silence, banning
all communication between convicts. Auburn's captain promised to
turn inmates into "silent and insulated working machines" who would
work by day and spend the nights confined to their cells to reflect on
their crimes. Whipping, forbidden after the American Revolution, was
reinstated by the New York legislature, allowing every guard to mete
out a summary lashing of any convict. Anyone caught talking, making
hand signals, or shirking work was whipped.

In 1831 Alexis de Tocqueville and Gustave Beaumont, sent by the French monarch to assess America's new penitentiary system, praised the Auburn model. Forcing inmates to labor for private contractors, they said, relieved taxpayers of the cost of imprisoning them and helped transform them into productive, laboring citizens. The lash was a superior form of punishment, Tocqueville and Beaumont wrote after visiting New York's Sing Sing prison, because "it effects the immediate submission of the delinquent; his labour is not interrupted a single instant."

Penitentiary discipline was dramatically transformed at Auburn. "[T]he silence within these vast walls . . . is that of death," Tocqueville and Beaumont commented. "We felt as if we traversed catacombs; there were a thousand living beings, and yet it was a desert solitude." As a result of this new level of control, local manufactures set up their equipment in the penitentiary and its factory produced tools, rifles, shoes, clothes, and more. For a day's labor, contractors paid the state about half of what they would pay a free worker. By 1831 Auburn was making a profit.

The Auburn model convinced other states to reinvent rather than abandon the penitentiary system. States could take out loans to build penitentiaries, and the prison factories would eventually repay the cost through contract labor. By 1831 Connecticut's Wethersfield prison, modeled after Auburn, brought in nearly $8,000 in profit (about $220,000 in 2018). For the first three years after it was founded, the Baltimore penitentiary brought the state of Maryland $44,000 in profits (about $1.2 million in 2018). For the contractors themselves, prison labor was as good as it got. Some reported profits as high as 150 percent over three years.

This privatization of prison production allowed for America's first prison boom. In the 25 years after Auburn opened, at least fourteen states built penitentiaries modeled after it. For the first time in the history of the world, imprisonment became the regular mode of punishment for the majority of crimes, and in almost every state, incarceration meant forced labor for private contractors. Most penitentiaries came to resemble the great textile factories for which American industry was becoming known.

Despite their support of forced convict labor, Tocqueville and Beaumont warned against the temptation to hand the penitentiaries over to private interests entirely. France had privatized its prisons. There, contractors who benefited from inmate labor were tasked with feeding, clothing, and caring for them. Under full privatization, they wrote, "The contractor, regarding the convict as a laboring machine, thinks only how he can use him to the greatest advantage for himself." He "sees nothing but a money affair in such a bargain" and "speculates upon the victuals as he does the labour; if he loses upon the clothing, he indemnifies himself upon the food; and if the labour is less productive than he calculated upon, he tries to balance his loss by spending less for the support of the convicts, with which he is equally charged."

Tocqueville and Beaumont's warning went unheeded. It would not be long before American penitentiaries were controlled entirely by private companies.

Welcome to the hellhole, a female CO greeted me the first time I visited Winn's segregation unit. *Welcome to the dungeon.* A few days later I'm back at Cypress with Collinsworth and Reynolds to shadow some guards. The metal door clicks open and we enter to a cacophony of shouting and pounding on metal. An alarm is sounding and the air smells strongly of smoke.

On one wall there is a mural of a prison nestled among dark mountains and shrouded in storm clouds; lightning striking the guard towers; and an enormous, screeching bald eagle descending with a giant pair of handcuffs in its talons. At the end of a long hall of cells an officer in a black SWAT-style uniform stands ready with a PepperBall gun. Another man in black is pulling burnt parts of a mattress out of a cell. Christian is walking up and down the hall with his German shepherd, stepping in and out of empty cells. *Christian is high as fuck right now,* an inmate shouts. Cypress can hold up to two hundred prisoners; most of the eight-by-eight-foot cells have two prisoners in them. The cells look like tombs; men lie in their bunks, wrapped in blankets, staring at the walls. Many cells don't have functioning lights and are only dimly il-luminated by the light from the hallway. In one, an inmate is washing his clothes in his toilet.

I turn on my watch camera to record these moments, but its memory is full. I forgot to delete yesterday's material. Fortunately I have a note-book in my breast pocket. Our teachers advise us to carry one at all times, to keep track of all the things prisoners ask us for. I go into the bathroom periodically to jot things down.

How are you doing? says a smiling man dressed in business casual. He grips my hand. *Assistant Warden Parker. Thank you for being here.* He is new to CCA, but he was once the assistant warden of a federal prison complex in Florence, Colorado, that includes the nation's most restric-tive supermax prison. *I know it seems crazy back here now, but you'll learn the ropes. We are going to win this unit back. It's not going to happen in an hour. It's gonna take time, but it will happen.* Apparently the segregation unit has been in a state of upheaval for a while, so the corporate headquarters sent in an emergency response team of so-called SORT (Special Operations Response Team) officers from out of state to bring it back under control. SORT teams are trained to suppress riots, rescue hostages, extract in-mates from their cells, and neutralize violent prisoners. They deploy an array of "less-lethal" weapons like plastic buckshot, electrified shields, and chili-pepper-filled projectiles that burst on contact.

I get a whiff of human feces that quickly becomes overpowering. On one of the tiers a brown liquid oozes out of a bottle onto the ground. Food, wads of paper, and garbage are all over the floor. Amid the detri-tus I find a Coke can, charred black, with a piece of cloth sticking out of it like a fuse. *I use my political voice!* an inmate shouts to the unit man-ager. *I stand up for my rights. Hahaha! Ain't nowhere like this camp. Shit, y'alls disorganized as fuck up in here.*

That's why we are here, a SORT member says. *We are going to change all that.*

Y'all can't change shit, the prisoner yells back. *They ain't got shit for us here. We ain't got no jobs. No rec time. We just sit in our cells all day. What you think going to happen when a man got nuttin' to do? That's why we throw shit out on the tier. What else are we going to do? You know how we get these officers to respect us? We throw piss on 'em. That's the only way. Either that or throw them to the floor. Then they respect us.*

I ask one of the regular white-shirted COs what his average day looks like in Cypress unit. *To be honest with you, normally we just sit here at this table all day long,* he tells me. They are supposed to walk up and down the eight tiers every thirty minutes to check on the inmates in their segregation cells, but he says they never do that.*

Collinsworth is walking around with a big smile on his face. He's learning how to bring inmates out of their cells for disciplinary court, which is inside Cypress. He's supposed to cuff them through the slot in the bars and then tell the CO at the end of the tier to open the gate remotely. *Fuck nah, I ain't coming out of this cell!* an inmate shouts. *You go' have to get SORT to bring me up out of here. That's how we do early in the morning. I'll fuck y'all up.* The prisoner climbs up on the bars and pounds on the metal above the cell door. The sound explodes down the cement hallway. My shoulders tense up to the point of pain.

They ain't go' do shit, one of the white-shirted guards says to me. *They just a bunch of babies. They talk but they ain't go' do shit.* An officer is pacing back and forth inside the key, calling COs over to her. A pair of handcuff keys went missing and she's beginning to panic. She looks frazzled, exhausted in a deep, years-long kind of way.

Collinsworth and the CO he is shadowing move an inmate from his

---

* CCA says it had no knowledge of guards at Winn skipping security checks before I inquired about it.

cell. *If that motherfucker starts pulling away from me like that again, I'm gonna make him eat concrete*, the CO says to Collinsworth.

I kind of hope he does mess around again, Collinsworth says, beaming. *That would be fun!*

An inmate yells at Collinsworth from a nearby cell. *Why don't you cut off that facial hair and come back here so I can fuck that ass. I'll rape the fuck out of you, boy.* A few prisoners cheer.

A CO passes a cuffed inmate off to me and tells me to take him to disciplinary court. I put my hand around his elbow, and as we walk, he pulls against my grip. I remember this game. I played it when I would walk down the hall in Evin prison in Iran. Whenever a guard tried to push me along faster, I slowed, maintaining a slight resistance, a tactile reminder that I wasn't pliant. But I'm not pushing this guy. He keeps pulling, so I stop. *Why you pulling on me, man?* he shouts and spins around, standing face to face with me. A SORT officer rushes over and grabs him. My heart races.

One of the white-shirted officers pulls me aside. *Hey, don't let these guys push you around*, he says. *If he is pulling away from you, you tell him, 'Stop resisting.' If he doesn't, you stop. If he keeps going, we are authorized to knee him in the back of the leg and drop him to the concrete.*

The scene prompts the same inmate who heckled Collinsworth to shout to me as I walk back down the tier. *He has a little twist in his walk. I like them holes in your ears CO. Come in here with me. Give me that booty!*

A SORT officer pulls me aside, taking the cuffs from my hands. He tightly grips an open cuff link and holds it to my jugular. *This here is a weapon*, he says, looking at me intensely. I need to make sure the cuffs are closed when I'm not using them.

At lunchtime Collinsworth, Reynolds, and I go down the walk back to the training room. *I love it here*, Collinsworth says dreamily. *It's like a community.*

. . .

When inmates are written up for breaking the rules, they are sent to inmate court, which is held in a room in the corner of Cypress unit. One day our class files into the small room to watch the hearings. Miss Lawson, the assistant chief of security, is acting as the judge, sitting at a desk in front of a mural of the scales of justice. *Even though we treat every inmate like they are guilty until proven innocent, they are* . . . She pauses for someone to fill in the answer.

Innocent? a cadet offers.

That's right. Innocent until proven guilty.

This is not a court of law, but it often issues judgements for felonies such as assault or attempted murder. Typically, in publicly run prisons, an inmate who stabs another will be referred to a criminal court to face new criminal charges. Here, it often remains in the hands of the company. The inmate may be transferred, yet prisoners and guards say inmates who stab other inmates typically are not even shipped to a higher security prison. The consequences of less serious offenses are usually stints in seg or a loss of "good time," sentence reduction for good behavior.

Inmate counsel, has your defendant appeared before the court? Miss Lawson asks a prisoner standing at the podium.

No ma'am, he has not. The inmate counsel represents other prisoners in the internal disciplinary process. Every year he is taken to a state-run prison for intensive training. Miss Lawson later tells me that inmate counsel never really influences her decisions.

The absent inmate is accused of coming too close to the main entrance. *Would the counsel like to offer a defense?*

No ma'am.

How does he plead?

Not guilty.

Mr. Trahan is found guilty. The entire "trial" lasts less than two minutes. This seems to be typical: Winn inmates charged with serious rule violations are found guilty at least 96 percent of the time.

Decisions made in this room can directly impact CCA's bottom line. In 2008 Kelsey Benoit was rushed to the hospital in Winnfield after he overdosed on his antipsychotic medication and Tylenol. After examining Benoit and learning how he'd been saving up his medication, the doctor concluded that he had attempted suicide. This was no surprise to Winn's social worker, because Benoit had made several attempts in the past. But when Benoit was brought into disciplinary court days later, the court ruled that he had not attempted suicide at all. Instead he had "self-mutilated." This was an important distinction: Suicide attempts were not punishable. Self-mutilation was, and it allowed for the company to recover damages from the inmate. In a trial that lasted just a few minutes, Winn's disciplinary court found him guilty and charged him $2,304, the cost of his hospital trip. Kelsey appealed to the DOC, but the department upheld CCA's decision, so Kelsey sued. In a hearing, DOC attorney Jonathan Vining said Kelsey took all those pills "basically to go to the hospital and cost CCA money." The judge didn't buy it, and Winn's decision was eventually overturned.

Miss Lawson calls the next defendant.

He is being considered for release from segregation. *Do you know your Bible?"* Miss Lawson asks.

Yes ma'am.

Do you remember in the Gospel of John, when the adulteress was brought before Jesus? What did he say?

I don't remember that, ma'am.

He says, "Sin no more." She points for him to leave the room.

Miss Lawson calls in the next inmate, an orderly in Cypress. He is charged with being in an unauthorized area, because he took a broom from the broom closet to sweep the tier during rec time, which is not the authorized time to sweep the tier. He begins to explain that a CO gave him permission. Miss Lawson cuts him off. *He's getting in too deep already*, she says. *How would you like to plead?*

Guilty, I guess.

You are found guilty and sentenced to thirty days loss of good time.

Man! Y'all—this is fucked up man. Y'all gonna take my good time?! He runs out of the room. *They done took my good time!* he screams in the hall. *They took my good time! Fuck them!* There is an uproar of pounding from the cells. For taking a broom out of a closet at the wrong time, this inmate will stay in prison an extra thirty days, for which CCA will be paid more than $1,000.

A week later, I am told to show up at six a.m. to learn about inmate transportation. I go to the infirmary, where a guard hands me a set of leg irons and tells me to get to work. I try to remember the rules about how to do this: Tell the inmate to lift his foot up to you; if you bend down you could get kicked in the face. Try not to close the cuffs all the way down, but if the inmates howl about them being too tight, don't worry about it. They'll be fine. I walk over to a fiftysomething white inmate. He has throat cancer and he makes this trip every day to get radiation. I fumble with the leg irons, forgetting which side is supposed to face up and how exactly to make sure they don't tighten on their own as he walks. The inmate looks at me, smiling, while I pause for a moment to remember the next step. I reach for the belly chain, but he corrects me, pointing to the handcuff box on the table. I slip the box over the short chain that connects the cuff links. "There ya go," the inmate says like a father who is teaching his son how drive a stick shift. I string the belly chain through the box and slowly, awkwardly through his jumpsuit. "There ya go," he says soothingly.

We drive for an hour and a half to the hospital in Shreveport. When we arrive, the guard who is supposed to be training me drops me off at the hospital with the inmate. I am not sure what to do, but the inmate leads the way. Despite his shackles and orange jumpsuit, he acts like a free person, greeting random people we walk by. When we find the receptionist desk empty, he complains to bystanders as though he is in a hurry to attend to his errands. In my guard suit, people say hello to me more than usual, but never to him. When the receptionist does arrive, she addresses questions about him to me as though he weren't there. I don't answer for him, letting the silence linger, watching her grow visibly uncomfortable with the prospect of having to speak to this shackled man. Eventually she does, and he responds politely.

He leads the way to radiation. I follow and wonder if he is going to take me somewhere that he's not supposed to.

I unshackle him and he gets on the radiation table. "Sleigh Ride" by the Rosettes is playing on the radio. He lies there, staring at the pictures of mountains on the ceiling, and the technician and I leave the room. These minutes, while he is being saturated with radiation, is the only time he has to himself each day.

When we are done we go to the hospital basement, where prisoners wait in holding cells to see a doctor. I sit in a dark room in which Mr. Tucker, the Winn SORT commander, is watching *Gun Smoke* on a tablet. A cop is playing a hunting game on his phone. Other officers sleep, several talk about fishing, and some just stare ahead blankly. After a couple of hours, a guard enters. "Who the hell left their gun in the bathroom?" he says, holding up a pistol wrapped in a paper towel. The cops all check their holsters. They have theirs. "That's bad man, that's real bad," one cop says. It was in the same bathroom that prisoners use.

A cop comes in a couple of minutes later. "Ooooh, Lord," she says. "Thank y'all you got it."

Mr. Tucker says it's not a big deal. It happens. He left his gun hanging on a wall in the prison once.

"Did you ever get the gun back?"

He says yes. "After the inmate told us where it was." He smiles sheepishly. The cops guffaw.

"Oh my Lawd!"

"You're lucky he didn't grab it," one says.

"Some of 'em ain't got it in 'em," says another.

"Noooo. Not that one," Mr. Tucker says. "That scared the shit out that inmate." He points up at the wall as though he was the inmate pointing at the gun, trembling in fear.

A Winn captain told us a story once. One day an inmate was rushed to a hospital for dislocating his shoulder. Transport officers are required to carry a sidearm, and when the officer signed his out at the front gate, he didn't holster it like he was supposed to. Instead he left it in the box on the floor of the van. While they drove to Shreveport, the inmate fished the box under the barrier to the back of the van. As they drove, the prisoner held the gun and the twelve rounds. Later, back in the prison, the inmate told the captain about it. "I said, 'No, you lying,'" the captain recounted to us. To prove his story, the prisoner gave the captain the serial number of the gun and handed him a bullet. He told the captain to go to the front gate, look in the gun, and find a piece of toilet paper he had shoved into the empty cylinder. "I went to the front gate, pulled that gun out, and pulled the toilet paper out of that cylinder."

Two weeks after I begin training, Chase Cortez* decides he's had enough of Winn. It's been nearly three years since he was locked up for theft, and he has only three months to go. But in the middle of a cool, sunny December day, he climbs onto the roof of Birch unit. He lies down and waits for the patrol vehicle to pass along the perimeter. He is in view of the guard watchtowers, but the company unmanned them

---

* His real name.

around 2010 to save money. Now a single CO watches the video feeds from at least thirty cameras.

Cortez sees the patrol van pass, jumps down off the back side of the building, climbs the razor-wire perimeter fence, and then makes a run for the forest. He fumbles through the dense foliage until he spots a clean white truck left by a hunter. Lucky for him, it is unlocked, with the key in the ignition.

In the control room an alarm sounds, indicating someone has touched the outer fence, a possible sign of a perimeter breach. The officer reaches over, switches it off, and goes back to whatever she was doing. She notices nothing on the video screen, and she does not review the footage. Hours pass before the staff realizes someone is missing. Some guards tell me it was an inmate who finally brought the escape to their attention. Cortez is caught that evening after the sheriff chases him and he crashes into a fence. CCA says nothing publicly about this escape. I heard about it from guards who had investigated the incident or been briefed by the warden.*

When I come in the next morning the prison is on lockdown. Staff are worried CCA is going to lose its contract with Louisiana. "We were already in the red, and this just added to it," Miss Blanchard's assistant tells me. "It's a lot of tension right now."

She tells us to work on our computer lessons while she figures out what to do with us. I take a course on insider training, which warns that were we to learn in a meeting that the state was going to revoke its contract with CCA, we would not be allowed to tell anyone, at least not any shareholders, until the company announced it. To do so would be illegal.

---

* The company later told me it conducted a "full review" of the incident and fired a staff member "for lack of proper response to the alarm." When I asked CCA about its decision to remove guards from Winn's watchtowers, its spokesman replied that "newer technologies . . . are making guard towers largely obsolete."

Because an escape could potentially hurt the value of shares, would it be illegal for me to tell someone about that too? And who would I tell? The only person here who is permitted to interact with reporters is the prison spokesperson, but even he is not allowed to speak freely. Miss Blanchard told us all statements are written in the corporate office. "He could not elaborate any more than what was on that paper," she said.

Later in the day Reynolds and I are called in to help with the lockdown. Because the inmates can't go to the chow hall, the captain needs extra people to push carts of food to the units. When we bring lunch to Birch unit, Collinsworth is there, grinning and swinging a big skeleton key at the end of a chain, doing his on-the-job training. Ten minutes after we begin passing out trays, an inmate comes to the bars and calls to me. "I got razors in my food, man," he says. He opens his mouth and a little piece of a razor is jammed in between his front tooth and lateral incisor. His front lip is bleeding a little. He shows me the mashed potatoes, and there are little bits of razor mixed into it.

I tell the case manager in the unit. "Go get him please," she says to the CO on duty. "'Cuz you know I'm go' hit him. I'm gonna tell him he's fucking dumb and I'm go' hit him."

She tells me she thinks he put razors in his own food because he is trying to get transferred out of here. "Nobody told him to eat it," she says. "That was just stupid on his part. I would have just found them in there. You know what I'm saying? Just throw 'em in there and stir it up. Don't fucking eat it you big dummy."

"Isn't that the one whose fiancée died?" a CO asks.

"His fiancée didn't die," the case manager says.

"Oh, she lost her memory?"

"But it came back."

"Oh, didn't his baby die?"

"His baby died."

From another tier an inmate shouts, "Everybody didn't get they food over here!"

"Most of 'em did," a sergeant replies.

"We didn't get enough trays," Collinsworth shouts to the inmate. "Can't do nothing about it."

Reynolds and I leave the unit with the food cart. I tell him to grab the front. *Man, it's an empty cart*, he snaps. *You can't take it?*

I push it and we walk silently, tension lingering between us. As I round a corner the cart lists to the side. I tell him to grab the front again. *Man, push the fucking cart!* he says.

What's your problem? I say. He won't help. I leave the cart on the walk and follow him back toward the empty chow hall, seething. When we reach the cafeteria, he says, *Man, why you staring at the back of my head? Why you looking at me?* He tries to stare me down. *You don't want to mess with me, man.* The other day he rolled up his sleeve and showed me two scars, one on each arm. One, he said, was from a shoot-out he got involved in with his drug dealer friends in Baton Rouge. The other is from when he got in a street fight in Winnfield. He elbowed someone in the face, and next thing he knew, he got knifed from behind. *It was some gang shit*, he said.

I go inside the chow hall. It's empty aside from the inmates working in the kitchen and the female guard that oversees them. For two hours Reynolds and I sit at separate tables and ignore each other.

A short black man with a wide forehead enters. His name is Sergeant King, and he talks with a group of inmates wearing hairnets and the female guard who oversees the kitchen. As soon as the woman leaves, King licks his finger dramatically, pretends to slap an invisible ass, and thrusts his pelvis into it explosively. The inmates bust up laughing and bump fists with him.

Later, Reynolds and I bring food to Cypress, the segregation unit.

He pushes the cart and we don't speak. It's dinnertime, but the inmates haven't yet had lunch. The unit smells like sulfur; some prisoners lit fires to protest the late meal. A naked man is shouting frantically for food, mercilessly slapping the plexiglass at the front of his suicide watch cell. In the cell next to him, a small, wiry white man is squatting on the floor. His arms and face are scraped with little cuts. A guard tells me to watch him.

It is Cortez. I offer him a packet of Kool-Aid in a Styrofoam cup. He says thank you and then asks if I will put water in it. There is no water in his cell.

| 8 |

August 1840. A steamship moved slowly up the Mississippi in the heat, floating past white mansions, palm trees, oaks, and sugar and cotton plantations that stretched out to bearded cypress forests on the horizon. A white man named Dr. David Hines sat aboard the ship in shackles. The other passengers, unaccustomed to seeing a white man in chains, looked at him sympathetically. Some may have recognized him from the newspapers. In the coverage of his trial, reporters treated him like a celebrity, detailing his black frock coat, his pantaloons, his fancy silk vest, and fine muslin frills. He was a master at swindling people of their money. He'd posed as women's lovers, aristocratic planters, and lawyers. He was a renowned outlaw, the type that white Southerners were coming to lionize in the mid-nineteenth century: Vilified for his deeds but admired for busting out of jails throughout the South, refusing to be caged. As he floated past the clusters of slave shacks on the riverbank, did he reflect on the dark irony of his situation? Dr. Hines had just been convicted of stealing a slave and selling him in Mississippi. Now, after trading in enslaved people, he himself was headed for fourteen years of forced, unpaid labor.

No one in the state had ever served that much time; the Louisiana State Penitentiary had only been open for five years. Before the penitentiary opened, white men in the South were rarely held in bondage. Penitentiaries were a Northern invention. On the few occasions when penitentiaries were put to a public vote in the South, they were rejected. Whites were uncomfortable with the challenges penitentiaries posed to their ideology of racial supremacy. "[U]nder the Penitentiary system, the free-born citizen is made to labor directly under the lash as a slave," railed a North Carolina commentator in 1846 when the state considered opening a penitentiary. "Is this not worse than death?" Some Southerners simply argued that penal reformers' claims that penitentiaries were more humane was false. "How is this pretended humanity to be exercised?" a state representative of Tennessee asked in 1826. "It is by taking a man who by the present law can only be sentenced to have a few stripes, and a few weeks imprisonment, and shutting him up in the penitentiary, there to be kept at hard labour, and to be whipped and driven at the whim and pleasure of his master." Others were skeptical of a system that made crime profitable to the state. "The community should never derive benefit from crimes," one correspondent said during a debate over the penitentiary in North Carolina, "because that makes it directly interested in their continuance and increase."

The penitentiary movement was also strongly associated with the Northern antislavery cause. Leading abolitionists like William Lloyd Garrison and Wendell Phillips viewed penitentiaries as a necessary part of the fight against capital punishment. They believed imprisonment at hard labor was fundamentally different from slavery because convicts could improve themselves and be rewarded with emancipation.

Early advocates of the penitentiary in Louisiana resisted the abolitionist association. In 1806 Governor William Claiborne argued that a penitentiary was necessary to prevent poor whites from fraternizing with slaves in the New Orleans jail. The main purpose of the jail was to hold people until they could be tried and punished, but like jails throughout the South, the one in New Orleans also acted as a holding pen and torture chamber for enslaved people. Planters could bring their unruly human property to be whipped by guards: up to twenty-five lashes for a fee of twelve and a half cents. And if slaveholders were traveling, they could drop their chattel there to be watched and disciplined. If the slaves were fit enough, the city would pay their owners twenty-five cents a day to use their labor in public works. People like Governor Claiborne worried that whites, kept in the same miserable quarters as enslaved African Americans, might naturally sympathize with their plight and become potential recruits for the abolitionist cause. A penitentiary would help prevent that.

Meanwhile, New Orleans was on track to surpass New York as the country's economic capital. The world's cash crop—cotton—flowed through its port, the second largest in the country. The city was also home to the country's largest slave market. As New Orleans boomed amid a sea of poverty, property crime rose, and the jail became overcrowded. Alexis de Tocqueville visited the New Orleans jail in 1831 and described it as a place where men are thrown together "with hogs, in the midst of all odors and nuisances. In locking up criminals, nobody thinks of rendering them better, but only of taming their malice; they are put in chains like ferocious beasts; and instead of being corrected, they are rendered brutal." Governor Andre B. Roman promised Tocqueville he would convince the legislature to appropriate funds for a penitentiary.

Legislators were hard to sway, but they were ultimately convinced after learning that other states were profiting from their penitentiaries. As the New Orleans jail grew more crowded, it became increasingly financially burdensome, so the idea of an institution that could actually generate revenue was irresistible. The penitentiary would be modeled after New York's Auburn penitentiary, functioning as a state-run factory. It would manufacture cheap clothing and shoes for slaves, subsidizing the slavery system while undercutting Northern domination in textile manufacturing. A penitentiary wouldn't be a threat to white supremacy; it would support it.

When Dr. Hines arrived in Baton Rouge on his boat from New Orleans to begin his sentence, the air was fragrant with the white blossoms of magnolia trees and ornate floral gardens. Baton Rouge was a quiet river town, not yet the state capital. Horses clopped down the streets, pulling buggies. Men fished, blacksmiths pounded steel, and artisans made shoes and saddles. The penitentiary, known by locals as The Walls, towered over everything around it. It was like nothing Dr. Hines had ever seen. Armed guards walked on top of twenty-four-foot walls, which were five feet thick at their base. There were some 170 convicts inside.

When Dr. Hines entered, guards shaved his head and gave him a cold bath. An officer put him in a seven-by-three-and-a-half-foot cell, leaving him in pure isolation. In the morning a guard read the prison rules to him. "You must observe silence, unless spoken to by the wardens or officers; you shall not laugh, sing, dance, or make a noise; you shall not look at the visitors, unless by permission of the wardens; you shall not speak to the officers, unless about your work." Dr. Hines's days were controlled by a strict routine: A bell would ring at four in the morning to wake him. At daybreak he and the other convicts would march silently in chains to their work in the prison factory. At mealtimes they ate alone in their cells.

For a twenty-five cent entrance fee, visitors could come and watch the convicts spinning cotton, making cloth, and pounding steel. Citizens could buy prisoner-made products at a discount in a store across the street. Reporters marveled at the new institution: "The first thing that strikes one on entering the gates of the penitentiary is the cleanliness everywhere observable; next, the systematic order that obtains; and next, the silence." But not everything ran smoothly. In 1839 two convicts in the wheelwright and saddlers shop seized pistols from guards and shot at them, eventually taking them hostage until the local militia was called to put down the insurrection. White citizens of Baton Rouge protested too. They didn't have a problem with forced labor per se; the majority of people in Louisiana were enslaved. Their gripe was that the prison retail store was undercutting their businesses. The state eventually capitulated, closing its store, but conditions for the prisoners only deteriorated as a result.

The penitentiary moved away from artisanal-type production, and the state appropriated $10,000 to buy a steam engine to mechanize prison labor. The legislature also ended the eight-hour work day for inmates: Prisoners would be made to labor from sunrise to sunset. They would make shoes for slaves, sold to planters at rock-bottom prices, and they would take the planters' cotton and turn it into cloth.

In 1841, less than a decade into the Louisiana State Penitentiary's existence, the *Charleston Courier* featured it as a model for private slaveholders. No one had developed such a fully rationalized and flexible system of forced captive labor as the penitentiary. Each convict was earning the state fifty-five cents per day (fifteen dollars in 2018). In less than one year the penitentiary had profited more than $5,000 ($135,000 in 2018 dollars) with the production of cotton cloth. The article proposed that slaveholders might use the penitentiary's methods to maximize slave labor—women and children could be kept at work year-round at the cotton looms, at which they would be more productive than they were in the fields.

Yet the penitentiary was on shaky ground. Up till 1837, Louisiana's booming economy seemed bulletproof. The United States was growing more cotton than all other nations combined. The frontier was constantly expanding, opening up more land for cotton, and it seemed impossible to lose money on real estate. New Orleans had the densest concentration of banking capital in the country. Money was pouring in from Northern and European investors. "A man could borrow money from any bank on a cargo or crop of cotton, either actual or potential, on the strength of his or his grandfather's name, or just on his face." The massive scale of investments caused the cost of cotton and number of enslaved people to skyrocket. Between 1830 and 1836 the value of Louisiana imports doubled, as did the cost of slaves. Then, in 1837 the bubble burst. Cotton prices toppled, land values plummeted, banks failed, and the state's economic institutions fell apart. America entered its first great depression. The state needed money, and the penitentiary became a target for belt-tightening. Despite some profitable years, earnings from the penitentiary factory had stopped covering costs, and state control of the institution began to be seen as an "expensive luxury." From 1830 to 1844 the penitentiary had consumed $450,000 of state funds (roughly $12 million in 2018 dollars).

In 1844 the state privatized the penitentiary, leasing it to a company called McHatton, Pratt & Ward. Initially the state didn't take a fee from the company, but the company was responsible for the operations of the prison, including feeding and clothing inmates, and it could use inmate labor toward its own ends. By 1850 Louisiana would require the company to pay the state one quarter of its profits. Seven years later it would raise the fee to half of all profits. The lessees were allowed to use inmates to construct levees along the Mississippi, which were required to keep plantations from becoming swamps. The work was so arduous that many laborers died from overwork or exposure, so many Louisiana planters forbade their slaves from doing it. The lessees were not penalized for prisoners who were injured or who died, so they put them to work.

Most convict labor, however, remained in the penitentiary. Dr. Hines had been in the penitentiary for four years when it was privatized. "These men laid aside all objects of reformation," he wrote in his memoir, "and re-instated the most cruel tyranny, to eke out the dollars and cents of human misery." Dr. Hines remembers one convict, Dr. James Palmer, who was "evidently insane" and serving two years for a stabbing. He was put to work in the factory, "carrying bobbins." One day he collapsed under their weight and was then taken to a cell and beaten with "sticks, paddles, ropes, and kicks." From then on, guards would stand over him and strike him whenever he looked up from his work. He became deranged, laughing randomly and gathering things from the prison yard to store in his cell. One day a guard struck him in the head with an iron rod and killed him. "Like a dumb brute, he was carried to his cell, instead of the hospital, and buried with less ceremony than a favorite dog."

On another occasion Dr. Hines witnessed the punishment of Judge McHenry, a forty-two-year-old white man serving seven years for robbery and horse stealing. For a "trivial offense" McHenry was "stretched upon a ladder and ordered one hundred lashes with the cat," a multi-tailed whip. McHenry passed out after forty-seven lashes and, after whipping him several more times, they poured salt and brandy over his wounds and carried him naked to the hospital. A few days later they strapped him to the ladder again and, to silence his moans and cries, they gagged him and covered his head with a blanket. The lessee said the point was to "afford an example for others."

Louisiana's annual penitentiary reports from the time give no information about prison violence, rehabilitation efforts, or anything about security. Instead they deal almost exclusively with the profitability of the prison factory. The state Board of Control stressed that "the manufacture of cotton goods is the most lucrative employment at which prisoners can be engaged; indeed, experience has taught us that it is the only reliable source of profit, subject to fewer contingencies than any other."

A year after the penitentiary was leased, lawmakers declared privatization a success and authorized a loan of $15,000 to increase industrial capacity. The upgraded penitentiary factory caught the attention of the US military, which in 1846 contracted it to produce some twenty-four thousand horse and mule shoes for the Mexican War effort. But the lessees focused mainly on cotton, buying a ninety-horsepower steam engine and other laborsaving machinery to create a cotton bagging and rope factory that was said to "never have been before attempted." The factory was now capable of producing one thousand yards of bagging per day, but with just 194 inmates, it didn't have enough convicts to meet the scale of production.

The lessees criticized the courts and the legislature for imprisoning people in jails rather than in the penitentiary, thereby depriving them of labor "to which they [were] entitled under the contract." Six years after their complaint, the number of inmates increased more than 50 percent, reaching 300. The state's largest newspaper was hopeful that the penitentiary could pave the way for more manufacturing in the South: "The successful introduction of cotton manufacture into our State Penitentiary, shows how profitable this species of industry may be made at the South . . . the profits of the institution are large."

States throughout the South followed Louisiana's lead, opening penitentiaries of their own, many of which operated textile mills. Some were run by the state, others were privatized, but profit, rather than rehabilitation, became the guiding principle of all. "If a profit of several thousand dollars can be made on the labor of twenty slaves," posited the *Telegraph and Texas Register,* "why may not a similar profit be made on the labor of twenty convicts?" The head of a Texas jail suggested that a penitentiary could be an instrument of Southern industrialization, allowing it to push against the "over-grown monopolies" of the North.

The 1848 bill that provided for the construction of a Texas penitentiary required that it be built near a navigable body of water so as to permit "the transportation of articles made . . . by the convicts to a market." Five years after Texas opened its first penitentiary, it was the state's largest factory. It quickly became the main Southern supplier of textiles west of the Mississippi.

In the midst of the Southern prison boom, Dr. Hines was pardoned by the governor of Louisiana. He had served twelve years. As soon as he got out, he traveled to New Orleans, assumed an aristocratic-sounding name, forged deeds and business documents, persuaded a Texan to give him a $600 loan, and skipped town. He traveled around the country in elite circles, dining once in New York with the city's former attorney general, John Van Buren. He eventually returned to his hometown of Charleston, where, posing as a Louisiana planter, he received a tour of a jail he once inhabited. While walking the streets one day, he was confronted by the Texan he had swindled. Dr. Hines ran, jumping over several walls in an attempt to escape, and was ultimately arrested after being located hiding in a church yard, clutching an ax.

When Dr. Hines was freed from the Louisiana State Penitentiary, the institution was only two decades old. Penitentiaries, in Louisiana and elsewhere, were founded on the premise that they would rehabilitate criminals. Were they working? Penitentiary supporters maintained that regimens of silence and forced labor would turn convicts into productive members of society, but there was no evidence to support this. Louisiana policymakers didn't seem too concerned. By 1857, five years after Hines was released, the penitentiary was making $44,000 in net profit (about $1.2 million, or $4,000 per inmate, in 2018). When the penitentiary made money like this, did it really matter how the inmates turned out?

One day in class we take a personality test called True Colors that's supposed to help CCA decide how to place us. Impulsive "orange" people can be useful in hostage negotiations because they don't waste time deliberating. Rule-oriented "gold" people are chosen for the daily management of inmates. The majority of the staff, Miss Blanchard says, is gold—dutiful, punctual people who value rules. My results show that green is my dominant color (analytical, curious) and orange is my secondary (free and spontaneous). Green is a rare personality type at Winn. Miss Blanchard doesn't offer any examples of how greens can be useful in a prison.

The company that markets the test claims that people who retake it get the same results 94 percent of the time. But Miss Blanchard says that after working here for a while, people often find their colors have shifted. Gold traits tend to become more dominant.

I find this unsettling. I think of personality as something relatively fixed—the constant in our lives when other aspects like career and stability and relationships change. But other studies have shown that personalities can change dramatically when people find themselves in radically new circumstances. In 1971 psychologist Philip Zimbardo conducted the now-famous Stanford Prison Experiment, in which he randomly assigned a set of student to the roles of prisoners and guards in a makeshift basement "prison." The experiment was intended to study how people respond to authority, but it quickly became clear that some of the most profound changes were happening to the guards. When regular people put on their uniforms and reflective sunglasses and were left relatively unrestrained, some became sadistic, forcing the prisoners to sleep on concrete, sing and dance, defecate into buckets, and strip naked. The situation got so extreme that the two-week study was cut short after just six days. When it was over, many of the "guards" were ashamed at what they did, and some "prisoners" were traumatized for years. "We all want to believe in our inner power, our sense of personal agency, to resist external situational forces of the kinds operating in this Stanford Prison Experiment," Zimbardo reflected. "For many, that belief of personal power to resist powerful situational and systemic forces is little more than a reassuring illusion of invulnerability."

The question the study posed still lingers: Are the soldiers of Abu Ghraib, or even Auschwitz guards and ISIS hostage-takers, inherently different from you and me? We take comfort in the notion of an unbridgeable gulf between good and evil, but maybe we should understand, as Zimbardo's work suggested, that evil is incremental—something we are all capable of given the right circumstances.

One day during our third week of training I am assigned to work in the chow hall. My job is to tell the inmates where to sit, filling up one row of tables at a time. I don't understand why we do this. *When you fill up this side, start clearing them out,* he tells me. *They get ten minutes to eat.* CCA policy says they get twenty minutes. We just learned that in class.

Inmates file through the chow line and I point them to their tables. The supervisor and another guard keep an eye on me. One man sits at the table next to the one I directed him to. *Right here*, I say and point to the table. He doesn't move. The supervisor is watching. Hundreds of inmates can see me.

Hey. Move back to this table.

Hell nah, he says. *I ain't movin'.*

Yes, you are, I say. *Move.* He doesn't.

I get the muscle-bound captain, who comes and tells the inmate to move. He begins moving to a third table. He's playing with me. *I told you to move to that table!* I say to him sternly.

Man, the fuck is this? he says and sits at the table I tell him to. My heart is pounding. *Project confidence. Project power.* I stand tall, broaden my shoulders, and stride up and down the floor, making enough eye contact with people to show I'm not intimidated but not holding it long enough to threaten them. I tell inmates to take their hats off as they enter. They listen to me, and a part of me likes that.

For the first time, for just a moment, I forget that I am a journalist. I watch for guys sitting with their friends rather than where they are told to. I scan the room for people sneaking back in line for more food. I tell inmates to get up and leave while they are still eating. I look closely at people as they sit to make sure no one has an extra cup of Kool-Aid.

Hey man, why you gotta be a cop like that? the inmate who I moved asks me. *They don't pay you enough to be no cop.*

What am I doing? Am I here to observe or to police Kool-Aid?

Hey Bauer, go tell that guy to take his hat off, Collinsworth says, pointing to another inmate. *I told him and he didn't listen to me.*

You tell him, I say. *If you're going to start something, you got to finish it.* Another CO looks at me approvingly.

I come back to myself. I stop telling people to take their hats off, and I let them sit at the wrong tables. *Hey Bauer*, Collinsworth says. *You need to start clearing people out*. I don't do anything. They leave when they are ready.

As I walk through the front door of the prison, I am not only wearing my camera watch but I'm also carrying my pen recorder. I've never brought it inside the prison—I've been feeling too nervous that a pen with electronics inside would raise suspicion from the guard running the X-ray machine. But the other day I noticed Collinsworth go through security with a pen that doubles as a flashlight and no one asked him any questions. I decide the risk is worth it—unlike my camera watch, the pen has enough memory to record audio all day long, allowing me to capture everything.

Kenny passes through the scanner ahead of me. My heart speeds up. On the other side, he puts his shoes back on and sits in a chair. As usual I feel like he's watching me, waiting to see what happens. I go through the metal detector and it beeps. "What you got in there?" the guard says, running the wand over my leg. I pull the pen out and show her. She waves me through.

From now on I will keep the pen with me always, hit Record when I come to work, and try not to turn it off until I clock out.

We file into a classroom attached to the armory. Winn's NRA-certified instructor, a cowboy-looking white man, is sitting at the front. He crumples up a paper towel, stuffs it into a Styrofoam cup, shoves a wad of tobacco into his bottom lip, and walks across the front of the classroom. "We are going to be going over our deadly force policies," he says.

Most people in the class are guards taking their mandatory retraining. He admonishes one for not taking her firearms refresher since the time she shot at the warden during a chase. "I didn't know it was the warden!" she says. "I saw a movement—"

"That was Warden Ehrlich?" Cowboy says.

"Uh huh."

"Lord what I thought about Warden Ehrlich back then."

"You wish I shot him?"

"I didn't say that!" The other guards laugh.

"The first thing we always talk about when it comes to firearms training is our use-of-force policy," Cowboy says. "Deadly force. When you can use it and when you cannot. Now y'all have seen the TV lately. Y'all see how controversial the use of deadly force can be and how easily it can be turned around." A few weeks ago, protests erupted after a grand jury declined to charge a police officer for choking Eric Garner to death when he found him selling loose cigarettes in New York. Four months ago Ferguson exploded with riots after a police officer shot Michael Brown to death. "And see, y'all in the line of duty could be put in a position like that and be doing your jobs and get caught up." He spits into his Styrofoam cup.

He passes out the quiz we are meant to take at the end of class to prove that we understand firearm rules. "Alright we got some multiple choice here," Cowboy says. "Instead of goin' through all the bullshit answers I'll just go straight to the correct answer. Imminent danger must be present before using deadly force. True or false?"

"True," everyone says in unison.

"What is imminent danger? Imminent danger is a level of danger that justifies the use of deadly force." The perfect circular definition. He tells us to write it down on the test and says the paper will be kept in our file, so that if we end up using deadly force, we can show that we went through the proper training.

"If you are armed and someone attacks you, do you shoot or not shoot, even if the guy is unarmed?"

People in the class look at one another uncertainly. No one offers an answer.

"Shoot or don't shoot?" he asks again. "Whether it's a free person or a' inmate."

"Shoot," one person says, and the rest join in.

"There you go. Where does the imminent danger come in? I am armed. That's where that imminent danger comes in. That he's attacking me, and he sees my gun, and he knows I'm armed. Why would he attack me? You have to assume that he don't care that you're armed, and he's gonna get your weapon. And you'll be justified in protecting yourself in such a manner, okay?"

If we encounter a situation in which deadly force is called for, "You got to engage that threat. That's legal terminology for shooting him so full of lead he can use his peter for a pencil. We don't shoot single rounds, we shoot multiple rounds."

"There you go!" says a sergeant sitting in the back of the class.

"You fire until the threat goes down. If the threat tries to get up, fire again on him. He's still a threat."

There are several reasons someone might be denied the right to possess a firearm, including having a past felony conviction or having been admitted to a mental institution. "What do y'all think is the most common [reason] for correctional officers?"

"Domestic violence."

Cowboy says that's correct. "Let me tell you how easy that can happen to you: You stop by a bar there one evening drinking a cold beer wit' your buddies and not being doin' nothin' wrong. Then you get home. The wife starts shouting at you about where you been? She snatches up your cell phone and sees a number she ain't never seen before, and it's actually one of your buddies' numbers. Y'all getting around. She's mad at ya'. She stomps yer phone. You push her. She pushes back. She slaps you. You slap her. The neighbors hear all that crap and call the police. Next thing you know the police is there and they're obligated under law, for being called for somethin' like that, to write up a domestic charge.

Wasn't no gun involved, just a slap back and forth. A slapfest! Did you know that once you get a domestic charge even if there's no firearm involved, you just lost your rights, right there, to carry a firearm?"

"It can happen to anybody," the sergeant says.

"It can happen *easily* to anybody," Cowboy says. "It almost happened to me once. So, keep that in mind. Your better half starts raising hell, just get in your vehicle and leave. That'd probably be the safest thing to do, till she simmers down." He pauses. Then, in a menacing voice to his absent wife: "Ohhhh, you ain't talkin' to me like that."

The sergeant: "Haha!"

"A-pushin' and a-shovin' and a-carrying on."

He teaches us how to load a revolver and a shotgun, and the proper way to aim. "I'm gonna go home and use my wife as target practice!" the sergeant says. Some people chuckle. I focus all my energy into keeping my face blank, holding back any indication of disgust.

Out in the back of the prison, not far from where Chase Cortez hopped the fence, there is a barn. Miss Blanchard, another cadet, and I step inside the barn office. Halters, leashes, and horseshoes hang on glossy walls made of pallet boards. Country music is playing on the radio. Three heavyset white COs are inside. They do not like surprise visits. One spits into a garbage can.

The men and their inmate trustees take care of a small herd of horses and three packs of chase dogs. The horses don't do much these days, mostly just range on the pasture out behind the housing units. The COs used to mount them with shotguns and oversee hundreds of inmates who would leave the compound every day to tend the grounds, trimming trees, hoeing, and chopping wood. "Back then when you heard 'Goons are coming!' it meant the field team was coming down," one of the men recalls. The shotguns had to be put to use when, occasionally, an inmate tried to run for it. "You don't actually shoot to kill, you shoot to stop," a longtime staff member told me one day. "Oops! I killed him," she said sarcastically. "I told him to stop! We can always get another inmate though."

Prisoners and officers alike talk nostalgically about the time when the men spent their days working outside, coming back to their dorms drained of restless energy and aggression. CCA's contract requires that Winn inmates are assigned to "productive full-time activity" five days a week, but few are. The work program was cut around the same time that guards were taken out of the towers. Many vocational programs at Winn have been axed. The hobby shops have become storage units; access to the law library is limited. The big recreation yard sits empty most of the time: There aren't enough guards to watch over it.*

"Things ain't like they used to be," Chris, the officer who runs the dog team, tells us. "It's a frickin' mess."

"Can't whoop people's ass like we used to," another officer named Gary, says.

"Yeah you can! We did!" Chris says. He then sulks a little: "You got to know how to do it, I guess."

"You got to know *where* to do it also," Miss Blanchard says referring, I assume, to the areas of the prison the cameras don't see.

"We got one in the infirmary," Chris says. "Haha! Gary did. Gary gassed him and I was whipping him."

"You always using the gas, man," a third officer says.

"I'm like this here," Gary says. "If one causes me to do three or four

---

* When I asked about the lack of classes, recreation, and other activities at Winn, CCA insisted that "these resources and programs were largely available to inmates." It said the work program was cut during contract negotiations with the Louisiana DOC, and it acknowledged some gaps in programming due to "brief periods of staffing vacancies."

hours of paperwork, I'm go' put somethin' on his ass. He's go' get some gas. He's go' get the full load. He ain't go' get just a half a load. The reason why is that I'm go' sit there for two hours doing paperwork. So I ain't go' do just a light use of force on him, I'm go' handle my business with him. Of course, y'all the new class. I'm sitting here telling y'all wrong. Do it the right way. But sometimes, you just can't do it the right way. You have to do what you can to maintain."

With no work program to oversee, the men's job is to take the horses and packs of bloodhounds anywhere across thirteen parishes to help police chase down suspects or prison escapees. They've apprehended armed robbers and murder suspects.

When we step inside the kennel, the bloodhounds bay and howl. Gary kicks the door of one cage and a dog lunges at his foot. "If they can get to him, they're going to bite him," he says. "They deal with 'em pretty bad."

When we go back to the barn office, Christian is there. Gary pulls a binder off the shelf and shows us a photo of a man's face. There is a red hole under his chin and a gash down his throat. "I turn inmates loose every day and go catch 'em," Chris says, rubbing the stubble on his neck. "And that was the result to one of 'em."

"A dog, when he got too close to him, bit him in the throat," Gary says.

"That's an inmate?" I ask.

"Yeah. What we'll do is we'll take a trustee and say we'll put him in them woods right out there." He points out the window. The trustee wears a "bite suit" to protect him from the dogs. "We'll tell him where to go. He might walk back here two miles. We'll tell him what tree to go up, and he goes up a tree." Then, after some time, they "turn the dogs loose."

He holds up the picture of the guy with the throat bite. "This guy here, he got too close to 'em."

"That looks nasty," I say.

"Eh, it wasn't that bad," Christian cuts in. "I took him to the hospital. It wasn't that bad."*

Gary, still holding the picture out on display, says, "He was a character."

"He was a piece of crap," Christian says. "Instigator."

"I gave him his gear and he didn't put it on correctly. That's on him," Chis says with a shrug.

"He got a piece of it," Miss Blanchard says.

On my last day of classroom training, Miss Blanchard tells me to go help out in the chow hall. While I stand and watch inmates eat, a young black guard comes up to me. "What you think about it so far?"

"It's cool," I say. "Interesting."

"You ever worked in something like this?" he asks.

"No."

"Have you ever wanted to be a police officer or anything?" he asks.

"No."

"It's just a job?" He's been working here for four or five months. "I want to be a police officer," he says. "That's why I'm doing this. It's kinda hard because I was smoking marijuana. God I love marijuana. I had to clean my system out for this. It was hard but I did it. I'm proud of myself. I'm trying to get it so I can retire. So I can go back what I used to do."

"What's that?" I ask.

"Smoking marijuana," he says and laughs. "I'm gonna be a cop, get a restaurant opened up, and when I'm about fifty I'm gonna go back to the shit I was doing when I was eighteen, nineteen—smoking weed and

---

* CCA says the inmate's injuries were "minor."

playing video games." He pauses. "There is that moment when you just need a joint," he says wistfully.

"Especially with a job like this," I say. "It's so stressful."

"Yes! Yes! And you can't hit nobody!"

I go back to the classroom to take our final test. It's intimidating. Ninety-two questions ask us about the chain of command, what to do if we are taken hostage, the warning signs of a suicidal inmate, the proper way to put on leg irons, what kind of search to conduct on an inmate before he is transported, the use-of-force policy, and the color designation for various chemical agents. We went through most of these topics so cursorily that I normally would not be able to answer half of them. Miss Blanchard's assistant tells us we can go over the test together to make sure we all get the answers right.

"I bet no one ever doesn't get the job for failing the test," I say.

"No," she says. "We make sure your file looks good."*

---

* CCA says this comment was not consistent with its practices.

| 10 |

abor wasn't the only way Louisiana made money from its prisoners before the Civil War. It also sold inmates' children into slavery. At the time, the vast majority of prisoners in the South were white men. White women were considered too delicate for prison and slaves were generally punished on the plantations. But Louisiana, unlike most Southern states, did imprison enslaved people for "serious" crimes, generally involving acts of rebellion against the slave system. A number of these imprisoned slaves were women. One named Azaline tried to poison someone and was sentenced to life in 1839. The historical record doesn't show who she was trying to kill, but more than likely it was her master. Other enslaved women would get life for the same thing: Susan, Elie, Lucinda. Some were locked up for arson. Others got life for "assaulting a white." When they were sentenced, their masters were compensated $300 by the state for the loss of their property.

The legislature insisted the penitentiary be racially segregated, but the lessees had resisted, saying it was impractical and would reduce productivity. So black women were mixed with male prisoners and subsequently some became pregnant. It's not clear whether their children's fathers were other inmates or prison officials, but this detail was not important to legislators who, in 1848, passed a new law declaring that all children born in the penitentiary of African Americans serving life sentences would become property of the state. The women would raise the kids until the age of ten, at which point the penitentiary would place an ad in the newspaper. Thirty days later, they would be auctioned on the courthouse steps "cash on delivery." The proceeds were used to fund schools for white children.

No recorded details remain about what it was like to raise a child in the prison or to have her taken away forever. We don't know what became of the children or their mothers. The only prison documents remaining are sparse penitentiary logs showing the particulars of the sales. Sometimes the mother herself isn't even noted. What was the mixture of the feeling of devastation over losing one's child along with the twisted hope that life as a slave might be an improvement over life in a prison?

It is possible the mothers got word from time to time of their children after they left, because many of them were purchased by prison officials. Maybe the children's new "owners" assuaged their own guilt by giving mothers updates on the kids. Or maybe not. The first men to buy imprisoned children were heads of the company that ran the penitentiary. Two, Charles and James McHatton, were brothers who co-owned a plantation and 107 enslaved people. At the first auction, Charles McHatton purchased thirteen-year-old Celeste and ten-year-old Fredrick for a total of $696. Three years later he'd purchase ten-year-old Alfred for $580. His brother and co-lessee James McHatton would purchase ten-year-old Joseph, whose mother, Azeline, would have two children sold into slavery from the prison.

William Pike, another lessee of the prison, would buy ten-year-old Clara Williams for $1,025. A penitentiary clerk and a member of the

prison board would each buy a child. Other children would go to builders, farmers, and small-time slaveholders. From the time the prison was
opened in 1835 to its takeover by Union troops in 1862, at least thirty-
three enslaved women were held there, the largest number of any state
penitentiary in the South. At least eleven of their children were sold into
slavery by the state. In total, Louisiana made $7,591 from the enslaved
offspring of incarcerated mothers, roughly $200,000 in 2018 dollars.

When, in January 1861, Louisiana declared its secession from the United
States, the penitentiary became a Confederate war machine. Prison production tripled over its normal levels, producing brogans, carriages,
wagons, wheelbarrows, tents, uniforms, sheet iron, and bullet castings
for war. The penitentiary became the largest single textile producer for
the state, manufacturing most of the state's cloth for soldiers and civil-
ians. Profits skyrocketed.

In April 1862, Union ships fired mortars on Confederate forts in
New Orleans and sailed into the port. Before fleeing, Confederates
torched hundreds of bales of cotton, warehouses full of tobacco and
sugar, and steamboats anchored in the harbor. Clouds of black smoke
rose toward the rainy sky. Throughout the city the "poor broke open
warehouses and carried away baskets, bags, and carts spilling over with
rice, bacon, sugar, molasses, corn, and other foods." What they couldn't
carry, they dumped into the river, burned, or tossed into the gutters,
leaving little behind for their Union enemies. People fled the city by
foot, horse, carriage, and army wagon. The roads and towns leading to
Texas became clogged with tens of thousands of slaves, driven on by
masters who were desperate to save their human property. Three thousand Confederate troops retreated from the port city.

Soon afterward, Union ships sailed up the river and took Baton
Rouge with little resistance. Union General Benjamin Butler

immediately took control of the penitentiary and forced the inmates to make clothes and tents for the Northern army. To keep the factory going, General Butler ordered that all cotton in the area be supplied to the penitentiary.

It didn't take long for the Confederates to return. In August 1862, the citizens of Baton Rouge woke to the fire of musketry and the deep booms of cannons. Confederate troops from Louisiana, Mississippi, Kentucky, Tennessee, and Alabama stormed the city. Families poured out of Baton Rouge, some crying, some praying, in the mounting heat and dust. Some raided plantation storerooms in the countryside, gorging themselves.

A third of the city was left in ruins from the battle. General Butler decided to withdraw from the city and concentrate his Union forces in New Orleans. To prevent the Confederacy from taking advantage of the penitentiary, his men destroyed the machinery and released the prisoners, ordering them to join the Union army. The penitentiary—the state's most important factory—was reduced to a burned brick shell.

Three years later the Civil War ended, and 4 million African Americans were freed. Before the war began, seven of the eight wealthiest states in America were in the South. The American brand of slave labor was the most productive system of nonmechanized cotton production the world had ever known, but now the South's economy was in ruins.

In Louisiana, one pear-shaped civil engineer with muttonchop whiskers wondered whether there was a way he could use the end of slavery to his advantage. His name was Samuel Lawrence James, and he was an innovator. He'd built the first streetcar lines in New Orleans and gained some notoriety leading a brigade of Irish volunteers during the war. He paid attention: The Thirteenth Amendment of the US Constitution abolished slavery for everyone "except as punishment for a crime." The state had leased convicts to businessmen before the war. What was to stop it from doing the same now, when it needed to save money more than ever? Half of Louisiana's population was newly liberated and many of them were now jobless. Surely the prison population would rise. Could he get those convicts to work for him, for free—like slaves? James dreamed big: He could resurrect the penitentiary and turn it into the largest factory in the state. He could build a plantation empire that put the prewar slaveholders to shame. If he could corner the market, he could have more men under his control, still driven by the whip, than anyone in Louisiana ever did during slavery. The whole prison system could be run as a business. And it would all be for him.

During my last days off before Christmas, I sit by the Cane River, which flows through Natchitoches. Unlike run-down Winnfield, the town I live in is the picture of Southern quaintness: Families lick ice cream cones while window-shopping on brick-paved Front Street. Local tourists visit Kaffie-Frederick General Merchantile, "the oldest general store in Louisiana." Men in hunting camo scoot from their trucks to Mama's, a bar that serves fried oysters and deep-fried alligator tail. Front Street flanks the Cane River, and through the month of December, light displays of crosses and nutcrackers and trains illuminate the opposite bank after dark. Nearly everyone I meet in Natchitoches tells me two things about the town: It was the setting for the film *Steel Magnolias*, and in 2013, Yahoo.com named it as having the third-best Christmas light display in the country after Rockefeller Center in New York and Walt Disney World in Florida.

The light display is, frankly, a little underwhelming, but on my days off I sit on a bench and stare at the water. Occasionally a pontoon meanders downriver with a plastic Santa or inflatable reindeer on it. Small fishing boats and rafts carry men dangling lines in the water in hopes of catching a white perch or catfish. They float through town, into the quieter stretches of the river where plantation houses stand above the cattails. These plantations were once at the heart of the local economy, sending bales of cotton downstream to New Orleans. Now, in 2014, mostly white local tourists visit them to marvel at the finer points of antebellum architecture. In the summer, one plantation hosts a music festival and couples get married under stately oak trees, out of view of the sheds where enslaved people once slept.

My fellow cadets have been talking up the Christmas parade, the biggest event of the year for this part of the state. For a day, the town of twenty thousand people grows to five times its size. As a contribution to the community, CCA sends the SORT team and a group of prisoners to help with cleanup. Inmates pick candy wrappers and Mardi Gras beads off the ground while people drink beer and eat turkey legs and meat pies. When I head downtown that day, the air smells faintly of barbecue from families grilling in their front yards and in the beds of pickup trucks. Some turn their lawns into parking lots, charging visitors five dollars for a spot. The parade is an endless procession of school dance troupes, Santas, elves, and people throwing candy from Corvettes and semi trucks.

There's Abe Lincoln! a black girl shouts, pointing at a white man in a top hat who is rolling by on a float.

I'm not Abe Lincoln! he replies, sounding insulted. A banner beside him reads, Sons of Confederate Veterans. Three rows of white men and boys walk ahead of the float, dressed in gray Confederate military uniforms. Some carry swords over their shoulders. A few carry the rebel flag. In unison the group stops, aims its muskets into the air, and fires.

Why don't y'all wear y'all white hoods next time? a black man in front of me shouts at the group. The parade rolls on, puffs of gun smoke rising into the air every few minutes.

. . .

During Christmas week I am stationed in the prison's mail room with a couple of other cadets to process the deluge of holiday letters. The person in charge, Miss Roberts, is a matronly black woman who dresses in a peacoat. She demonstrates our task: Slice the top of each envelope, cut the back off and throw it in the trash, cut the postage off the front, staple what remains to the letter, and stamp it: Inspected. The activity feels like knitting, the perfect monotony for idle conversation.

Miss Roberts tells us how much she loves Christmastime. She watches Hallmark movies and listens to the Chipmunk's Christmas album on her way to work. It brings tears to her eyes.

"Did you get your hundred dollars?" Miss Roberts asks a cadet.

"Ma'am?"

"From the Christmas party. They drew your name!" Almost no one went to the company party.

"Really? Well aren't I lucky. Today *is* a good day."

"I'm still waiting on my fifty dollars," Miss Roberts says. "The other day I found some drugs in someone's legal mail. They are supposed to give us fifty dollars when we find drugs. I ain't got it yet. They supposed to give it to me, but getting it is another story."

Miss Roberts teaches us the kinds of things to look for in the letters by mentioning them as they arise. As she flips through a stack of photos, she pulls one out. No pictures should have anyone making a hand sign, "not even a peace sign," she says. She opens a letter with several pages of colorful drawings from a child. "Now, see like this one, it's not allowed because they're not allowed to get anything that's crayon." I presume this is for the same reason we remove stamps; crayon could be a vehicle for drugs. There are so many letters from children—little hands outlined, little stockings glued to the inside of cards—that we rip out and throw in the trash.

One reads:

> *I love you and miss you so much daddy, but we are doing*
> *good. Rick Jr. is bad now. He gets into everything. I have not*
> *forgot you daddy. I love you.*

Around the mail room there are bulletins posted of things to look out for: an anti-imperialist newsletter called *Under Lock and Key*, an issue of *Forbes* that comes with a miniature wireless internet router, and a CD from a Chicano gangster rapper with a track titled, "Death on a CO." I find a list of books and periodicals not allowed inside Louisiana prisons. It includes *Fifty Shades of Grey*; *Lady Gaga Extreme Style*; *Surrealism and the Occult*; *Tai Chi Fa Jin: Advanced Techniques for Discharging Chi Energy*; *The Complete Book of Zen*; *Socialism vs Anarchism: A Debate*; and *Native American Crafts & Skills*. On Miss Roberts's desk is a confiscated book: Robert Greene's *48 Laws of Power*. Other than holy books, this is the most common text I see in inmates' lockers, usually tattered and hidden under piles of clothes. She says this book is banned because it's considered "mind-bending material," though she did enjoy it herself. Donald Trump and Bill Gates did, too, so much that they coauthored *The 48 Laws of Power and Their Impact on My Life*. There are also banned books on the list about black history and culture, like *Huey: Spirit of the Panther*, *Faces of Africa*, and *Message to the Blackman in America* by Elijah Muhammad, and an anthology of news articles called *100 Years of Lynchings*.

Cracking down on black political consciousness in prison is common nationwide. In Texas, Adolf Hitler's *Mein Kampf* and David Duke's *My Awakening* are allowed, but books by Sojourner Truth, Harriet Beecher Stowe, Langston Hughes, and Richard Wright are banned. Alabama banned Douglas Blackmon's Pulitzer Prize–winning *Slavery by Another Name: The Re-Enslavement of Black Americans from the Civil War to World War II*, which chronicles the convict lease system in

Alabama. According to a lawsuit, a prison official told an inmate the book was "too incendiary" and deemed it a "security threat." In California, men are kept in long-term solitary confinement for simply having books in their cells about the Black Panthers. I reported on one California inmate who had spent four years in solitary for possessing a news article written by another inmate, having a cup in his cell with an image of a dragon on it, and keeping a notebook that contained what investigators called "Afrocentric ideology": references to Nat Turner, the nine Scottsboro Boys, the number of blacks executed between 1930 and 1969, and quotes from figures like W. E. B. Du Bois and Malcolm X. California prison officials claimed such material was proof of affiliation with a prison gang. In one case prison officials justified the long-term solitary of an inmate in part because he possessed a pamphlet titled The Black People's Prison Survival Guide, which advised inmates to read books, keep a dictionary handy, practice yoga, avoid watching too much television, and stay away from "leaders of gangs."

Miss Roberts makes a face at the letter she holds in her hand. "That's the craziest girl I ever seen," she says. She is familiar with many of the correspondents from reading the intimate details of their lives. "She's got his whole name tattooed across her back all the way down to her hip bone. When his ass gets out—*whenever* he gets out, he's got thirty or forty years—*if* he ever gets out, he ain't going to her. But he's gonna have a bankroll when he gets out of here. She sends him all that money. Every once in a while he'll send something back to her. *Every once in a while.*

"She has his name tattooed all the way down her arm and all the way across her chest."

"That's love right there," Reynolds says.

"That's foolishness," Miss Roberts says. "That ain't love."

As I pull each sheet of paper out of its envelope, I feel like a voyeur, but the letters draw me in. One woman wrote her husband of twenty-five years, who was soon to be released.

What woman want to feel like she is dirt under your fingernails. . . . You know beyond a shadow of a doubt I am your dirt. But you know I love you. . . . You should be saying life is short. I have missed all this time. I want to love the family I have left. I want to love my wife. . . . I need to be a better man to her. I need to show her what she mean to me but you—you show me an angry and bitter little boy. . . .

Pat, Jay, and Beatrice said they are okay with you coming back with the understanding you will not be hitting or slapping me.* They said you are family so they welcome you back. But I am to be treated with love and kindness. . . . I am going to give you six months to get it together. Find out what you really want.

I am surprised by how many of the letters are from former inmates with lovers still at Winn. I read one from a recently released inmate to his lover:

Hope everything is going well with you. Very deeply in love with you. Well I am still in the same place. Sorry I missed your call—trying to get me a free government phone. They give you 500 minutes free. I thought the people in prison was crazy. There are a lot of homeless people just as crazy. Almost been in 20 fights because of the crazy nuts here. . . . There are a couple homosexual girls I talk to, but I mostly stick to myself. . . . If I could do construction work I could have a job today. They got all kinds of construction work going on here. . . . But I don't know how to drive a fork lift. And my health prevents me from standing on my legs for long.

---

* Names used in the letters have been changed to protect privacy.

I won't be able to spend x-mass with my family either. Baby my heart is broken and I am so unhappy. I never thought I would be homeless. I always had a great fear of being homeless. I think I was born to experience everything life has to offer. Some of it I wish that I could have missed. My dad had heavy equipment. I should have learned to drive it and work on it. Then at least I could have had some skills to use when I got older. Those skills would come in handy now. [T]here a lots of jobs driving an 18 wheeler. But I don't have a CDL and my DUIs keep me from that. And even if I did find a job and had to work nights or work the evening shift, then I wouldn't have anywhere to sleep because the shelter won't let you in to sleep after hours. In order to get my bed every night I have to check in before 4pm. After that you lose your bed so the program is designed to keep you homeless. It don't make sense.

I want to go to apply for SSI and disability. That could take up to 4 months to get. Well baby I will be spending x-mass here at the shelter. . . . It will be hard and unhappy not to spend x-mass with you.

I bet that this is a sad letter. I wish that I had good news. This will be a short letter because I don't have a lot of paper left.

Merry Christmas baby. Very deeply in love with you.

Another is from Angola prison:

Where did we go wrong? There were the vows we made. "Blood in, Blood Out." So what happen? What's the sudden change of mind? Love doesn't just fade away that easily Fat Man unless you never loved me in the beginning. Bae, what do you expect me to do without you in my world? Just forget about you?

Well, I'm not! I refuse to give up without a fight we are for life I have nothing if I don't have you. Bae, I truly love you and I can love you better than any of them other hoes you so called left me for. Our anniversary is in 13 more days on Christmas and we could have been married for 2 years why can't you see that I want this to work between us?

Bae, [remember] the jeans, the first pair of Jordans you ever got me and I ever owned in my life, the chain that you bought for my B-day, that says "My Fat Man 4 eva," the picture frame that says "Run DMC," the engagement ring you proposed to me with on the yard, most importantly the tattoo on my left tittie close to my heart that won't never get covered up as long as I have a breath in my body and I'm about to get your name again on my ass cheek. I'd gonna say property of Dyonte G. Bates 4 Life or Fuck Me Dyonte G. Bates 4 Life which ever you want.

A corrections counselor from Cypress walks into the mailroom. DOC officers showed up by surprise and shook down the whole prison with dogs. He says the inmates are pissed. "There's going to be a lot of ARPs"—Administrative Remedy Procedures, or inmate grievances—" for lost property claims tomorrow."

"De-nied!" Miss Roberts says, and laughs.

"De-nied!" he repeats. They both laugh.

"They all go' be that same thing," Miss Roberts says. "De-nied. Ah ha!" The man leaves.

"Oh my goodness, y'all, I feel like taking a nap," Miss Roberts says. "I didn't get any sleep last night. I got this dog. She was just in a foul mood last night."

"God made dogs just for people, boy," Reynolds says.

"I think he did," Miss Roberts says. She tells us about a dog she once had. "I go ar ar and she goes ar ar. We were just having a conversation then all of a sudden I go aaaaoooo and she goes aaaaaaoooo. Yes indeed. That was my baby."

The front of one card reads, "Although your situation may seem impossible . . ." and continues on the inside of the card, "through Christ, all things are Him-possible!" It contains a letter from the wife of an inmate:

> *Here I am once again w/ thoughts of you. I hate it here*
> *everything reminds me of you. I miss u dammit! It's weird this*
> *connection we have its as if I carry you in my soul. It terrifies*
> *me the thought of ever losing you. I pray you haven't replaced*
> *me. I know I haven't been the most supporting but baby seriously*
> *you don't know the hell I've been through since we got torn apart*
> *And I guess my family got fed up w/ seeing me kill myself slowly*
> *I attempted twice 90 phenobarb 2 roxy 3 subs. I lived. 2nd after*
> *I hung up w/ you 60 Doxepin 90 propananol I lived wtf? God*
> *has a sense of humor i don't have anyone but u, u see no one*
> *cares whether I live die hurt am hungry, well, or safe. . . . So*
> *I've been alone left to struggle to survive on my income in and*
> *out mental wards and running from the pain of you bein*
> *there . . .*
>   *Your my everything always will be*
>
>   *Love your wife.*

This note, with its list of pills, haunts me as I go through my normal after-work routine. First I upload the files from my pen recorder and wristwatch camera onto my laptop. I try to make sense of the scrib-blings in my notebook, in which I keep track of each audio file I create by sliding the pen's clip up and down throughout the day. I shower, I eat, and I sit in front of my laptop and make some notes. Then I sit in front of the camera that is set up at my kitchen table and talk about the day. What if she commits suicide?

I want to talk to someone other than myself, but no one back home really understands and no one here knows who I really am. I don't hang out with the other cadets after work; it feels wrong to enter their personal lives when they don't know I'm writing about them. I need to get out of my head, so I pull out my phone and text the one person in Natchitoches I know—Anthony.

I met Anthony playing pool at the only club in town, a corrugated steel shed called the Body. He told me he was an Afghan war veteran and showed me a gunshot wound on his white chest. His eyes were hardened and a little wild. The bill of his hat was tightly curved; a generic-looking tribal tattoo was wrapped around his forearm. We drank shots out of little plastic salsa cups and played pool. Even though he called Northerners "Yankees," he didn't seem to mind that I was from there. When I told him I worked at Winn, he told me he'd been a prisoner there. *You met Billy Bob yet?* he asked me. *He's in the SORT team. Don't fuck with him. He was a marine. Ask him about the fifty caliber wound in his calf.*

He texts me back and tells me to come out to his trailer park. They are going to have a party.

Anthony's trailer is cramped and rundown. Socks hang from a light fixture to dry. Plastic takeaway cups are strewn around. A table is stacked with large boxes of fireworks. Inside, I greet Matt, a lanky white truck driver. I meet Anthony's little brother, two sisters, a nephew, and a friend who introduces himself as the "token black guy." Anthony doesn't have a job besides doing maintenance in the trailer park. He and his mom also own two other trailers. "That's what keeps us out of jail," he says. Anthony asks if I play beer pong. I told him I've never played. They all look at me curiously.

"You don't know how to play beer pong?" a white man named Bubba says.

"No, I'm not from here."

"They don't play beer pong in California?" Bubba says. "Never goin' there!"

"They can't have fireworks there either," Anthony informs him.

"Huh?! Fuckin' stupid! They're missin' out on everything." I offer them the pale ales I bought at the gas station. They all decline and stick to Bud Light. A debate ensues about beer pong house rules. Are we playing where, if the ball bounces off several cups and then goes in one, the opponent has to drink every cup the ball touched? Are we playing where, when a team is down to four cups, it gets to rerack them? Are we playing Death Cup where, if someone is holding a cup in his hand and another team lands a ball in it, that team automatically wins?

We toss a Ping-Pong ball into plastic cups of beer. Did the woman who wrote that letter really take all those pills, or was she lying to get a reaction from her boyfriend in prison? How desperate would someone have to be to cry for help from someone who is locked up and can do nothing? I struggle constantly to understand what my role should be. How much should I engage? Is it wrong for me to be here, in this trailer park and in the prison, with people who don't know I'm a reporter or that they might someday show up in the page of a book? My editors and I agreed that I should do my job as a prison guard as best I can. But we never talked about what to me is a bigger ethical concern: Is it okay for me to participate in the prison system? I will soon be locking men up, day in, day out. Some of them have been incarcerated since they were children. Some are in prison for using drugs; others are poor people who committed crimes to stay afloat. I've been telling myself that to really investigate, we sometimes have to get our hands dirty. But what happens if I see a guard beating someone? Do I try to stop him, or do I film it? What if the woman who wrote the letter actually was serious and I just ignored it? What if she killed herself?

Bubba and I lose the game and have to drink six warm cups of Bud Light. He downs his and walks away. I pour mine on the ground and find Anthony, who is staring at the table full of fireworks. He and Matt are scheming. "We're gettin' the black guy," Matt tells me and hands me a bottle rocket. "You go left and I go right." I don't follow. The two chase the black man around and shoot bottle rockets at him.

"You know, Shane, the military is fucking fun dude," Matt says. He, like Anthony, is a veteran. He tells Anthony to grab him another beer and strips down to his underwear. Nearby, a pit bull is leaping into the air as it tries to bite the fire spraying from a sparkler that someone is holding just above its reach. Anthony strips too. A woman asks what they are doing. "Military," Matt says. "It's the only way to do it." He grabs a large firework. It's the kind you'd normally stand on the ground, light, and get back before it explodes, but he holds it against his leg and braces himself. Anthony lights it—"Fire in the hole son!"—then huddles behind Matt's back. Boom!

Anthony, excited, grabs another. "Light this one nigga!" Boom!

"Shane, you want to go a round?"

"Nah, I'm good."

"Yeah Shane," Matt says. "The military is fucking fun dude."

Anthony and Matt become drunk and continue pretending that they are at war. When the fireworks run out, Matt says he wishes the fireworks shop was still open. He says he would spend the $300 he has. No, he would get a payday advance and buy even more.

During the weekend I decide I need to tell Miss Roberts about the suicide letter, but when I return for work, I sit in the parking lot and have a hard time summoning the courage. What if she tells someone else? What if word gets out that I'm soft, not cut out for this work?

After I pass through the scanner, I see her. "Hey Miss Roberts?" I say, walking up behind her.

"Yes," she says sweetly.

"I wanted to check with you about something. I meant to do it on Friday, but uh . . ." She stops and gives me her full attention, looking me in the eyes. "When we had a class by the mental health director, she told us to report if there was any kind of suicidal—"

She cuts me off, waving her hand dismissively, and begins walking away.

"No, but it was like a letter thing—"

"Yeah don't even worry about that," she says, still walking toward her door.

"Really?"

"Mmmhmmm. That's if you see something going on down there," she says, pointing toward the units. "Yeah don't worry about it. Alright." She enters the mail room.

Today is my first of three days of on-the-job training, the final step before becoming a full-fledged CO. The captain tells an officer to take me to Elm unit. We move slowly down the walk. "One word of advice I would give you is never take this job home with you," he says. He spits some tobacco through the fence. "Leave it at the front gate. If you don't drink, this job will drive you to drinking." Research shows that, on average, about one third of prison guards suffer from post-traumatic stress disorder, more than soldiers returning from Iraq and Afghanistan. Suicide hotline posters are taped up for staff around the prison—on average, COs commit suicide two and a half times more than the population at large, revealed a study that was conducted on corrections officers and law enforcement working in Florida. Corrections officers also have shorter life spans. Those who don't kill themselves die about a decade earlier than most.

The walk is eerily quiet. Crows caw, fog hangs low over the basketball courts. The prison is locked down. Programs have been canceled. With the exception of kitchen workers, none of the inmates can leave their dorms. Usually lockdowns occur when there are major disturbances, but today, with some officers out for the holidays, guards say there just aren't enough people to run the prison. The unit manager tells me to shadow one of the two floor officers, a burly white US Marine veteran. As we walk the floor an inmate asks him what the lockdown is about. "You know half of the fucking people don't want to work here," the marine tells him. "We so short-staffed and shit, so most of the gates ain't got officers." * He sighs dramatically.

"It's messed up," the prisoner says.

"Man, it's so fucked up it's pitiful," the marine replies. "The first thing the warden asked me [was] what would boost morale around here. The first two words out of my mouth: pay raise." He takes a gulp of coffee from his travel mug.

"They *do* need to give y'all a pay raise," the prisoner says.

"When gas is damn near four dollars a gallon, what the fuck is nine dollars an hour?" the marine says.

"That's half yo' check fillin' up your gas!"

We walk slowly around the unit. He tells me he served in Africa, the Caribbean, and Eastern Europe. In 1996 he left the US Marines and joined as a reservist. He got a job in the oil fields and worked there till they closed in 2003. Then he got a job at Winn. "I learned the old-school way," he says. He left the prison when the US National Guard

---

* CCA says Winn was never put on lockdown due to staffing shortages and that it has "no knowledge" of gates going unmanned at Winn.

was called to fight in Iraq. Now he's back. Back when they could hit prisoners, he says, things were a lot easier. He points to a security camera. "They get on your nerves. I used to drag motherfuckers to the tier. You can't do that now."

An inmate, who the marine calls the "unit politician," demands an Administrative Remedy Procedure form. He wants to file a grievance about the lockdown—why are inmates being punished for the prison's mismanagement?

"What happens with those ARPs?" I ask him.

"If they feel their rights have been violated in some way, they are allowed to file a grievance," he says. If the captain rejects it, they can appeal to the warden. If the warden rejects it, they can appeal to Department of Corrections. "It'll take about a year. It goes through here pretty quick, but once it gets to DOC down in Baton Rouge, they throw it over in a pile. I've been to DOC headquarters. I know what them sonsabitches do down there: nothin'."*

I do a couple of laps around the unit floor, and then see the marine leaning against the threshold of an open tier door, chatting with a prisoner. They are both laughing.

I walk over to them. "This your first day?" one of the prisoners asks me, leaning up against the bars.

"Yeah."

"Welcome to CCA boy. You seen what the sign say when you first come in the gate?"

"Knowledge is perfection?" the marine says. "Perfection *bull*shit." He and the two inmates laugh.

"No, not that sign," the inmate says. "It says 'the CCA way.' Know

---

* Miss Lawson, the assistant chief of security, later told me that during the fifteen years she worked at Winn, she saw only one grievance result in consequences for staff.

what that is?" he asks me. There is a pause. "Whatever you make it, my boy."

The marine titters. "Some of them down here are good," he says. "I will say dat. Some of 'em are jackasses. Some of 'em just flat out ain't worth a fuck."

"Just know at the end of the day, how y'all conduct y'all selves determines how we conduct ourselves," the prisoner says, his head cocked back, fingering the stubble under his bottom lip. "You come wit' a shit attitude, we go' have a shit attitude."

"I have three rules and they know it," the marine says, leaning his weight against his arm as he grips the bars. "No fightin'. No fuckin'. No jackin' off. But! What they do after the lights are out—I don't give a fuck 'cuz I'm at the house."

The next day I'm stationed in Ash, a general population unit. The unit manager is a black woman named Miss Price, who is so large she has trouble walking. She is brought in every morning in a wheelchair pushed by an inmate. Inmates call her "the Dragon." It's unclear whether her jowls, her roar, or her stern reputation earned her that nickname. Prisoners relate to her like an overbearing mother—afraid to anger her and eager to win her affection. She's worked here since the prison opened twenty-four years ago, and one CO says that in her younger days, she was known to break up fights without backup. Another CO says that last week an inmate "whipped his thing out and was playing with himself right in front of her. She got out of her wheelchair, grabbed him by the neck, threw him up against the wall. She said, 'Don't you ever fucking do that to me again!'"

In the middle of the morning, Miss Price tells us to shake down the common areas. I follow one of the two COs into a tier and we do perfunctory searches of the TV rooms and tables, feeling under the ledges, flipping through a few books. I bend over and feel around under a water fountain. My hand lands on something loose. I get on my knees to look. It's a smartphone. I don't know what to do—do I take it or do I leave it? My job, of course, is to take it, but as a former prisoner, I suddenly feel like the worst kind of snitch. It is one thing to play the role of a turnkey, but how can anyone who has been locked up deliberately take from someone the little bit of freedom he has managed to carve out for himself—his ability to contact the outside world unsurveilled, to access the internet, to slip away from the totalitarian control of prison? Sure, the inmate might use it to help bring drugs into the prison, but do I care? When I was locked up, I hoarded antianxiety pills in hopes of an occasional night of blissful detachment, and I would have died for a joint to smoke or anything to take me away from that place.

But the question of whether or not to take the phone is also a practical one. I know by now that being a guard is only partially about enforcing the rules. Mostly it's about learning how to get through every day safely, which requires that decisions like these are weighed carefully. A prisoner is watching me. If I leave the phone, everyone on the tier will know. I will win inmates' respect. But if I take it, I will show my superiors I am doing my job. I will alleviate some of the suspicion they have of every new hire. "Those ones who gets along with 'em—those are the ones I really have to watch," SORT commander Tucker told us. "There is five of y'all. Two and a half are gonna be dirty." If I take the phone, they will assume I'm not selling them. If they assume I'm not bringing in contraband, they will pay less attention to me. If they pay less attention, I won't blow my cover.

I take the phone.

Miss Price is thrilled. The COs couldn't care less. The shift supervisor calls the unit to congratulate me. I loathe myself. When I do count later, each inmate on that tier stares at me with the meanest look. Some step toward me threateningly as I pass.

. . .

Later, at a bar near my apartment, I see a man in a CCA jacket and ask him if he works at Winn. "Used to," he says.

"I just started there," I say.

He smiles. "Let me tell you this: You ain't go' like it. When you start working those twelve hour shifts, you will see." He takes a drag from his cigarette. "The job is way too fucking dangerous." I tell him about the phone. "Oh, they won't forget your face," he says. "I just want you to know you made a lot of enemies. If you work in Ash, you gonna have a big-ass problem because now they go' know, he's gonna be the guy who busts us all the time."

He racks the balls on the pool table and tells me about a nurse who gave a penicillin shot to an inmate who was allergic to the medicine and died. The prisoner's friends thought the nurse did it intentionally. "When he came down the walk, they beat the shit out of him. They had to airlift him out of there."* He breaks and sinks a stripe.

When I come in for my third and final day of on-the-job training, I am shepherded into the conference room, where guards are brooding over their coffee and Monster energy drinks. Shortly after Cortez escaped, the warden decreed that the security staff should meet at the beginning of every shift. Assistant Warden Parker stands in the front of the room, dressed in khaki cargo pants and a windbreaker. "If y'all don't mind, if you can open your eyes," he says to a few people in the middle row. "Some of y'all are lookin' at me with your eyes closed." He leans his elbow against the podium, the picture of a guy-next-door, we're-in-this-together type of boss. "It's a good thing we are having these

---

* CCA says it has no knowledge of this incident.

meetings, because I guarantee you these inmates are meeting in their little organizations so that they can team up against us," he says.

"That's what this is really, really, really all about. The inmate population for a period of time here, for whatever reason, have actually had the opportunity to keep us running and constantly chasing our tail. But we're doing good. Have y'all noticed the three wardens from DOC? We got these three wardens from DOC coming in giving us wonderful insight on what we are doing wrong." He sounds a little hurt. The Department of Corrections, which has ultimate authority over prisons in the state, has been taking a closer look at Winn's day-to-day operations since Cortez escaped.* Guards also tell me there was a rash of stabbings over the summer that CCA didn't report to the DOC like it was supposed to.† The DOC wardens have appeared out of nowhere, watching over COs as they work, asking them questions. The newer guards fret about losing their jobs. Old-timers shrug it off—they say they've seen Winn weather tough times before.

"What they are failing to see is how far we've come," Parker says. Do we have things we need to improve on? We have *a lot* of things we need to improve on, but the wheels are getting back on the track here at Winn. We've come a long way. I'm not gonna say we're gonna stop every fight and suddenly there's gonna be rainbows over this place and puppy dogs and butterflies are gonna be everywhere. I'm not saying that.

"What is Parker's game plan for today? I want us to start focusing on this homemade clothing." He says we, the officers, need to begin confiscating altered uniforms and any hat that looks too much like a "free person's hat."

---

* According to DOC documents I later obtained, the department had just written to CCA about "contract compliance" and areas where Winn's "basic correctional practices" needed improvement.
† The company's spokesman says it reported all assaults.

"Bagging and sagging. If you got a guy who continues to bag those little jeans they buy? If they want to bag and sag even though they have a belt, obviously they don't fit. If they don't fit"—he snaps his fingers—"confiscate 'em. Let's start cleaning up some of this riffraff clothing.

"I plan on being the lord of the do-rags here this year. This is gonna be my whole thing—getting do-rags off the yard. But I can't be the only person out there confiscating this stuff." I wonder how this is going to cut down on violence or prevent escapes.

"Anybody got anything else? Come on, this is it! We got coffee in this room for a reason! To wake us up and help us get going! You guys like that coffee?" The coffee is a new perk. It tastes like shit.

I am sent to Ash where Miss Price gives me a key. She says nothing of it and nor do I, but we both understand the significance of the gesture: As a trainee, I am not meant to hold a key. It is six inches long, weighty, smooth, and brass. When it's time for inmates to go out for morning chow, I slide it into a lock and turn it to the left. The bolt releases with a satisfying report. I stand at the gate while inmates pass, gripping the key in my pocket, feeling its rounded teeth press into my palm. After the last prisoner leaves, I grip a bar on the door and yank it along its track until it hammers closed. I walk, swinging the key in circles on the end of a thin chain.

| 12 |

A few years after the Civil War ended, Samuel Lawrence James bought a plantation on a sleepy bend of the Mississippi river in West Feliciana Parish. It was known as Angola, named for the country of origin of many of the people who were once enslaved there. Before the war, it produced thirty-one hundred bales of cotton a year, an amount few Southern plantations could rival. For most planters, those days seemed to be over. Without slaves, it was impossible to reach those levels of production.

But James was optimistic. Slavery may have been gone, but something like it was already beginning to come back in other states. While antebellum convicts were mostly white, seven out of ten prisoners were now black. In Mississippi, "Cotton King" Edmund Richardson convinced the state to lease him its convicts. He wanted to rebuild the cotton empire he'd lost during the war and, with its penitentiary burned to ashes, the state needed somewhere to send its prisoners. The state agreed to pay him $18,000 per year for their maintenance, and he could keep the profits derived from their labor. With the help of convict labor, he would become the most powerful cotton planter in the world, producing more than twelve thousand bales on fifty plantations per year. Georgia, whose penitentiary had been destroyed by General Sherman, was leasing its convicts to a railroad builder. Alabama had leased its convicts to a dummy firm that sublet them for forced labor in mines and railroad construction camps throughout the state.

There was no reason Louisiana couldn't take the same path. African Americans were flooding the penitentiary system, mostly on larceny convictions. In 1868 the state had appropriated three times the money to run the penitentiary as it had the previous year. It was the perfect time to make a deal, but someone beat James to it. A company called Huger and Jones won a lease for all of the state prisoners. Barely had the ink dried on the contract before James bought them out for a staggering $100,000 (about $1.7 million in 2018 dollars). James worked out a twenty-one year lease with the state, in which he would pay $5,000 the first year, $6,000 the second, and so on up to $25,000 for the twenty-first year in exchange for the use of all Louisiana convicts. All profits earned would be his. He immediately purchased hundreds of thousands of dollars of machinery to turn the state penitentiary into a three-story factory. One newspaper called it "the heaviest lot of machinery ever brought in the state." The prison became capable of producing 10,000 yards of cotton cloth, 350 molasses barrels, and 50,000 bricks per day. It would also produce 6,000 pairs of shoes per week with the "most complete shoe machinery ever set up south of Ohio." The factory was so large that the Daily Advocate argued it would stimulate Louisiana's economy by increasing demand for cotton, wool, lumber, and other raw materials.

James's industrial project was so ambitious that he didn't have enough prisoners to fill the demand. To keep hands operating the prison factory's two thousand spindles day and night, he imported 150 Chinese laborers in 1871. Brought by steamer from Alabama, they were likely the first Chinese to settle in Baton Rouge. They worked in the prison every night until six in the morning, earning $22 a month in gold (about $425 in 2018 dollars), roughly the equivalent of the cost of maintaining his convicts.

In 1873 a joint committee of senators and representatives inspected the Louisiana State Penitentiary and found it nearly deserted. "The looms that used to be worked all day and all night, are now silent as the tomb." The warden and the lessees were not at the prison. "It is pretty difficult to find out who are the lessees or, indeed, whether or not there are any," the inspectors wrote in their report. Where were the convicts? Almost as soon as James's prison factory was running, he'd abandoned it. He'd discovered that he could make a lot more money subcontracting his prisoners to labor camps where they were made to work on levees and railroads. A convict doing levee and railroad work cost one-twentieth that of a wage worker.

Some in Louisiana's Reconstruction legislature tried to reign in James. In 1875 it forbade convict labor from being used outside prison walls—senators and representatives were concerned it would deprive their constituents of jobs—but James disregarded the ban and kept his labor camps going. A Baton Rouge district attorney sued James for non-payment of his lease. James ignored him and made no payment for the next six years. He had become untouchable.

He wasn't the only one. Throughout the South, states were leasing to powerful politicians, Northern corporations, mining companies, and planters, and they imposed little or no restrictions on what type of work businesses could force prisoners to do or how many hours they could work them. In 1872 Mississippi transferred its lease to Nathan Bedford Forrest, first Grand Wizard of the Ku Klux Klan, who also leased convicts in Alabama and Tennessee. Georgia gave leases to seven contractors. The winners included Joseph E. Brown, the chief justice of the Georgia Supreme Court, and General John Brown Gordon, a former US senator who founded the state's chapter of the KKK. The two would work convicts in the mines for their new company, Dade Coal, and by 1880, Brown became a millionaire. Another lessee was Colonel James Monroe Smith, a Georgia legislator who "ran perhaps the largest family owned plantation in the postbellum South." Smith would lease around four hundred convicts a year, working most on his plantation and subleasing the rest to sawmills, railroad camps, and turpentine farms. Smith was so politically connected, and had financed so many of the buildings in his county, that he would joke to county officials, "You had better send me some more niggers or I will come down and take the courthouse away from you."

Most states were happy to keep the supply coming. In the early postwar years, legislators were satisfied with breaking even with lessees so long as they were rid of the penitentiary's drain on their treasuries. But once they realized how great the demand was for forced labor, they increased their prices. Georgia, Mississippi, Arkansas, North Carolina, and Kentucky were making between $25,000 and $50,000 each year. Alabama and Tennessee were bringing in around $100,000 annually. By 1886 the US commissioner of labor reported that, where leasing was practiced, the average revenues were nearly four times the cost of running prisons. Writer George Washington Cable, in an 1885 analysis of convict leasing, wrote that the system "springs primarily from the idea that the possession of a convict's person is an opportunity for the State to make money; that the amount to be made is whatever can be wrung from him; that for the officers of the State to waive this opportunity is to impose upon the clemency of a tax-paying public; and that, without regard to moral or mortal consequences, the penitentiary whose annual report shows the largest case balance paid into the State's treasury is the best penitentiary."

By 1890 some twenty-seven thousand convicts were performing some kind of labor in the South at a given time. States had enacted new laws that ensured that thousands of black men were being sent to labor camps. In 1876 Mississippi passed its "pig law," which defined theft of any property over ten dollars in value, or cattle or swine of whatever value, as grand larceny, with a sentence of up to five years. After its adoption, the number of state convicts quadrupled from 272 in 1874 to 1,072 three years later. Arkansas passed a similar law, as did Georgia, whose numbers increased from 432 in 1872 to 1,441 in 1877. Nearly all of these "new" convicts were black. Some states ensured more years of work by charging convicts for the "cost of conviction." In Alabama, for example, those who could not afford the fee were made to work it off at the rate of thirty cents a day. Abe McDowell of Wilcox County was sentenced to two years for stealing a pig valued by the jury at one dollar. For the "cost of conviction," he had to work nearly four years. James Jackson of Greene County, whose three misdemeanor sentences aggregated seventy days, had to work more than four years for the costs. Dennis Wood of Monroe County got a two year sentence for a felony, and more than nine years for the costs.

As a rule, convicts worked the most arduous jobs in the most dangerous reaches of the South, often where free laborers refused to work. In North Carolina most of the thirty-five hundred miles of railroad tracks built between 1876 and 1894 were laid by convicts. It's no coincidence that the number of black prisoners increased nearly 150 percent in that period. In Mississippi the railroad owners subleased convicts to build through the canal swamps. A legislative committee discovered in 1884 that the convicts were "placed in the swamp in water ranging to their knees, and in almost nude state they spaded caney and rooty ground, their bare feet chained together by chains that fretted the flesh. They were compelled to attend the calls of nature in line as they stood day in and day out, their thirst compelling them to drink the water in which they were compelled to deposit their excrement." When a grand jury inspected the penitentiary a few years later, it reported seeing twenty-six inmates recently brought in from farms and railroads, "many of them with consumption and other incurable diseases and all bearing on their persons marks of the most inhuman and brutal treatment. Most of them have their backs cut in great wales, scars, and blisters, some with the skin peeling off in pieces as the result of severe beatings. . . . They are lying there dying, some of them on the bare boards, so poor and emaciated that their bones almost come through their skin, many complaining of want of food. . . . We actually saw live vermin crawling over their faces, and the little bedding and clothing they have in tatters and stiff with filth"

By using convicts, the labor was cheaper, didn't strike, and it could be driven at a pace that free workers wouldn't tolerate. One Mississippi report claimed its convicts do "thirty percent more work than free laborers, being worked long, hard, and steadily." The South's "penitentiaries" had become large rolling cages that followed railroad building or ramshackle stockades deep in the forests, swamps, and mining fields.

There are no substantive memoirs by prisoners during the convict leasing era. The most detailed account of a convict labor camp was J. C. Powell's *The American Siberia*, published in 1891. Powell spent fourteen years guarding convicts for a Florida railroad company and a major turpentine firm. At the time all of Florida's convicts were leased to private companies; its penitentiary had been converted into an insane asylum. Powell was tasked with establishing a camp in the pine forests of Northern Florida. Shortly after he arrived in the fall of 1876, a crowd gathered in the town of Live Oak to witness the arrival of some thirty convicts, most of whom were black. As the prisoners stumbled off the freight train, the crowd recoiled. The convicts "were gaunt, haggard, famished, wasted with disease, smeared with grime, and clad in filthy tatters," Powell wrote. "Chains clattered about their trembling limbs." The convicts had been working for a railroad company, building a line through the tropical marshes and palmetto jungles of Lake Eustis. The company provided neither food nor shelter, so they built huts out of whatever they could find, sometimes waking up "half submerged in mud or slime." To eat, they were allowed brief intervals to scour the woods to dig up roots and cut the tops from "cabbage" palmetto trees.

Two of the men who got off the train had hands that "resembled the paws of certain apes, for their thumbs, which were enormously enlarged at the ends, were also quite as long as their index fingers, and the tips of all were in a line." The deformity was caused by a punishment called "stringing up," in which a cord was wrapped around the men's thumbs, flung over a tree limb, and tightened until the men hung suspended, sometimes for hours, their feet dangling off the ground. It was a punishment used throughout the South, as was "watering," a form of torture dating to the Spanish Inquisition, in which a prisoner was strapped down, a funnel forced into his mouth, and water poured in so as to distend the stomach to such a degree that it put pressure on the heart, making the prisoner feel that he was going to die. Another common punishment was "sweating," in which a man was closed up in a tin or wooden "sweat box," sealed except for a hole two inches in diameter at nose level and placed under the sweltering sun. The temperature often rose so high that a man's body would swell and sometimes bleed. Mississippi was still using this method of torture 1925, when its official Punishment Record Ledger showed that four hundred prisoners served four thousand hours in the sweatbox.

Powell refused to use such forms of punishment; he fancied himself a reformer. Under his rule, men would be punished by kneeling down, placing their palms on the ground, and pulling their pants down to be whipped by a foot-and-a-half-long leather strap below their loins. Unlike the railroad company these convicts had labored for, the turpentine company that employed Powell would finance a crude log house with two platforms on each side for the prisoners to sleep on. At night, a long chain was stretched down the middle, to which the convicts were strung by smaller chains attached to the shackles on their ankles. After a day's work, the men would sit on the platforms, get chained up, and eat a dinner of salt pork, cowpeas, and corn bread. Sometimes Powell would remove "a literal stratum of gnats" from the top of the pan before feeding the prisoners. After dinner a bell would ring and they would lie down. If a man wanted to adjust his position in the night, he would have to ask a guard for permission.

Prisoners, convicted of everything from larceny to murder, were forced to spend the day running from one pine tree to the next at a trot, hacking wedges into them so their sap could be collected. The men were all connected by a "squad chain," which made them effectively pull one another along. Powell frequently saw men drop of fatigue, to be dragged through the dirt a dozen yards by the other men on the squad chain. The men would slow down briefly and the fallen man would "stagger up, dash the dirt out of his eyes, and go reeling and running on." The work was so grueling that a one-eyed druggist sentenced to seven years for school record forgery drove a needle into his only working eye to avoid more toil. Another man drove an ax through his foot. It left a severe gash, but he could still hobble so Powell made him chop wood. The man put his foot on the chopping block and used his ax to reopen the old wound. His foot swelled from gangrene and he died.

To track down the frequent runaways, Powell kept foxhounds, which he raised at the camp. To train them, he'd order a "trustee" to run a few miles into the forest, and then he'd put the dog on the trustee's track, much like CCA would do 140 years later. Unlike CCA, however, Powell's dogs were not trained to bite the prisoner when they found him; they merely led the guards, who followed on horseback. But many of the escapees were never caught. Convict leasing was so unpopular among the larger population that locals would often hide the fugitives.

Distain for convict leasing became so high that when two convicts ran off, Powell's guards refused to chase him, "regarding it as an open invitation to assassination."

At one point Powell and his employees were brought to trial for their brutality; citizens who lived near the camp testified against the lessees, but neither Powell nor the company was convicted.

In Louisiana, Samuel L. James didn't leave behind such details about his railroad and levee camps. Rather, history recorded more about how he himself lived than the people forced to labor for him. James kept a second home in New Orleans where he and his wife would receive the city's elite. Their "very elegant toilets and cordial hospitality" would be noted in the paper's gossip columns. After visits to New Orleans, the James family would ride his steamboat back to Angola, eating delicious meals and playing poker on deck, while transporting convicts in the cargo below. On the plantation the family kept around fifty prisoners in an ill-ventilated fifteen-by-twenty-foot shack located a half mile from their nine-bedroom mansion. During the day, some convicts would tend to the expansive yard, its oak, pecan, and fig trees, and the family's stable out back.

James's granddaughter, Cecile James Shilstone, grew up on the farm and, in her brief memoirs, recalled her childhood on Angola fondly. "We had plenty of servants and plenty to eat," she wrote. She and her brother would ride a donkey around their yard and when it became stubborn, she would call a convict "yard boy" over to push it along. She remembers taking "little Negro children to the store for candy" and seeing her brother scamper around with black children as his "guardians and play-mates," hunting birds and snakes with slings they called "nigger shooters."

When James's daughter gave birth, the baby was raised by a "faithful Negro nurse" who had been convicted of murder. "Papa always chose the murderers in preference to the thieves to act as servants," Shilstone wrote. "A thief is a sneak and not to be trusted in one's house. Once a thief, he's apt to steal again. Whereas, a murderer is hot-headed, [he] committed a crime which he is usually sorry for later and will not do so again."

In the mornings, the convict houseboys would bring James coffee in bed and saddle up his horse, which he'd ride out into the fields at daybreak to see that the work had begun. Shilstone's idyllic descriptions of plantation life differed greatly from the few scant accounts reporters recorded from prisoners, which described a dawn to dusk work regimen, whippings, and being forced to sleep in muddy clothing. While the fieldworkers ate "starvation rations," James would return to the big house in the morning to a spread of bacon, eggs, grits, biscuits, battercakes, syrup, coffee, cream, and fruit. At lunchtime, a "little Negro boy" would sit on the stairs and pull a rope that would spin a fan to keep the family cool. The fieldwork continued through the day, but during the hottest hours, the James family slept, rising later to take a ride around the plantation in their carriage.

One day, in 1894, James was doing his rounds when he was struck by a sudden brain hemorrhage. He died soon after, and his body was laid out in the Big House for a viewing. When the estate was passed on to his son, it was valued at $2.3 million, the equivalent of some $63 million in 2018.

A convict under James's lease was more likely to die than he would have been as a slave. In 1884 the editor of the *Daily Picayune* wrote that it would be "more humane to punish with death all prisoners sentenced to a longer period than six years," because the average convict lived no longer than that. At the time, the death rate of six prisons in the Midwest, where convict leasing was nonexistent, was around 1 percent. By contrast, in the deadliest year of Louisiana's lease, nearly 20 percent of convicts perished. Between 1870 and 1901, some three thousand Louisiana convicts, most of whom were black, died under James's regime. Before the war, only a handful of planters owned more than one thousand slaves, and there is no record of anyone allowing three thousand valuable human chattel to die. The pattern was consistent throughout the South, where annual convict death rates ranged from about 16 percent to 25 percent, a mortality rate that would rival the Soviet gulags to come.* Some American camps were far deadlier than Stalin's: In South Carolina the death rate of convicts leased to the Greenwood and Augusta Railroad averaged 45 percent a year from 1877 to 1879. In 1870 Alabama prison officials reported that more than 40 percent of their convicts had died in their mining camps. A doctor warned that Alabama's entire convict population could be wiped out within three years. But such warnings meant little to the men getting rich off of prisoners. There was simply no incentive for lessees to avoid working people to death. In 1883, nine years before Samuel L. James's death, one Southern man told the National Conference of Charities and Correction: "Before the war, we owned the negroes. If a man had a good negro, he could afford to take care of him: if he was sick get a doctor. He might even put gold plugs in his teeth. But these convicts: we don't own 'em. One dies, get another."

---

* Gulag death rates during 1942 and 1943 were around 25 percent, according the Soviet Union's interior ministry records. Another particularly bad year was 1933, in which 15.3 percent of gulag prisoners died, likely from a famine that killed six to seven million "free" citizens as well. Aside from those years, mortality in the Soviet labor camps ranged between 0.67 percent and 15.3 percent, meaning that, overall, it was more likely for a prisoner to die under convict leasing than in a Soviet gulag.

On my first official day as a corrections officer, I am stationed on suicide watch in Cypress unit. In the entire prison of more than fifteen hundred inmates, there are no full-time psychiatrists and just one full-time social worker: Miss Carter. In class she told us that one-third of the inmates have mental health problems, 10 percent have severe mental health issues, and roughly one-quarter have IQs less than seventy points. She said most prison mental health departments in Louisiana have at least three full-time social workers. Angola has at least eleven. Here, there are few options for inmates with mental health needs. They can meet with Miss Carter, but with her caseload of 450 prisoners, that isn't likely to happen more than once a month. They can try to get an appointment with the part-time psychiatrist or the part-time psychologist, who are spread even thinner. Another option is to ask for suicide watch.

A CO sits across from the two official suicide watch cells, which are small and dimly lit and have plexiglass over the front. My job is to sit across from two regular segregation cells that are being used for suicide watch overflow, observe the two inmates inside, and log their behavior every fifteen minutes. "We never document anything around here on the money," Miss Carter taught us a month ago. "Nothing should be 9:00, 9:15, 9:30, because the auditors say you're pencil-whipping it. And truth be known, we do pencil-whip it. We can't add by fifteen because that really puts you in a bind. Add by fourteen. That looks pretty come audit time." One guard told me he just filled in the suicide watch log every couple of hours and didn't bother to watch the prisoners.*

For one inmate, I jot down the codes for "sitting" and "quiet." For the other, Damien Coestly,† the number for "using toilet." He is sitting on the commode, underneath his suicide blanket, a tear-proof garment that doubles as a smock. "Ah hell nah, you can't sit here, man!" he shouts at me. Other than the blanket, he is naked, his bare feet on the concrete. There is nothing else allowed in his cell other than some toilet paper. No books. Nothing to occupy his mind.

This is all intended to be "a deterrent as well as protection," Miss Carter said. The sparse conditions discourage people from falsely claiming they want to kill themselves. Some inmates claim to be suicidal because, for one reason or another, they want out of their dorms and don't want to go to protective custody, where they would be labeled as snitches. Inmates on suicide watch don't get a mattress; they have to sleep on a steel bunk. They also get worse food. The official ration is one "mystery meat" sandwich, one peanut butter sandwich, six carrot sticks, six celery sticks, and six apple slices per meal. I calculate that eating it three times a

---

* CCA's spokesman says the company is "committed to the accuracy of our record keeping."
† His real name.

day provides at least 250 calories less than the US Department of Agriculture's daily recommendation.*

Cost may also play a factor in why CCA tries to keep suicide watch the most undesirable place in the prison: Nowhere else does a single guard oversee one or two inmates. If more than two inmates are on constant watch for more than forty-eight hours, the prison has to ask the regional corporate office for permission to continue, Miss Carter told us.† Sometimes the regional office says no, she said, and the prisoners are put back on the tiers or in seg.

"Come on man, get the fuck out of here," Coestly shouts to me. "You know what I'm about to do is, get up on top of this bunk and jump straight onto my motherfucking neck if y'all don't get the fuck out from the front of my cell."

I look over to the cell to the right and see the other inmate sitting on his metal bed, staring at me and masturbating under his suicide blanket.

I tell him to stop.

"Move your chair then. I'm just doing my thing." He keeps going.

I get up and grab a pink slip to write him up, my first disciplinary report. On my way out, a white inmate with machine guns tattooed under his eyes looks at me through the food slot. "What the fuck are you looking at?!" he shouts.

"You making a mistake," the masturbator says to me. "You fuck with me like that, I'm gonna go all night."

"All right," I say.

---

* Specifically, it is 250 calories less than the USDA's daily recommendation for sedentary adult men under the age of forty-one. CCA says suicide watch meals are of "equivalent nutritional value" to general-population meals. It also says suicide watch is "designed for the safety of the inmate and nothing else."
† CCA says this is inaccurate.

"Write that bitch. I don't give a fuck. I'm on extended lockdown."
He tells me he's been in Cypress for years. He begins singing and dancing in his cell. *"All night, all niiiiiight."* Prisoners down the tier laugh.
"I'll add that to my collection. I have about a hundred write-ups. I don't
give a fuck!"

Coestly asks if same sex marriage is legal where I'm from. (It is not
yet legal nationally.) I say yes. "I knew it. I knew it. I knew it," he says.
"If you fuck a man in the ass down here, it's a crime. It's in the law
books. Sodomy. We ain't got nothing down here. They ain't go' legalize
pot. They ain't go' legalize motherfucking same sex marriage." He hands
a Styrofoam cup through his food slot, asking me to get him some coffee. I tell him I'll think about it.

Someone down the tier calls for me. He's not on suicide watch, just
regular segregation. "I'm having some mental health issues, man," he
says. He has a wild look in his eyes, and he speaks intensely but quietly.
"I'm not suicidal or homicidal necessarily, but it's hard for me to be
around people." There is another man in his cell with him, sitting on the
top bunk, shaving his face. "And, and, and the voices, demons, whatever
you want to call them, want me to wait till y'all come down here and
throw defecation or urine or something. I don't want to do that, okay?"
He says he wants to go on suicide watch as a preventive measure. "Until
I figure out what's going on here"—he taps the sides of his head with his
index fingers—"then that's where I need to be." His request is denied by
the unit manager. With four inmates on suicide watch, we are already
over capacity.

"We are going to have a Mexican standoff," Coestly says. "Ever seen
one of those? I'm gonna jump off this motherfucking bunk headfirst."
He says he's having a mental health emergency. When I tell the key officer, she rolls her eyes. In class Miss Carter told us that "unless he's
psychotic and needs a shot to keep him from doing the behavior, then I

just let them get it out of their system." It takes six hours for a psychiatrist to show up.

One man needs a mattress. "I'm having a medical emergency!" another shouts. I approach his cell. "Asthma attack," he says calmly. "I don't have my inhaler," he says. He looks to be breathing completely normally, but I report it to the key officer as I'm required to. She looks annoyed. "You know you're on suicide watch, right?" she says. "'Cuz it seems like you're over here more than you are down the tier." I look over at the regular floor officers who are supposed to be handling these things. They are sitting at a table next to the key, the control room in the middle of the unit, and they look bored.

I go back to my post, across from Coestly and the masturbator. The man who said he's having the asthma attack shouts from down the tier, enraged. "You are just going to sit there and do nothing?!" He grips the bars of his door and shakes them so hard it seems like the door might open. "Get me the fuck out of here!" A chorus builds of people shaming me for sitting in my chair while they need help.

One of the other inmates on suicide watch, who's been silent until now, begins yelling through the food slot. "Third world!" he shouts. "They are giving lethal injections now in the white man's prison." His voice has a demonic, possessed quality to it, and he hits the plexiglass to punctuate his sentences. "I'm the devil! I can smell your fear when you sleep at night, tossing and turning. Yeah. Play with me! Play with me!" He spits fiercely on the floor. The CO sitting directly across from him twiddles his thumbs and gazes straight ahead with a measured, unthreatening blankness.

In the neighboring cell the masturbator is staring at me, completely naked, jacking off vigorously. I pretend not to notice, but it becomes too obvious. I tell him to stop. He gets up, comes to the bars, and strokes himself five feet in front of me. I leave and come back with the pink sheet of paper, and he shouts, "Stop looking like that 'cuz you making my dick hard!" I don't respond, just write. "Stop looking like that 'cuz you making my dick hard! Stop looking like that 'cuz you making my dick hard!"

The seemingly schizophrenic man next to him hits the plexiglass repeatedly. "That's what the devil's doing to you, in the invisible world—sticking his invisible dick in your white or black ass and *fucking* you with it." My heart is pounding. For an hour I stare at a Styrofoam cup on the floor and study the blotches in the concrete. I try to take my mind anywhere but here.

To my relief, Sergeant King calls me out. Last time I saw him was in the cafeteria when he was pretending to slap a female guard's ass. He tells me I need to rewrite my report on the masturbator, because saying someone looked at you and masturbated is not enough. It's too open to interpretation and the charge will not stick. He coaches me: *On 1-15-2015, at 1245 hours, I, CO Bauer, witnessed inmate Carl Skeen holding his erect penis in his right hand and stroking it with an up and down motion while staring directly at me.*

At lunchtime Coestly demands a vegetarian meal from the SORT team. He doesn't get one, so he picks the meat out of his sandwich and eats plain slices of bread and carrot sticks. Afterward I watch him sleep, wrapped in his suicide blanket like a cocoon.

Hours pass and the tier becomes quiet. The masturbator calls down the hall. "Hey, cell thirteen. Send me down something." A couple of minutes later I see, down the hall, a hand pass a ball of toilet paper to another hand. It moves from one cell to the next, all the way to the masturbator. He opens it up and pulls out a cigarette rolled in an inmate request form. "Anyone got any Bible paper?" he shouts down the hall. No one responds. He takes a match out of the bundle and lights it. He takes a couple of puffs, leaning back against the wall, and passes the cigarette under his cell door to the schizophrenic man. He takes a few drags and passes it to the guy with the machine guns under his eyes. Each enjoys the cigarette privately. The CO and I pretend not to notice.

A few hours later a SORT officer walks a cuffed man onto the tier. His eyes are tightly closed and snot is dripping off his upper lip. He was pepper sprayed after punching my old instructor Kenny in the face as Kenny sat in his office doing paperwork. Kenny's in the hospital now—after he confiscated another inmate's cell phone, the prisoner put a paid hit out on him.

Kenny is gone for days, recovering from his busted nose. The message his assailant sent was clear: Keep your hands off our phones. Meanwhile, the fact that I took the phone in Ash unit showed Miss Price that I'm a strong officer who plays by the rules, so she asked the warden if I could be posted there permanently. Now I work there, on the floor, almost every day. I barely see the other cadets. About one third of the trainees I began with have already quit. Collinsworth is stationed in Ash on the night shift. Miss Doucet decided she couldn't risk an asthma attack, so she quit too. The others are stationed around the prison, in different units and different shifts.

In Ash, I immediately try to smooth over the phone thing with the inmates. I tell a few of them that I took it because I didn't have a choice and suggest they should try to hide their contraband better.

"You ain't no police?" one asks me.

"Nah. I ain't here to be police," I reply. "If people ain't fucking with me, I ain't got a problem with them."

Don't be like your partner Bacle,* they say. In some units and on some shifts, the pairing of floor officers changes day to day, but for whatever reason, CO Bacle and I become a regular pair. I tell the inmates

---

* Bacle has allowed me to use his real name.

I'll never be like him, all that shouting and hollering. If he were not a squat, hobbling sixty-three-year-old, Bacle's occasional fantasies about putting shock collars on inmates or shoving his keys down their throats might not seem so harmless. But he hates the company too. "All you are is a fucking body to 'em. That's the way I feel," he says. He counts the days until his Social Security kicks in and he no longer needs to work here to supplement his retirement checks from the coast guard.

Every day I come to know him better. He is a reader of old westerns and an aficionado of Civil War reenactments. He uses words like "gadzooks" and phrases like "useful as tits on a boar hog." Back before the hobby shops closed, he liked to buy his wife gifts made by prisoners. Once he bought her a handmade saddle for her toy unicorns. "When she seen it, she was tickled pink. We are still fat, dumb, and happy over it!" His breath smells perpetually of menthol chewing tobacco, a fleck of which is always stuck in the corner of his mouth.

Bacle becomes a teacher of sorts. "You got to have what I call a *rapport* with some of the inmates," he says. Mostly he is referring to the orderlies, the prisoners selected for special roles inside each unit. When an orderly passes out toothpaste, Bacle tells me to follow the inmate's lead. "I just kind of modify it from when I was in the service. I might have rank over someone, but I don't want to step on their toes."

Without the orderlies, the prison would not function. Each unit has a key orderly, whose job is to keep the key clean and pack up the property of any prisoner sent to seg. Count-room orderlies deliver the tallies from each unit to the room where they're tabulated. Tier orderlies, floor orderlies, yard orderlies, walk orderlies, and gym orderlies keep the prison clean. Orderlies typically maintain a friendly relationship with the guards, but they take every opportunity to make it clear to other inmates they are not snitches. And they rarely are. It is much more likely for them to be movers of contraband. They cozy up to guards who will bring it in, and their freedom of movement allows them to distribute the goods. I will see some of the most trusted orderlies get busted while I'm here.

Bacle regularly gives his lunch to the muscular key orderly. We are not allowed to do this, so he does it discreetly. "It's a habit I got into when I started," he says. Bacle isn't afraid to bend the rules to keep things under control. When one inmate begins marching around angrily, saying "fuck white people," and we're too afraid to try to get him into his tier, Bacle buys cigarettes from another inmate, gives them to the agitated prisoner, and says, "Why don't you go have a smoke on your bed to calm your nerves?" And it works.

Instructors like Kenny preached against giving concessions to inmates, but in reality most guards think you have to cooperate with them. Frankly there just aren't enough staff members to do otherwise. Bacle and I don't have time, for example, to keep watch over the corrections counselor when she is in her office, where there are no security cameras, so she uses two inmates as her bodyguards.* COs are always under pressure to impress on the supervisors that everything is under control. We rely on inmates for this, too, letting some stand out in front of the unit to warn us when a ranking officer is coming so we can make sure everything is in order. When Miss Price isn't watching, Bacle lets a guy called Corner Store off his tier so he can run deodorant and chewing tobacco and sugar and coffee between inmates on different tiers. They aren't allowed to trade commissary items, but they do anyway, so when we let Corner Store handle it, they stop pestering us with ploys like faking medical emergencies to get off the tier.

Corner Store is a thirty-seven-year-old black man who looks fifty-five. His hair is scraggly, his uniform tattered, his face puffy. He walks with the clipped gait of a stiff-legged old man who is late for a meeting he doesn't really want to attend. He's been in prison for half his life,

---

* CCA says this action violated its policy.

though I don't know what for. I rarely know what anyone is in for. I do know that he used to sell crack, that he saw his friend get shot to death when he was eight, and that he once exchanged gunfire with some white men in Mississippi who called him a "nigger." At least that's what he tells me. Fourteen of his eighteen years behind bars have been at Winn.

Corner Store does not inspire fear, yet he is confident. He tells COs to open the tier door for him; he does not ask. On his pluckier days, he flaunts his status by sitting in the guards' chairs and smoking. He talks to us as if we are office colleagues from different departments. And unlike the floor orderly who protects his reputation by loudly proclaiming that rats deserve to get stabbed, Corner Store doesn't need to make a show of his loyalty to inmates, yet it is unwavering. When I ask him to teach me some prison lingo, he refuses gently.

The first time I meet Corner Store, he walks through the metal detector at the entrance of the unit. It beeps, but neither Bacle nor I do anything; its sound is one of the many we tune out. The device was installed not long before I began working here, in an effort to cut down on the number of inmates carrying shanks, but functionally it is a piece of furniture. We never use it because it takes at least two officers to get inmates to line up, walk through it, and get patted down whenever they enter or exit the unit, which leaves no one to let inmates into their tiers. When Corner Store makes it beep, he calls over to me: "Hey, watch this here! I'm going to go back through this thing and it won't go off." He jumps through it sideways, and it doesn't make a sound. I laugh. "This is something my granddaddy taught me years ago," he says. "Anything that a man makes can always be altered. Always. That's just like this paint," he says, pointing to the wall. "I can take a chisel and take all the paint off this door. I guarantee you I can make fifty pairs of dice and put them in the store and sell them. All I need is water, paint, and toilet paper and it's going to come out hard as a rock."

He learned to hustle because he had no money or support from his family. For his courier services, inmates kick him cigarettes, coffee, and ramen packets. He doesn't take charity; he learned early that little comes without strings in prison. Sexual predators prey on needy inmates, giving them commissary or drugs, seemingly as gifts, but eventually recalling the debt. If you don't have money, the only way to pay is with your body. "When I first come to prison, I had to fight about five times for my ass," Corner Store says. "This is how it starts: You're scared of being in prison because of the violence or whatever. You go to people for protection. But this is the number one thing you don't do. You have to be a man on your own." He tries to discourage vulnerable inmates from seeking help, and says he's gotten into fights to stop new prisoners from being sexually assaulted. "It just hurts me to see it happen. A kid who really don't even understand life yet, you turn and fuck his life up even more?"

He says there have been periods when he's had to pack a shank. "Sometimes it's best, because you got some bullheaded people in prison who don't understand nothin' *but* violence. When you show them you can get on the same level, they gettin' on, they leave you the fuck alone."

"They always talking about how prison rehabilitates you," he says. "Prison don't rehabilitate you. You have to rehabilitate yourself." When Miss Price is around, Bacle and I are careful not to make it obvious we are letting Corner Store out, and he makes sure to stay out of her sight.

In the morning meeting, the captain and Assistant Warden Parker are frustrated. Why is no one cracking down on sagging pants and homemade clothing? In private, the officers say that if the assistant warden doesn't want inmates to wear bleach-stained jeans, he should take them himself. Why should they put themselves on the line? The other day Bacle was warning inmates to hide their hats when Parker is around.

"Does anybody know why we don't want them to wear individualized clothing?" the assistant warden asks us all. "We want them institutionalized. You guys ever hear that term? We want them *institutionalized* not *individualized*. Is that sort of a mind game? Yup. But you know what? It's worked over the couple hundred years that we've had prisons in this country. So that's why we do it. We don't want them to feel as though they are individuals. We want them, for lack of a better term, to feel like a herd of cattle. We're just moving them from point A to point B, letting them graze in the dining hall and then go back to the barn. Okay?"

His tone softens. "I apologize if it seems like we're coming down on y'all, but unfortunately, due to a series of events that took place in 2014, culminating with that escape, there is a high, high level of scrutiny on how you do your job." He says the wardens have been pestering him. "'Are they scared, Mr. Parker? Are you not providing the adequate training that your staff members need, Mr. Parker, to be tolerable enough and strong enough to take clothing away from an inmate? Are they that scared, Mr. Parker?'

"Someone said this place has been sliding down for a long time. Here's what we have before us: We have to climb up that hill extremely fast."

Guards are constantly getting frustrated about Parker's "game plans" for turning Winn around: keeping inmates away from the bars at the front of their tiers, getting them quicker to chow, keeping them off the floor, finishing count faster. The plans always mean more work for us, but we never discuss the problem that both guards and inmates complain about most: There aren't enough employees. Corporate has tried to mitigate the problem by bringing officers in from out of state. The economics of this are never clear to me—it seems more expensive to pay for transportation and lodging than to hire more locals or raise wages. There are an average of five guards, filling in for a month or so at a time, from places like Arizona and Tennessee.

As Parker talks, I count the number of people in the room. I recently began making this a habit. It's the only way for me to know how many guards there are in the prison. According to CCA's contract with Louisiana, thirty-six guards are expected to show up for work at six a.m. every day. Twenty-nine of them fill mandatory twelve-hour positions that require a body in them at all times—these include unit floor officers, front-gate officers, perimeter patrol, shift supervisors, and infirmary officers. Some days I count twenty-eight, some days twenty-four, but there are almost always fewer than twenty-nine total. It's possible that employees working overtime from the night shift aren't there or that others trickle in late. But it still appears there are often fewer people on the shift than contractually required to keep the prison open, let alone running smoothly.* I later get hold of a letter between CCA and the DOC that shows that while I work here, Winn has forty-two vacancies for regular guards and nine vacancies for ranking officers. Miss Lawson, the assistant chief of security, says that when officials from the DOC were scheduled to visit, "we would be tripping over each other, but it was just because we were paying people overtime to come in and work extra."

Often the only guards in a 352-inmate unit are the two floor officers and the key officer. There is supposed to be an officer controlling the gate that connects each unit walk to the main walk, but often there isn't. From nine a.m. to five p.m. on weekdays, every unit should have two case managers who manage rehabilitation and reentry programs, two corrections counselors who are in charge of resolving inmates' daily issues, and a unit manager who supervises everything. Not once do I see all these positions filled in a unit.

During my time at Winn, I witness corners cut daily. Key officers,

---

* CCA's spokesman later tells me I was too low on the totem pole to have an accurate understanding of staffing at Winn. He adds that "security is everyone's job" and a "team effort" involving even employees who are not guards.

who are charged with documenting activities in the units, routinely record security checks that do not occur. I hear that these logbooks are audited by the state and are the only evidence of whether guards walk up and down the tiers every half hour. I almost never see anyone do such a security check unless DOC officials are around. Collinsworth tells me that when he worked in the key he was told repeatedly to record security checks every fifteen to thirty minutes, even though they weren't being done. Miss Lawson later says she was once reprimanded by a warden for refusing to log checks that did not occur. "I'm just going to write down that you are doing your security checks every thirty minutes," a ranking officer once told me. "That's just how it's been done, so until someone up top tells me different, that's how we'll do it."*

The company also compensates for the shortage by requiring us to work extra days, which means that for up to five days in a row, I have just enough time to drive home, eat dinner, sleep, and come back to prison. Sometimes I have to stay longer than twelve hours because there is no one to relieve me. A guard I relieve one morning is ending a four-day stretch; in a forty-eight-hour period he had worked for forty-two hours at the warden's insistence, he says. He didn't sleep the whole time.†

Assistant Warden Parker tells us the DOC has required CCA's corporate office in Nashville, Tennessee, to report what CCA is doing to fix the mess at Winn. An obvious remedy would be to raise the pay of non-ranking officers to the level of DOC officers—which begins at $12.50 per hour, $3.50 more than ours—and reinstate rehabilitative and recreational programs for inmates. Miss Lawson told me such requests hit a roadblock at the corporate level. "There were years that the wardens

---

* CCA's spokesman says the company had no knowledge of security checks being skipped or logbooks being falsified.

† CCA says no such incident occurred.

would beg for more money, and it was like, 'Okay, on to the next subject,'" she said.

Instead, corporate takes a different approach to show it means business: A few days after I worked suicide watch, it removed the local officers from Cypress and turned the unit entirely over to members of the company's national SORT team. These are guys who "use force constantly," Parker says. "I believe that pain increases the intelligence of the stupid, and if inmates want to act stupid, then we'll give them some pain to help increase their intelligence level." He tells us that, just the other night an inmate wouldn't hand over a bag he was given by another inmate. "So he went through the pain of chemical spray and the employment of chemical munitions. So if we have to increase their intelligence level, then by all means, let's do it.

"I don't know when it dawned on me in the last couple weeks," Parker says to us. "I care about this institution and I care about all of you. I'm tired of people telling me that people at Winn aren't doing their jobs. A term used a couple of weeks ago that was very embarrassing to me was: They don't even understand basic prison management at Winn." Some of the guards shake their heads silently. "Anybody feel good about that one? I know I sure as hell don't."

After the meeting, everyone moves slowly down the walk. "I'm tired of this kumbaya shit," says Edison, a big white CO dressed all in black with a bull neck and a red bulbous nose. He hasn't been in a great mood lately: He was removed from his post in Cypress when the SORT team took it over, and it wounded his pride. Suggesting he can't handle his own is about the worst insult you could give him. "I'm sick and tired of doin' this shit," he says. "The security in this place is pathetic. They need to tighten up on the tier doors, re-man the towers, and reinstitute the inmate work out in the field and the inmate programs, and give these fools something to do besides sit in their beds, eat, watch TV, and figure out how to fuck with us." He blames the "ivory tower" in

Nashville—CCA's corporate headquarters—for Winn's problems. "Those fools ain't got nothing in their mind but the bottom line."

Today the captain assigned Edison to join me and Bacle in Ash. Having a new guard come to Ash is like having a visitor to our twisted household. Bacle likes to complain to outsiders about how the inmates in Ash "take stupid pills by the quart jar." As we stand around on the floor, waiting for the day to begin, he complains about the most mundane of issues: how some inmates don't sit on their bunks during count like they are supposed to.

"How are your fighting skills, Bauer?" Edison asks me. The question makes me nervous. This is the opposite of the approach I'm trying to take in here.

"Alright," I say.

"You're with me," he says. "We're going to give these motherfuckers an eye-opener today. I don't play that bullshit. You get your ass on the bunk."

"You're not into this playing shit," Bacle says sympathetically.

"That's right," Edison says.

"You're a grade A-1 asshole when it needs to be," Bacle says.

"I'm a grade A-1 drill instructor when I have to be."

"That's what this place needs!"

"I know it does," Edison says. "It needs to go back to about 1960. Give a goddamn PR-24"—a police baton—"and hand a can of gas to everybody."

"Mmmhmm."

"You get stupid, you get beat down. You get big and stupid, you get gassed and beat down. Either way you learn your fucking place."

Edison has been at Winn for a year and a half. I ask why he's working here. "With my skill set, it was the only thing open," he says. He is a US Army Rangers veteran and was once a small-town police chief. He says he retired when "the city council got afraid of me." "When I was a cop, I knew damn well that I would shoot your ass. I didn't carry two extra clips, I carried four. When I went to work, I went to war. When I got off, I still went to war. I carried two clips on me regardless of what I was wearing. I carried *at least* my Glock forty underneath my arm and usually I had a Glock forty-five on my ankle. Go ahead, play with me."

His brow is furrowed and his fists are clenched. "Parker knows I'm pissed off. When I know that I've got another position, I'm going to stop holding my tongue at these meetings. When they ask if there are any more questions, I'm going to ask, Do you foresee us going from an *allowance* to a living wage in the immediate future, like before 2035? With the bullshit we gotta put up with from the ivory tower and the lack of living wage, nobody is going to put up with this shit forever." He, like me, like the nonranking guards who've been here since 1991, makes nine dollars an hour.

We walk the floor. He stops. We stop. "You know what is stupid?" he says. "I see murderers. I see rapists. I see robbers. And then I see, the vast majority is in here for bein' stupid enough to smoke a joint too close to a school. Twenty-five years, federal mandatory. Then you got somebody that slaughtered a whole fucking family serving twenty-five to life and he's out in six to eight." (About one-fifth of Winn inmates are in for drug-related crimes. Getting busted with a joint near school will typically land you about six years, not twenty-five.) Edison's indignation about drug criminalization surprises me. "Now, where's the fucking justice? And we're paying how much per inmate per day?"

"President George Washington had a bottom forty of the hemp plant!" Bacle says. When you smoke weed, "you want to sit around the campfire or in your house." He laughs hysterically.

"Exactly, the only thing you want to do is eat, fuck, or sleep, or listen to music while you eat fuck or sleep, but that's pretty much it."

Edison pulls a banana out of his bag. "Potassium," he says. "Keeps the muscles from tensing up."

"Count time!" the key officer, Miss Calahan,* yells. I unlock the door of B1 tier and Edison walks in. An inmate is standing at the sink, brushing his teeth. "Get on your bunk," Edison barks. The inmate keeps his back turned to Edison. "Or would you like to do it in Cypress?" Edison steps in toward him. "Step out!" Edison shouts, pointing to the door. He's seriously sending a prisoner to seg for this?

The inmate walks out, still brushing his teeth. "This man is going on about some bullshit," he says, waving his toothbrush around. A spot of toothpaste lands on Edison's jacket, which is hanging on a nearby chair.

"Go ahead! Be dumb! Let's go!" Edison yells, turning his hat backward. "I'm already taking your ass to Cypress. *Please* be stupid enough to touch me." The inmate continues to brush his teeth.

I walk down the tier and do count. "That Crip boy is going to tear his ass up," one inmate says as I pass. "Your work partner going to get stabbed." I can't keep count straight in my head. I just want to get off the tier.

When we leave the tier everyone comes up to the bars and yells at Edison. "You want to go next?" he shouts. "Behind the wall!" They don't budge. "Every one of y'all is going to Cypress."

"Suck my dick!"

"White man!"

The captain and Sergeant King enter the unit. The captain tells Edison to step aside so he can talk to the inmates and try to ease the tension. "This pacification bullshit," Edison mutters to me. "Yeah we knew how to pacify 'em in Vietnam! We dropped a fucking five-hundred-pounder on 'em. That pacifies." The captain tells Edison to

---

* Miss Calahan has allowed me to use her real name.

come with him. "It's not warm and fuzzy enough," Edison says to me as he leaves.

Sergeant King pulls me aside. "I'm here for you, bro," he says. He reminds me that he had my back when the inmate was masturbating in front of me while I was on suicide watch. "Don't ever think I'm against you. 'Cuz I'm gonna knock one of 'em out if I have to. And we go' write that report like he was trying to kill me and it was self-defense. Haha-haha!"

King has been working at Winn for five months, but he's been in corrections for eight years. He knows some of the prisoners here from his childhood. One inmate in Ash was his neighbor. As a kid, King spent time in juvenile hall. Like Edison, he's an army vet, and he credits the military for correcting his delinquent ways. After twenty-two years in the service, he got a job in a juvenile correctional facility in Texas. One day he told a boy to get off the basketball court, and the kid grabbed his throat and tried to strangle him. "I damn near beat the piss out of him. Sixteen years old, six foot three. As soon as you put your hands on me, you're not a teenager, you're a man. I put that uppercut on his ass and the superintendent said, 'I strongly suggest that you resign, sarge.' I fucked him up pretty good."

"Oh well!" Bacle says.

"All of this I shattered," he says, pointing to his jaw and mouth.

"Oh well!" Bacle says.

| 14 |

n the decade before Samuel L. James's death at his Angola plantation, convict leases were becoming increasingly concentrated in the hands of large corporations rather than with individual businessmen. There was probably no lessee that controlled more convicts than the Tennessee Coal, Iron and Railroad Company (TCI), the largest steel enterprise in the South. The company operated coal mines in Tennessee and Alabama. In Alabama alone, some fifteen thousand state and county convicts labored in the mines at a given time. Most spent the bulk of their waking days underground, sweating in the suffocating warrens of coal mines. They crawled into narrow crevices, laid on their backs, and hacked at the walls, trying to free huge slabs of coal. The state did not penalize TCI when inmates were killed, and the chances of death were high. In 1889, 18 percent of Alabama's convict laborers perished. Coal slabs, weighing half a ton or more, sometimes fell on top of the inexperienced convict miners. After weeks or months of sweating in suffocating warrens, convicts sometimes killed each other with their picks. Other times they were shot by guards. In one instance, 123 men were killed by an explosion and fire inside a mine. In a gamble to escape death in Alabama's massive Pratt mines, a convict would sometimes try his luck escaping through the great maze of pitch-black, abandoned tunnels, some of which were filled with escaping methane gas or toxic runoff from active shafts. On a number of occasions, convicts set fire to the mine in hopes of breaking free during the chaos. One man was found dead in the Pratt mine after feeling his way in the pitch darkness for two or three weeks. Dysentery frequently swept through TCI's labor camps, killing many. When a prisoner died, he was typically buried among the mine's refuse.

An Alabama state health inspector described conditions at one camp, run by a smaller coal company. Prisoners drank water piped in from the river, the same river that other convicts located upstream used as a toilet. "[I]t is a water that no population of human creatures inside or outside of the prison walls should be condemned to drink," the inspector wrote. Rows of coke ovens outside their barracks turned the coal into the carbon-rich fuel coal companies used to produce the steel for the railroad tracks it was laying throughout the South. Convicts breathed gas, carbon, and soot from the stoves every night. The emissions killed the trees for hundreds of yards around. Yet according to a report by Alabama's inspector of convicts, the high mortality rates were based not on the conditions of their incarceration but on the "debased moral condition of the negro . . . whose systems are poisoned beyond medical aid by the loathsome diseases incident to the unrestrained indulgence of lust . . . now that they are deprived of the control and care of a master."

Alabama and Tennessee state officials saw little reason to hinder mining operations by handwringing over the lives of mostly black convicts. The two states may have run two of the most brutal convict lease systems in the South, but they also made the most money. Between 1880 and 1904, Alabama's profits from leasing state convicts made up 10 percent of the state's budget. Tennessee's convict leasing profits contributed a similar amount to state coffers. Convict labor directly contributed to the success of their mining industries. In the twenty-two years leading up to 1900, Alabama's coal production leapt from 224,000 tons to 8,500,000 tons. More than one-quarter of miners in the Birmingham district were prisoners and upward of half of all Alabama miners learned the work as unpaid convicts.

The person to thank for bringing convict labor to American coal mines was newspaper editor and former slaveholder Arthur Colyar. After the Civil War ended in 1865, he sold his plantation and put his former slaves to work mining coal for TCI, his new company. At a time when the economy of former slave states was based almost entirely on agriculture, Colyar quickly became the leader of a Democratic faction pushing for industrialization of the South. For him, finding a way to use forced labor was key. He worried that if the incipient mining industry had to rely solely on free labor, the mining regions would become an "outpost for Pennsylvania tramps whose principal business was to strike."

Colyar lobbied Tennessee to lease convicts to the emerging industrial elite, and by 1871 his work had paid off. For $150,000 the state granted a five-year lease for all of its convicts to a professional card gambler named Thomas O'Conner, who put them to work laying tracks and mining coal all over the state. Even children were leased to him. In 1874 Tennessee leased 123 convicts under eighteen years of age; fifty-four of those were under sixteen, three were twelve, and one only ten years old. He extracted money from his prisoners every way he could, even collecting their urine and selling it to local tanneries by the barrel. When they died from exhaustion or disease, he sold their bodies to the Medical School at Nashville for students to practice on.

Colyar's TCI took over the Tennessee lease in 1883, acquiring thirteen hundred convicts. "One of the chief reasons which first induced the company to take up the system," he explained, "was the great chance which it presents for overcoming strikes." Labor disputes were so strong at the time that militiamen, federal troops, and mercenaries regularly became involved. Five years before TCI won the lease, railway workers nationwide paralyzed the railway system in protest of wage cuts, and the eight-hour work day was becoming a central demand of labor unions around the country. As long as TCI had convicts working in the mines, free miners understood that if they pushed too hard for higher wages, they could easily be replaced. From the beginning of convict leasing after the Civil War to 1890, the earnings of free miners in Tennessee dropped by half.

Borrowing from the antebellum practice of pricing slaves based on their classification as "full hands," "half hands," and "dead hands," TCI's divided convicts into four classes depending on their level of fitness, and paid the state accordingly. For a "first class man" who could mine four tons of coal per day, TCI paid $18.50 per month, while it charged $13.50 for a second class man. For a forth class man who mined a ton or less, the company only had to pay the cost of keeping the prisoner fed, clothed, and guarded. Compared to free laborers, who earned $45 to $50 per month, this was a steal. Any convict who didn't meet his quota was whipped. An Alabama government inspection showed that in a two-week period in 1889, 165 prisoners were flogged. "Nearly all the whipping was done for failure to get task, or for getting slate or rock in the coal," an investigator said. A former guard recalled: "The whipping was done with a two-ply strap as wide as your three fingers, tied to a staff. The convicts were face down with their pants off. They were whipped on the hands and legs five to twelve lashes."

As brutal as it was, an 1886 report by the US commissioner of labor in Alabama defended the system. "Convict labor [is] more reliable and productive than free labor," it said. "Mine owners say they could not work at a profit without the lowering effect in wages of convict-labor competition." Alabama went to some lengths to justify its practices to the rest of the country. In 1890, Alabama Inspector of Convicts W. D. Lee told the annual congress of the National Prison Association in Cincinnati, "We have difficulties at the South which you at the North have not. We must not be held to too strict an accountability. We have a large alien population, an inferior race. Just what we are to do with them as prisoners is a great question as yet unsettled. The Negro's moral sense is lower than that of the white man. We say that he has been degraded by three or four generations of slavery. I will not consent to that. While slavery is degrading, the Negro in slavery has reached a higher state of civilization than he ever reached anywhere else. What would become of him away from the white man, I do not know." Another inspector, Dr. Albert T. Henley, added, "It is almost impossible to reach the Negro by means applied to the white convicts. We waste time in trying to make a Negro think he needs reformation." Like with slavery, racist ideology and the profit motive went hand in hand. If reformation of black criminals was impossible, the logic went, we might as well make use of them in the mines.

Tennessee was so hooked on the income it drew from its TCI lease that it literally went to war for the company. In the 1890s free miners were beginning to agitate for better working conditions. The issue of convict competition had long been a sore issue for miners there. As early as 1877 they had exploded three kegs of powder under a convict barracks in protest of the company's use of convict scabs. By 1890 their grievances encompassed other issues. The company had been paying workers in scrip that could be used only in overpriced company stores, and workers began to organize with national mining unions to demand that TCI pay them in cash. The company viewed union organizing as a serious threat. To quell the agitation, TCI closed one of its largest mines, in Briceville, for "repairs," in April 1891. When it reopened two months later, management required workers to sign an "iron-clad" contract that included a no-strike clause, a presumption of right on the company's part in any dispute, and an illegal requirement that workers be paid in scrip. When miners refused to sign it, the company ordered its prisoners to tear down the workers' houses and build stockades for the additional convicts it would bring in to replace them. The miners were evicted, but a week later on Bastille Day, three hundred of them returned, armed with everything from rocks to rifles. They took some forty convicts from their stockade, put them in boxcars, and sent them to the prison in Knoxville. The state militia escorted the convicts back soon afterward, and 130 troops occupied the makeshift prison.

What began as a strike over worker grievances turned into a war against convict leasing. The miners returned a second time with fifteen hundred armed men, some coming from as far as Kentucky. They surrounded the Briceville stockade and, without a shot being fired, the militia commander surrendered. The prisoners, their guards, and the militiamen were transported by train back to Knoxville. Again, the convicts were returned to the mines days later, but this time the governor agreed to the miners' demand that a special legislative session be called to repeal convict leasing. It seemed like a major victory for the miners, but the legislature only used the session to fortify the prisoner labor system. Now TCI could call in the militia not only for actual unrest but also any time the company considered mob action "imminent."

Up to this point the miners had been careful not to set prisoners free, but on Halloween 1891, one thousand masked miners laid siege to the Briceville stockade, fed and clothed the prisoners, burned buildings down, and set the convicts free. Some convicts fled for Kentucky while others marched with the free miners to Coal Creek and Oliver Creek where they liberated more prisoners, burned company property, and looted company stores. All told, some 450 convicts were set free. About one-third were never recaptured.

To ensure there would be no further challenges to convict labor, the state built a militia fort outside the Coal Creek mine, complete with trenches and a Gatling gun. With military backing, TCI cut the free miners to half time while keeping 360 convict laborers working full time. Throughout the summer of 1892, pitched battles were fought between free miners and the militia, and stockades were burned and rebuilt.

The rebel miners were losing the military war, but they succeeded in taking away the state's economic incentive to rent out its prisoners. "The state really made no money," a governor would later say, "but rather lost by leasing of convicts on account of riots, outbreaks, and invasion." Before the rebellion, convict leasing had been making the state around $75,000 per year (about $2 million in 2018 dollars), but now taxpayers were paying an extra $200,000 for the militia to fight the miners and guard prisoners ($5.5 million in 2018). "That was a strong argument among the mass of the voting population," said Tennessee reformer P. D. Sims. "Now came the demand from the people, 'We must cut down this expense; we must abandon the lease system for one that will cost us less money.'" In 1893 Tennessee became the first state in the South to abandon convict leasing.

In 1907, nine years after TCI set up shop in Alabama, the company was bought out by the titan of Northern industry, the US Steel Corporation (USS). USS was the world's first billion-dollar company, and its buyout of TCI was one of the biggest transactions in the history of US capitalism to that date. The merger, brokered by J. P. Morgan, created a virtual monopoly for USS. In his biography, the head of the corporation, Elbert H. Gary, said he was outraged when he learned that the mines he acquired were using forced labor. Gary was regarded at the time as a national leader of business ethics and progressive labor practices. "Think of that!" his biographer quoted him as saying. "I, an abolitionist from childhood, at the head of a concern working negroes in a chain gang, with a state representative punishing them at the whipping post!"

If Gary was indeed troubled by his company's use of forced labor, he did nothing to change it. In fact, USS was even more aggressive at acquiring convicts than TCI had been before the buyout. Three weeks after USS took over TCI, it signed a new lease for four hundred more prisoners. In 1908 the company signed a contract with Jefferson County, in which it paid nearly $60,000 to acquire every prisoner arrested that year. TCI continued to use convict labor for another twenty years. When USS published a commemorative book to celebrate TCI's one- hundred-year history, dating to the 1860s, it said nothing of the tens of thousands of men forced to work in its mines, nor the hundreds who died there. When Douglas Blackmon, author of *Slavery by Another Name*, contacted USS, executives told him it was "not fair" to assign responsibility for a corporation's actions so long ago. The company told Blackmon it could not locate records having anything to do with its history of leasing prisoners. Company officials said they knew almost nothing about the bodies buried at the Pratt mines, land still owned by USS, even though it obtained a cemetery property tax exemption for one of the burial fields in 1997. "Are there convicts on that site?" a spokesman said to Blackmon. "Possibly, quite possibly. But I am unable to tell you where they are."

15

On my mandatory overtime day, I am sent to suicide watch. It's been several weeks since I was last there, and this time it feels like I'm accessing a top-secret world. Cypress has become a place we walk past, but no longer enter. Since CCA put the out-of-town SORT members in charge, the only regular guards that enter are those stationed on suicide watch. The sun has not yet risen when I am buzzed into the unit, and as soon as I enter, my eyes burn and snot immediately begins to flow out of my nose. The peppery air makes me cough. The officer in the key, a portly blonde woman, is sitting at her desk, doing paperwork in a gas mask.

"Take long, slow breaths," a SORT member with a crew cut advises as I cough. He was a machine gunner in Afghanistan. He asks if I need a gas mask. I know better than to show such weakness, so I decline.

In a shower, caged and secured with a bolt lock, a naked man is moaning in panic, rocking from side to side and waddling forward and back. SORT had reports that the man had a shank in his cell, so they surprised him early in the morning to do a cell search and sprayed him when he pulled his covers down. "It burns, it burns," the inmate says repeatedly. His breath is labored. His fingers, held out from his sides, extend and contract. SORT members in black uniforms walk past as if they don't notice him. Cockroaches run around frantically to escape the burning.

A voice from the suicide watch row calls me over. It's the man who was raving schizophrenically when I did watch three weeks ago. His cell is empty except for his suicide blanket and a couple of normal blankets they gave him. He asks if I can open a door for ventilation to get the pepper spray out of the air. I ask the machine gunner, who looks at his watch to give himself a second to contemplate the answer. "Nah, they'll be fine," he says with a laugh. "They can breathe it in."

The schizophrenic man asks if I'll give him my prison-issued lunch today. He says he got doused with two cans of pepper spray last week because he wanted more food and was kicking his door to get the guards' attention. "They said they ain't never seen nobody take that much spray," he tells me. During the next four months, Winn will report using chemical agents some eighty times, a rate seven times higher than that reported by Angola. During a ten-month period, it will report twice as many "immediate" uses of force* as the eight other Louisiana prisons combined. After Collinsworth is stationed in the key here, he'll tell me about an inmate who insulted a SORT officer's mother. The officer cuffed him, stood him in his underwear out of view of the cameras, and covered his whole body with pepper spray for "about eight seconds or so." When Collinsworth filed a use-of-force report, which is standard procedure following the event, he says he was ridiculed by members of the SORT team, who told him that "I should have said I didn't see anything." He says an assistant shift supervisor admonished him for "tattling."†

---

* "CCA expressly forbids retaliatory force," its spokesman tells me.

† CCA says the officer who sprayed the inmate was fired.

I notice an Oklahoma SORT member give a quick series of hand signals to his partner across the floor, who responds to him similarly. He tells me they are using the sign language of the Sureño prison gang. They learned it from prisoners transferred from California to Oklahoma. When the US Supreme Court ruled in 2011 that the overcrowding of California prisons was so severe that it constituted cruel and unusual punishment, the state contracted with private prisons located around the country to take thousands of its inmates. Oklahoma got an influx of California prison gangs, which the SORT member tells me was a "good thing" because gang culture is highly disciplined. "With their politics, they *have* to clean their cells. They *have* to maintain cleanliness. If they don't, they get stabbed. If they acted the way these guys act, they'd get stabbed."

There are no gangs at Winn, but that has more to do with Louisiana prison culture than the management of the prison. In most prisons nationwide, the racial divide is stark and internal politics are determined by racialized prison gangs like the Aryan Brotherhood and the Mexican Mafia. But Louisiana is an anomaly. Here, there are no prison gangs. White inmates will make racist comments to me when no one is around, but the overt hate that is common in prisons elsewhere is rare here. Attempts by individual prisoners to organize prisoners along racial lines ultimately fail. In a prison that is 75 percent black and less than 25 percent white, people of different races sit together in the chow hall, hang out on the yard, and sleep in the same dorms.

In Idaho CCA was accused of ceding control to prison gangs to save money on wages. A lawsuit filed in 2012 by eight inmates at the Idaho Correctional Center alleged there was effectively "a partnership between CCA and certain prison gangs," in which gang members were used to discipline inmates. A subsequent FBI investigation found that employees had falsified records and understaffed mandatory positions. A confidential Idaho Department of Correction memo shared with CCA that was disclosed in the case showed that by August 2008, inmate-on-inmate assaults and other incidents of violence had "steadily increased to the point that there are four incidents for every one that occurs in the rest of the Idaho state-operated facilities combined."* No charges were brought against CCA, nor were any sanctions levied against it. But the state ended automatic renewal of its contract and reopened it to bidders. "It was a lot better than this place," an out-of-state guard who worked in Idaho at the time told me.

The head of the SORT team enters Cypress about two hours after I arrive. He looks at me suspiciously, asks what I'm doing here, and tells me I have to leave.

Sometimes, as a prisoner, you are uprooted without warning. Settled into your routine and niche in the prison power structure, a guard may tell you suddenly that it's time to go. They ship you to another prison across the state and you begin from scratch. Often you don't know why. It's usually jarring and unwelcome, but when a guard at a prison up north tells Johnny Coestly to pack his stuff, it's the best news he's heard in a long time. He is being shipped to Winn, where his little brother is locked up. Johnny hasn't seen him in thirteen years.

His brother is Damien Coestly, one of the men I had monitored on suicide watch during my first day on the job. Johnny has no idea Damien had been in and out of suicide watch since he's been locked up. The last time he's seen Damien, they were in a hotel room in a New Orleans suburb, laughing and joking as a hurricane raged outside. Damien, then twenty years old, was on the run. A few months earlier, three men had

---

* CCA points to a later analysis by an independent monitor that concluded that the rate of violence at Idaho Correctional Center during the entire first eight months of 2008 was not disproportionate to that of other facilities.

confronted him in a club. One was angry because Damien had been "messing" with his girlfriend. The man spit in his face. Damien shot all three, killing one. Not long afterward Damien was arrested, sentenced to thirty years, and sent to Winn. As a former felon, Johnny was never allowed to visit him. He and Damien frequently talked on the phone, but the calls ended when Johnny got locked up for selling drugs. It will be great to hear his little brother's voice again.

Johnny hasn't yet finished the intake process at Winn when a guard takes him into a room where the warden and the prison's social worker are waiting. They have bad news: Damien has been sent to the hospital. He is unconscious. Johnny's world suddenly stops. Before the information can sink in, Johnny is put back on a bus and shipped to another prison across the state.

Damien had just come off two weeks of suicide watch. A SORT officer had decided to put him in a regular segregation cell with an elderly man who was severely mentally ill. State policy allows inmates to be removed from suicide watch only with the approval of a mental health professional or a physician, but SORT didn't bother with that. An inmate who had been a few cells down from Damien in Cypress saw a SORT member take him out of his cell to make a phone call. Damien told the officer he was feeling suicidal, and the officer said he would come back to get him, to put him back on watch. No one came, and Damien repeated several times that he was going to kill himself. According to prison policy, that should have gotten him automatically placed on suicide watch.

Guards were supposed to check on inmates in seg every thirty minutes, but an hour and a half passed and no one had come. Then an inmate pounded the metal above his cell door. SORT officers came storming down the tier with pepper spray in hand, shouting, "Who the fuck is beating?"

"Dude is hanging himself!" the inmate shouted.

The SORT officers found Damien's cellmate, sedated by sleeping medication, struggling to hold Damien up to relieve the pressure from the sheet he was hanging from. As the cellmate was asleep, Damien had tied a sheet to the top of his cell's bars, looped it around his neck, and jumped off the bunk.

When Damien's mom, Wendy Porter, arrived at the hospital, she found her son unresponsive, skin peeling from his shackled ankles. What shocked her most was his size. He'd always been slim—six months ago, he weighed in at 121 pounds—but he liked to work out and he was always muscular. Now he was a shadow of himself. She sat with him for much of the nineteen days he remained on life support. When he died at age thirty-three, he weighed seventy-one pounds.

I reach out to Damien's mom to see if I can learn more about her son. I wrestle with whether to tell her about the video I secretly shot of him the day I was stationed on suicide watch. I know I'll write about her son's death and probably publish some of the video online. She tells me she has no video of him, not even from his childhood. The least I can do is give her the opportunity to watch this footage of her son, suicidal in an empty cage, before the world sees it. I send her my snippets: Damien nibbling carrot slices; Damien trying to hand me a Styrofoam cup through his food slot, asking if I'll sneak him some coffee; Damien telling me he's going to jump from the top bunk and break his neck; Damien, quiet, wrapped in his suicide blanket like a cocoon; Damien leaning up against the bars. "This dumb-ass motherfucking CCA, this tops the charts in nonrehabilitation," he says. "This Winnfield, man. This type of shit ain't gonna change till you shut it down." After she watches it, she calls me, her voice somber. She didn't realize it was that bad, she says. "If I knew it was that bad, I would have *walked* to Winnfield. That keeps playing in my head. It hurts me to see him sitting there crying out for help and no one would help him."

Wendy calls me periodically, mostly to vent about wanting to sue

CCA and to fret over how to pay the bill the hospital had sent her for Damien's medical records. One day, when I answer the phone, she says, *You say you writing for a magazine? My son say I should be compensated for this.* I explain that it is considered unethical for journalists to pay their sources. *Maybe I should write a book*, she says. *Could you help me write a book? I got this bill from the hospital for $307.41. Then maybe if I wrote a book I could pay that.*

I learn that the prison sent her Damien's belongings, and I ask her if I can come to New Orleans and look through it. When I pull into her driveway, she is there, wearing a T-shirt with "God is Good!" on it and a floppy purple cap to cover the scars from her recent brain surgery. She isn't the broken woman I expected to find. Rather she gives the impression of someone who has weathered much in life, who has trained for this painful storm. Her two remaining sons are in prison. Their fathers and Damien's are either behind bars or dead. When we sit and talk in her living room, it becomes clear that she is navigating her loss while reckoning with the fact that she'd missed a lot of her boys' childhood because she'd been smoking crack. "When I would put the crack in a pipe, I would be looking in a mirror asking God to please help me," she says. When Damien got locked up, she was serving a short prison term. When he was five, she gave custody of her children to her aunt. Yet she is eager for me to know that she never stopped loving her kids. She quit using drugs and got back into their lives. Even when they were in prison, she would always send them what little she could scrape together.

She disappears into a room and comes back with a small cardboard box that contains everything he owned: letters from her, sugar packets, stacks of documents, photos. There is a picture of him sitting in a prison yard in front of a row of books—biographies of Malcolm X and Che Guevara and titles on astronomy, astrology, and health. There is a grievance form in which he claimed he'd mailed the gold caps from his teeth to his mom, but they went missing.* There is a printout from CCA's website on which he highlighted the phrase, "We constantly monitor the offender population for signs of declining mental health and suicide risk, working actively to assist a troubled offender in his or her time of need."

Damien's fragile mental state was no secret at the prison. He went on suicide watch at least seventeen times during the three and a half years before he died. He told a friend of his in the prison that he was not going to finish his sentence: When he was at peace with God, he was going to kill himself. He told his friend he regretted killing the man who'd spit on him and said he'd rather be in the same place as that man than do his time in prison. In Damien's files, Winn's part-time psychologist noted, "Inmate stated that he was feeling depressed and worried that he was going to kill himself, because he was hearing the voice of the person that he killed and that he was telling him to kill himself and join him." On another occasion a prison counselor wrote, "He says [he's] done with CCA and his life."†

As I read through the papers, I begin to see the contours of a person who not only was in desperate need of mental health support, but also wanted help so badly that he was battling the company in his attempts to get it. In the box I find a grievance in which he complained that the rehabilitative efforts at Winn were inadequate and that he'd been on a wait list for twelve-step and mental health programs for two years. "Just because I have twenty years left in prison doesn't mean that I'm nonexistent and that I don't matter," he wrote. There is one from 2014 in which he claims that while on suicide watch in Winn's Cypress unit, he was jolted awake by two guards who dragged him out of his bunk, cuffed him, made him stand naked in the hallway, and slammed him against the wall

---

* CCA turned down his complaint.
† CCA responded to one question about Damien Coestly's death. It never responded to the more than twenty additional questions I sent.

repeatedly. In another complaint Damien wrote that he and other inmates were left on suicide watch with no guards to monitor them. He claimed that two inmates then came into the tier and threw milk cartons full of feces on the inmates in the suicide watch cells while the guards stood by, doing nothing to stop them. "Check the cameras ASAP because this incident is going to ruin Winnfield's reputation with this criminal act," he wrote. "I fear for my life back here in Cypress because there's nothing but chaos back here."*

Damien had apparently been studying law in prison. After suing Winn over two pairs of shoes taken by guards, the Department of Corrections asked CCA to reimburse him $47.32. Was he preparing a more substantial case against the prison? Damien had collected documents from lawsuits brought on behalf of inmates who had committed suicide in custody. He had filed at least one grievance claiming that guards were putting him on suicide watch, naked, without consulting the mental health staff, which was against DOC policy. He had appealed to the DOC to review his claim, a necessary step before an inmate can file a federal civil rights claim. The DOC denied his appeal.

Damien didn't just protest on paper. He frequently went on hunger strike. At times it was because the prison would not give him a vegetarian meal as he'd often requested. The prison didn't offer vegetarian options, so he ate the regular meals without the meat. Other times he stopped eating to protest inadequate mental health services. Once, the prison psychologist reported in Coestly's medical records that Damien was on suicide watch and "upset because he felt that he was not getting the appropriate care from mental health." He wrote that Coestly complained that claiming to be suicidal was the only way to get a meeting with the psychiatrist. "Inmate has a long history of playing games and trying to manipulate the system," the psychologist wrote.

---

* It is not clear if CCA received or reviewed these complaints.

CCA claims the suicide rate in its prisons is lower than in public prisons. But is this true? CCA never reported Damien's suicide to the state. CCA's spokesperson will later insist to me that Damien did not commit suicide at Winn because he was no longer in CCA's custody when he died. After the hospital found Damien to be brain dead, CCA requested that DOC grant him a "compassionate release." Because he died after he left Winn, no suicide tarnished CCA's record.

While I read through Damien's papers, Wendy keeps offering me food: candy, chips, whatever she finds while searching through her cupboards. Eventually she sits down. "He suffered," she says. "That's why I kept sending money: He was hungry. Give him his food! That's all he wanted was his food. He didn't want no meat. He just wanted something like a fruit and a vegetable. He weighed seventy-one pounds. That was like somebody starving." Her voice cracks. "I keep food in my house. I *give* people food!" she shouts, weeping. "I would never turn nobody down for no food, and he weighed seventy-one pounds." She pauses and takes a deep breath. "It's all about a dollar. That's what you is, a dollar sign to them. You know what my son said? He said it over the phone. He said, 'When I get through with them, they're going to shut this place down. It ain't fit for an animal.'" When I say goodbye, she gives me a breakfast bar and a tangerine. I get in my vehicle, I eat them, and I drive.

| 16 |

The torture and slaughter of thousands of African American men was no secret during the six-odd decades of postbellum convict leasing. From the beginning, newspapers had published exposés, legislative investigations had revealed startling numbers of deaths, and penal reformers and individual legislators had pushed for abolition. But outcry over humanitarian concerns had never been enough to end convict leasing on its own. It was only when leasing stopped bringing enormous profits to powerful businessmen and state treasuries that the system came apart.

Things began to change in Texas, where the lease for all of the state prisoners had been controlled entirely by a man named Edward H. Cunningham. Thanks to the labor of more than a thousand black convicts who worked his Sugarland plantation at any given time, Cunningham was the richest sugar planter in Texas and one of the largest in the country. Convicts he didn't use on his own plantation were subleased to planters around the state. The fact that Cunningham's lease accounted for 3 percent of the state's total revenue was not enough to assure him that it would be renewed once it expired in 1883, so he began an aggressive lobbying campaign. He set up a private club for legislators stocked with "whiskey . . . cigars and other luxuries." To avoid the scandal of committing outright bribery, his club hosted games of "jack-pot poker," in which even bad players found they could win big.

The strategy backfired. Newspapers exposed his scheme, and to save his business and reputation in the face of public outrage, Cunningham was forced to withdraw his bid. The state would never again allow one contractor to monopolize the lease, but instead began granting leases to a variety of employers. Since these companies weren't controlling the entire system, they could be choosier about the convicts they accepted. Strong "first class men" were easy for the state to rent out to private mines, wood camps, and plantations, but "surplus labor" or "deadheads" were not. The prison administration had to figure out what to do with the men the contractors rejected, so, beginning in 1884, former slaveholder, Confederate officer, and prison superintendent Thomas J. Goree began an "experiment." The state bought two plantations of roughly two thousand acres each to "work second-class labor, negroes, boys, cripples, such men as we cannot hire out for first class labor."

The venture was a success. In the first year, the state earned about $10,500 (around $250,000 in 2018). Twelve years later, it was earning more than five times that amount. The prison system's financial agent calculated that the supposedly weaker prisoners working the state-run plantations were earning more profit per person than the "first class, able bodied negro convicts employed on contract farms." The government farm was earning $501.39 per inmate while the contract farms were bringing in just $178. The profits encouraged prison officials to ask the legislature for money to buy more prison farms. By 1910 the state of Texas owned more than twenty thousand acres of sugar property. The 1908 crop alone would pay half of the purchase price of the Imperial plantation and the entire purchase price of the Ramsey plantation, where

CCA cofounder T. Don Hutto would become warden nearly sixty years later. By 1928 the state of Texas would be running twelve prison plantations.

There is no indication that laboring for the state was any better for inmates than slaving for private businessmen. To avoid work on the state-run plantations, prisoners amputated their own feet, placed lye into razor cuts to create festering sores, injected kerosene under their skin, and fractured their arms and legs. Most commonly, however, they amputated three fingers from one hand or severed their Achilles tendons. When tendons were cut, they would be reconnected by doctors and the inmates would be sent back to the fields. From 1932 to 1951 there were nearly nine hundred recorded cases of self-mutilations in Texas prisons.

Nevertheless, convict leasing abolitionists began to present state-run prison plantations as a more humane alternative to privatized penal systems, and a more economical one. In the late 1880s and 1890s North Carolina, South Carolina, Georgia, Virginia, Mississippi, Arkansas, and Alabama all acquired plantations, most of which are still prisons today. When Louisiana abolished leasing in 1901, it bought Angola from the Samuel L. James family and turned it into the state's main prison, alongside several other plantations and levee camps. The governor said that in taking over the prison system, the penitentiary board was engaged in "not only handling a large prison as such, but in the establishment of a great industrial and business enterprise." State-owned prison farms became the main mode of incarceration for many Southern states.

For years convict leasing and state-owned plantations coexisted, but leasing wasn't making the profits it once did. Since multiple companies were now bidding on contracts rather than a single businessman monopolizing the convict work force, they were under pressure to pay closer to the going rate of free labor. Companies made higher and higher bids, forcing the cost of convict labor in Texas to rise steadily until, in 1908, the Texas Turpentine Company was paying forty-five dollars per convict per month, a rate which, when combined with the cost of maintaining and guarding convicts, equaled the price of free labor. A similar pattern unfolded throughout the South. In Georgia the price of convicts rose more than twentyfold in thirty years, reaching a free laborer's wage by 1904. As a result, convict leasing became less desirable to the businessmen who had fought so hard to maintain it. Free laborers, who could be laid off in slack times, began to seem like a more attractive option. In both Georgia and Texas, once leasing costs reached the level of free workers, leasing was abolished as soon as contracts expired.

In other states entrenched interests fought to maintain leasing, and abolitionists had to come up with creative ways to overcome them. One reform governor, George W. Donaghey of Arkansas, called for a law "abolishing the lease system under any form" in his 1908 inaugural address. Convicts, he argued, should be worked under state supervision on Cummins, a farm it purchased in 1902. Leasing had actually been "abolished" in Arkansas nearly twenty years earlier, but lessees and penitentiary officials justified continuation of the practice. They argued that the number of prisoners in the state was too large for them to all be cared for on Cummins, a farm it purchased in 1902. Donaghey realized that the system would not break until a final blow was struck against the companies perpetuating the system, so he decided to do it himself. During his lame duck period in 1908, Donaghey pardoned 360 prisoners, one-third of the state's convicts. Three convict camps were suddenly without workers, and Donaghey estimated it would take at least two years before the convict population reached the previous levels. The state abolished the system for good the following year.

. . .

Ironically, some of the strongest opponents of convict leasing were white supremacists. By 1900 Mississippi had become the nation's poorest state and thousands of whites found themselves falling into a labor system—sharecropping—that was designed for former slaves. One newspaper owner, James Kimble Vardaman, promised to save white men from the patrician planters who disenfranchised them and the "field niggers" who worked their land. In 1903 Vardaman, known by his followers as the "White Chief," ran for governor of Arkansas. He gained national attention when he blasted President Roosevelt as a "little, mean, coon-flavored miscegenationist" because he invited Booker T. Washington, whom Vardaman called a "nigger bastard," to dine with him in the White House. In his gubernatorial campaign, Vardaman promised to handle the "coon problem" by ending black education, curtailing voting rights for African Americans, and repealing "frivolous safeguards" relating to race. His campaign banner read, "A Vote for Vardaman Is a Vote for White Supremacy, the Safety of the Home, and the Protection of Our Women and Children."

When he was elected governor the following year, he immediately set to work to end convict leasing, claiming it enriched plantation owners and railroad barons at the expense of poor whites and the state. During a legislative session, Vardaman pointed to a legislative investigating committee report to show that by dividing its profits with Delta plantation owners, the state was not making as much money as it could from its convicts. "If the state can make money working a private individual's land and giving that . . . individual half of the [profit], it can . . . make more money working its own land and keeping the entire product."

Before Vardaman became governor, the state had bought more than twenty thousand acres to turn into prison farms. Vardaman personally supervised the construction of prison barracks and the draining and clearing of the land. He believed in a certain type of rehabilitation— black people should not be brutalized but taught proper discipline, strong work habits, and respect for white authority. This, he believed, could be accomplished only under the guise of the state. But Vardaman insisted he was "more interested in the salvation of men than I am in hoarding gold." Fortunately for Vardaman, forcing black men to pick cotton in the name of rehabilitation also created gold. In 1905, less than a year after the state put convicts on Parchman, it turned a profit of $185,000 (about $5 million in 2018). The following year, Mississippi ended convict leasing. Within ten years, state profits from prison labor would be around $600,000 ($14.7 million in 2018).

The final blow to convict leasing was the exposure of the torture and death of a twenty-two-year-old white man in Florida named Martin Tabert. Tabert was from a middle-class family in North Dakota, and in 1921 he set out on an adventure across the country. He traveled by train, working odd jobs to fund his trip through the West, Midwest, and eventually the South. By the time he got to Florida that December, he'd run out of money, and when his train stopped in Leon County, the sheriff pulled him off for not having a ticket and charged him with "stealing a ride on a railroad train." The sheriff fined Tabert twenty dollars for vagrancy, but he had no money, so he sent a telegram to his brother: "In trouble and need fifty dollars to pay fine for vagrancy. Please wire money in care of sheriff." His parents sent money right away, but the sheriff returned it to them stamped "Party Gone." Because he didn't have money on hand to pay the fine, Tabert had already been sold off to the Wisconsin-based Putnam Lumber Company for three month's work in a turpentine camp.

Little had changed in the turpentine camps since J. C. Powell, author of The American Siberia, had been a guard in one fifty years earlier. Tabert worked in swamp water all day in tattered shoes that didn't fit. His feet and legs swelled up and he asked the whipping boss, Walter Higginbotham, for a larger pair. Higginbotham ignored him. When Tabert later complained about an aching groin, a doctor gave him medicine, but Higginbotham still made him work. Some days later, he accused Tabert of shirking when he lagged behind the other convicts on a two-mile hike to the swamp. When they returned for the night, Higginbotham told Tabert to lie on the ground in front of some eighty convicts, pulled up his shirt, and gave him some thirty lashes with a seven-and-a-half-pound leather strap, dragging it through sugar and sand between each lick. Tabert lay twitching on the ground and begged Higginbotham to stop, prompting the man to hold his foot on Tabert's neck and whip him forty more times. "You can't work yet, eh?" Higginbotham taunted. Tabert struggled to stand up, and as he staggered around in a half circle, Higginbotham hit him over the head with the handle of the strap. Tabert, no longer able to stand, was laid down on a cot, where he perished the following night. The camp physician examined his body and pronounced that he died from "pneumonia with malaria complications."

The Putnam Lumber Company sent a letter to the Tabert family, saying their son had died of fever, expressing their condolences and notifying them they had buried his body. The family initially believed the company's story, but they began receiving letters from former convicts, telling them that their son had been murdered. The family convinced the North Dakota state attorney to go to Florida to investigate Talbert's death, and the evidence he collected substantiated every detail of the letters. The attorney said the Leon County sheriff was "little better than a slave-catcher": He had an agreement with the company that it would pay the sheriff twenty dollars for every convict sent to its camp for at least ninety days.

The Florida legislature ordered an investigation into Tabert's death and found that after the sheriff made his agreement with Putnam Lumber, the number of people arrested as vagrants for riding a train without a ticket multiplied eightfold. A former Leon County jailer testified that the sheriff was "railroading" laborers into the lease system for a sizable profit. Men charged with vagrancy were brought before "inebriated court officers," without lawyers, late at night, and they were regularly found guilty.

The Tabert family sued the Putnam Lumber Company, which settled out of court for $20,000 (some $140,000 in 2018) in exchange for a public statement from the family that the company was absolved "of all willful blame." Higginbotham, meanwhile, was tried for murder, found guilty, and sentenced to twenty years in prison. His conviction was later overturned on a technicality and the state supreme court ordered a new trial. Higginbotham was released on a $10,000 bail and, as he awaited retrial, he returned to his duties for Putnam at a different camp. Then, on October 19, 1924, he beat and shot to death a black turpentine worker named Lewis "Peanut" Barker. He was again indicted for murder. Meanwhile, Higginbotham was acquitted of all charges in the Talbert case. When it came time for his trial on the Barker murder, he was "physically unable to appear in court" because of an automobile accident. There was no further attempt to punish him for the crime.

In the history of convict leasing, no other case rose to the level of cause célèbre of the Martin Tabert story. The New York *World* covered the case closely, winning a Pulitzer Prize and prompting editorials in papers throughout the country that demanded an end to the lease system. Organizations as prominent as the American Agricultural Association began to refer to the convict lease system as "slavery." People countrywide boycotted Florida-made goods and the state's tourism began to suffer. In 1923 the Florida legislature abolished convict leasing.

When Alabama State Senator Walter S. Brower submitted a bill to abolish Alabama's leasing program in 1923, the Tabert case was prominent in his campaign. "The Tabert boy, who was killed in a Florida convict camp, was a short time man," he said. "He was convicted of riding a train. There can be a repetition of the Florida affair in Alabama." The following year, a white convict named James Knox was found dead in an Alabama coal mining camp and his death certificate, signed by a doctor, claimed that the cause of death was suicide. The attorney general later found that Knox had in fact been subject to the "watering" torture. Large amounts of water were poured into his mouth through a funnel for not working fast enough. "James Knox died in a laundering vat," the attorney general's report read, "where he was placed by two negroes. . . . It seems most likely that James Knox died as a result of heart failure, which probably was caused by a combination of unusual exertion and fear. . . . After death it seems that a poison was injected artificially into his stomach in order to simulate accidental death or suicide."

Florida and Alabama were the last two states to use convict leasing, and the Tabert and Knox cases pushed them to end it. For the thousands who had been through the system, the justice was perhaps bittersweet. Under the convict lease system, private companies had been torturing and slaughtering black men for decades. It took the murder of a white man for the country to pay attention.

| 17 |

Bacle, Calahan, and I stand in the key on Saturday morning. I rub my eyes—three more days until I get a break. Calahan looks worn out too. Bacle, however, is giddy and does a little dance, shaking his fists up and down and shimmying with his hips. He is excited because a twentysomething inmate, who is particularly difficult to corral into his tier, got locked up last night for masturbating at the woman working the key.

I can never bring myself to get excited with Bacle when people are sent to Cypress, but I am beginning to harbor a secret hope when I come into work that a small set of inmates will have disappeared. With all the people who get caught standing at the bars in the dead of night, staring at the woman in the key, jerking off, how is it never the guy with the facial tattoos? I dread doing count on B1 tier. It's almost routine now that when I open the door and shout "count time!" and everyone pours out of the TV room and goes to their beds, Tattoo Face goes to the toilet. Technically, they aren't allowed to do this during count, but it's one of the rules we ignore as a matter of practicality—who wants to fight with someone over when they can take a piss? I try to pretend like I don't notice that he stands over the toilet bowl and stares at me with his dick in his hand while Bacle is walking down the tier. But even when I don't look, I feel him there, watching me. Sometimes when I come up the tier, finishing up my count, I catch a glimpse of his erect penis and our eyes meet before he looks away. He knows I know what he is doing. Sometimes when I open his tier door for chow, he whispers things to me. "Today's gonna be a *real* nice day," he says, his eyes scanning me up and down. I don't know how to deal with him. If I called him out in front of everyone during count time, the entire tier would laugh at me. There is nothing more emasculating than getting "jacked off on." I could write him up, but I can't imagine another male guard citing an inmate for sexual harassment. What would the other officers think of me? And besides, Tattoo Face is careful to make it difficult. In the quiet parts of the day, for example, he stands at the bars with his hands in his pants watching me. He knows that if I did write him up, it wouldn't go anywhere, since no masturbation charge will stick unless I can write that "I saw the inmate holding his erect penis and moving his hand in a back and forth motion," and if I were to take liberties in my telling, the surveillance cameras could prove I was lying.

I know some of this is caused by my own rookie mistakes: I've given the wrong impression with all the smiling and doing favors. I try to address every request and respond to every inmate who yells "Minnesota," my new nickname. The microwaves on some of the tiers are broken, so I help out by carrying cups of water for soup or coffee to another tier, where other inmates heat them up. When Corner Store isn't working and people ask if I can let them off the tier for a minute so they can run and exchange a honey bun for a few cigarettes, I unlock the door. I let people out to see the corrections counselor when they need a mattress, or to call their lawyers, even when she tells me she doesn't want to field these requests, which is most of the time.

But people like Tattoo Face mistake kindness for weakness. How do I find the middle ground between appearing soft and being draconian? I need to set my terms and stick to them. Like they told us in training, the key is to be consistent: The inmates will test you, but if you are unwavering, they will fall in line. The easiest approach would be to follow Bacle's lead; charting my own path shows a gap between us that the prisoners can exploit. But I'm not like Bacle. When I write up one inmate after he runs off the tier against my orders, I think about it all weekend, wondering if he will get sent to Cypress. I feel guilty and decide I will only write up inmates for two things: threatening me and refusing to get on their tier after they enter the unit. The floor is where most assaults happen, and when a lot of inmates are out there, things can get out of hand. That's not why I choose to write them up for it though. I write them up because my main job is to keep inmates off the floor, and if I don't establish authority, I end up having to negotiate with each prisoner over how long he can wander the unit, which is exhausting.

I've been beginning to wonder whether I'm being too lenient when I let inmates out to Ash's small yard for rec time. It's a tiresome routine. We go around, tier by tier, shouting for anyone who wants to go outside. They are supposed to get ready and line up at the door for when we come around again to open it, but it never happens this way. Instead we open a tier door, people get up from their beds and trickle out, and then we close it and go to the next one. Once we finish all eight tiers, there are inevitably inmates calling for us to come back and let them out, each with his own excuse about why he wasn't ready earlier. I want to make sure everyone gets outside who wants to go, so I usually end up wandering around, letting out the stragglers. But I'm beginning to feel that even gestures like this are double-edged: I'm communicating to them that they can ignore me, and that later I'll respond to their commands.

Bacle opens the door of A2 tier, and a man on the toilet asks him to come back in a few minutes. "If you don't come out now you ain't coming out!" Bacle shouts at him and slams the door. After we go around to each tier, the inmate is standing at the bars and asks us to open the door. Bacle looks at me. "It's up to you," he says. Is Bacle testing me? I hesitate for a moment and then say no, he can't come out. The prisoner shouts as I walk away.

Once the floor is clear and the inmates are locked inside the yard, Calahan tells me to go to Ash gate. I need to fill in for the gate officer Childs who has to report to the count room to do his annual online training. These trainings have suddenly become a priority because the DOC wardens began showing up unannounced throughout the prison. At the gate I can see ten inmates in the small yard. A few are lifting twenty-pound dumbbells attached to the ground with chains. Others are doing bench presses and leg extensions on a rusty, clanging weight machine. The elderly gate officer hands me his keys and shuffles down the walk.

"Hey CO, you letting Bacle lead you wrong," one inmate shouts at me from the small yard.

"What you talking about?"

"I'm talking about how you don't want to let nobody out on the shitter." It's the guy who was on the toilet. How did he get out here? "The warden had just *told* us if we got a problem with y'all we should let him know," he says in a threatening tone. "Bacle goes busting our fucking ass and looking like he need to take a nigga down. So we coming to you with respect, bro."

"Hey!" the coach shouts at the inmate. He's standing outside the gym, across the walk from Ash gate. "That right there ain't respect young man!"

"I ain't even talking to you!"

"You know you disrespect!" the coach shouts.

"Shit, you ain't got no respect for nobody! I ain't trying to come at you! Shit, you getting all in my business. Be professional! You gonna get what you looking for!"

"Come and give me some of that partner!" the coach says. "I want your ass!"

"Shit you ain't even worth it!" the inmate retorts.

"Neither is you!"

"Make your little money and go on home."

"Make my little money? You don't how much fuckin' money I make." The coach goes into the gym. I walk over to the fence and call the inmate over.

"Hey, I hear you about the shitter," I say.

"Ain't no problem, we just trying to live together," he says.

Before count time rolls around, I unlock the yard gate and ask everyone whether they want to go back inside. Once count begins, they will have to stay put until it's finished. All but one go back into the unit.

I stand out on the main walk. A couple of gunshots ring out, muffled cracks in the surrounding forest. "They got a gun range 'round here?" the lone inmate on the yard asks me through the fence. He is in his late twenties, with a round, dark face, a gap in his front teeth, and eyes that are calm yet confident. His pecs are defined by his tattered, hooded gray shirt.

"People hunt out in those woods," I say. We can see the wall of yellow pines to the west beyond the perimeter fence.

"You like your little job right here?" Gray Shirt asks.

"It's alright," I say.

"See I be noticing somethin'. You be a little demanding on that floor, brah."

"Got to be," I say.

"Yeah but you be forcing people's hands into a little corner, brah. Niggas be trying to respect you, and treat you like a man. You be over-aggressive with dudes."

"I'm not like that with everybody," I say defensively. "Only people that don't respect me."

"You be doing that with me! I ain't never disrespected you. You be lookin' to *say* I disrespectin' you, brah. Yeah! You looking for it! And you might be putting yourself in an uncomfortable position because you might be dealing with a nigga that be like, 'Fuck it! You gonna call the captain? Well I'll pop the shit out you then.' You force a nigga hand."

"Nobody's gonna do nothing," I say.

"You serious?" He laughs. "You think I'm bullshitting. The captain will tell you: See six months ago I probably would have popped the fuck out you if you came fucking with me crazy." I become aware of the quiet. No one is around. Except for me, the walk is empty. "I'm in jail for killing police. I don't really like police. But I know I got to deal with y'all because I'm incarcerated. I got children. I ain't no stupid mother fucker."

Sometimes, he snaps. Once, he says, the SORT team shot him thirteen times with a PepperBall gun. He had been on suicide watch, naked in his cell for a month. "I lost my fucking mind in that bitch. I'm head butting the glass and all types of shit." Edison, the bullnecked former cop, was working in Cypress at the time. "I don't like that dude's walk, bro. He seem like he's top authority. He done been in the army. He done body guarded for Shaq. He done did all these types of things." He thinks Edison was intimidated by him. "I be like one of the only dudes back there working out. He saw my body progressing." Gray Shirt kept a water bottle in his cell, he says, because there was no running water in it. He would ask COs to fill up the bottle. One day, Edison took it. "I said, 'You bitch ass motherfucker.'

"'Somebody mace this motherfucker," Edison said.

"If they mace me I'm gonna dropkick you first, bitch," Gray Shirt replied.

When Edison passed by later, Gray Shirt threw a cup of piss on him. "Bitch! I'll beat your mother-fucking ass," Gray Shirt shouted. When the captain and others came to take him out of his cell, he refused. He just jogged in place, naked, as a SORT officer aimed the PepperBall gun at him. "I go in military mode. I don't give a fuck. I ain't worried about no pain or nothing. We go' hurt each other in this bitch, you heard me? I'm tryin' to get 'em to open the door. 'Y'all gotta do a cell entry. Come on in this bitch. I'ma take y'all paint ball and I'ma take this fucking mace, but I want to put my hands on one of these mother-fuckers.'"

"You are in here for shooting police?" I ask. "What happened?"

He tells me a stick-up man tried to rob his brother when he was moving pounds of weed from Texas to Baton Rouge. The man shot up his brother's truck in their neighborhood, but didn't get the drugs. The shooting drew the attention of the police, and he says he saw the cops sneaking around and taking pictures, trying to build an indictment against his brother. So he went after them and killed one officer. "I've been down now eleven years. Got nineteen more to go. I'm walkin' that shit down."

He's been imprisoned on that charge since he was seventeen. But he was locked up for manslaughter when he was thirteen, he says. When he got out on his first charge, "I had a probation officer, a little female. A little freaky ass probation officer. She'd suck my dick and let me eat her pussy and just, you know what I'm saying, freak out with her. I didn't ever fuck her till I got older." She was married to a deacon in a Pentecostal church, but Gray Shirt said their relationship was strained. She would take this inmate to her kids' baseball games, and he would be the only black man there. He would bring the kids toys, like giant incredible hulk gloves, and they grew fond of him. After he got locked up again, he says she came and visited him, but eventually she stopped. "She's still a PO now. She still sends me pictures and shit."

He tells me I need to restructure my priorities. What I really should be thinking about is money, not petty battles with inmates. "Believe it or not, there are ups and downs, but you can make a lot of money in this motherfucker. I've seen some of the crookedest motherfuckers who be acting like they be trying to stop the violence and shit. Half of them got rich off this motherfucker—dumb rich." He looks at me intensely. "You can beat 'em in the game. All this depends on how you make it. You can do a job that you risk your life for, that they really ain't paying you shit, or you can come in this bitch and get with the program."

He suddenly walks off toward the weights. I turn around and see a few white men coming down the walk. They are the evangelists, here now and then to talk to inmates and hand out pamphlets. I unlock the gym gate. They go inside and the prisoner comes back to the fence.

"This camp easy," he says. "I ain't lying. This is the best one I done been to. It's everything you got at this camp that you not supposed to have. Who wouldn't want to be in paradise where you can watch a fuck flick or you could talk on the phone to your people. Or you can just relax and be on drugs or whatever, you feel what I'm sayin'? And the people"— the Department of Corrections—"ain't tripping, because nine times out of ten the free people getting loaded too. They coming in here drunk, high."

He says the real problem is the stabbings—the *joogings*. "It's slowing money down, know what I'm sayin'? I done watched dudes make damn near fifty thousand dollars in this bitch. Niggas around this bitch, they got the game fucked up, know what I'm saying? If you could stop from joogin' each other, you could stop from making publicity. Now you got the people taking the camp over again. Every morning you got the DOC walking through this bitch. See what I'm saying? Just fight. Go out there and get a black eye. Get a little busted nose and call it what it is. They'll let you fight all day." I think of a time a cadet found a lock in a sock in an inmate's locker during a shakedown. "I don't give a shit about no lock in a sock," Mr. Tucker told the cadet. "They can beat the shit out of each other as much as they want with that."

The inmate sees Kenny coming down the walk. He stops talking, but there is no time to walk away. It would look too unnatural. Kenny eyes me suspiciously for the briefest moment and asks whether I saw the maintenance guys go past with the paint for Elm. He walks on.

"My rounder just whooped his ass about two weeks ago."

"Ash key to Ash Gate," Miss Calahan says over the radio.

"Go ahead," I say into my shoulder.

"Sir, what's your yard count?"

"I have one. Just one." I let go of the radio and lean up against the fence.

"So what was that about?" I ask the inmate.

Kenny, he says, is "a bitch." "He do shit by the book. He fair, don't get me wrong. When he ran the gym, you gonna get rec. You gonna get your hair cut. He be fair. He do everything by the book. But *fuck* the book. We need to live in this bitch. So alright, I done paid three hundred fifty dollars for a brand-new phone. Now you done came here and took my motherfucking shit. How the fuck you think I'm finna feel? My Momma just told me she ain't gonna buy no mo' 'cuz it cost too much money. My girl is saying I'm breaking they pockets 'cuz it's the second one they bought in one month. You gonna come and take this motherfucker? You gonna take this motherfucking ass-whooping then. That shit hurts. Shit."

"How much did he have to pay to get that guy to go after him?"

"I ain't go' lie, if I want a motherfucking CO ass bad enough, I'd pay about fifteen hundred for you. Watch a nigga tear your ass up." I'm sure he knows about the phone I took. It was on his tier. He knows I've been struggling too. He watches people like me come and go. He sees guards flounder. He sees us break. He sees us turn against the institution. He sees us harden. He sees what I do and where I fail. He, more than most COs, knows what it would take for me to make it. "It's all about how you carry yourself," he says. "Respect is earned, that shit ain't given. It's just about how you go about wanting your respect, know what I'm sayin'? You can go about it hollering and tripping and policing and shit. You going to get more disrespect than you get respect. Or you can go through this letting certain shit slide, you know. You might turn the other cheek too.

"On the real though, you got to realize that a lot of these dudes is young. A lot of them is seventeen, eighteen. They in here all day cooped up, bored, nothing to do, and it just so happens you are a person that's over them with authority so automatically you a target, you know what I'm sayin'?"

"Yeah, and that's why I gotta show them that they can't mess around with me. What do you think I should do? Ignore it?"

"Yeah! That's what you supposed to do."

"Nah, it doesn't work that way. Because you know what happens if I ignore it? It happens more." I don't know if I believe what I'm saying, but this logic pours automatically from my mouth. "'Cuz when I first came in here, that's what happened."

He laughs. "They ate you alive, huh?"

"People started thinking, Oh, he's scared, he's scared," I say. "So you gotta show people you don't mess around."

"People don't think you're scared man. A lot of people think you're gay, bro. You be wearing those tight-ass pants."

I look down at my pants. "These aren't tight!" I say, gripping the loosely hanging leg. This isn't the first time I've heard this.

"Well you know, nigga not lookin' at that, you heard me? Niggas talkin' about the glutes, know what I'm sayin'? Like you got them skinny jeans on, know what I'm sayin'? People say they are so tight they give you a suntan in the wintertime." We both laugh. "You got a woman's swag, brah. On the real! Everybody that move like you and act like you, they homosexuals. It's not a bad thing. See, I been down eleven years, and you know, you nice." I chuckle and kick the fence lightly with the tip of my boot. For some reason this guy doesn't threaten me like some others. "When they seeing you they like, yeah if he was in here, I'd be fucking the shit out of him! They looking at it like, Okay, you comin' through this motherfucker with these tight-ass pants on, lookin' good, and you don't want to admit you gay? You say you got a wife? That don't mean shit. I know about four people work here that's married that got wife and children that's gay."

"But how do you know they're gay? You just *say* that."

He looks at me sideways. "Nope."

"Like who?" I say.

"I can't say no names."

"I'm not gonna say nothing."

"I understand that, but if it was with you, you wouldn't want me to mention your name."

I notice the cirrus clouds streaking above us. When I took this job, I decided I would never tell an outright lie, but I wouldn't necessarily correct people's misperceptions about me. How far can I take this? Can I make myself an empty canvas for this prisoner, too, letting him believe I am naive, or even that I want something from him, so I can go deeper? I've been coming to believe that the barrier between prisoners and guards is insurmountable and that little is possible beyond stunted conversations and interactions, but this guy is frank and open in a way no other prisoner has been. Maybe he is the one to bring me across that barrier. Also, having inmates like him in my good graces helps me because younger, harder prisoners follow their lead. If he was on my side, maybe things would be easier for me.

"What's your name?" I ask.

He hesitates. "Derik."

"Derik what?"

"Ah, I don't really like doing all that shit here."

"It's not like I can't find out if I want to."

"Yeah you could find out, but see I'll make it harder for you."

"It's fine. You don't have to tell me."

"Derik Johnson, man. See I ain't really with that giving up information shit. I don't give a fuck. I'll probably pass a polygraph. I ain't never gonna tell on myself, you heard me? Let me tell you something: Even if you was bringing shit in for me, I'd always have that one thought in the back of my mind. There might come a time where we go to set some shit up and you might get me locked up. You better have the same thought about me."

"I do," I say.

"You'd be a fool if you don't. Everything that glitter ain't gold and everybody that talk real ain't real."

Childs comes back down the walk, back from his online training. "You ready to go back to work young man?" he shouts to me.

"You done?" I ask him.

"I gave up. I told her 'You do this shit. I don't know nothing about no computers.' I failed sexual harassment and I had to take it over." I hand him the keys, he unlocks the gate, and I go back into the unit.

After lunch, the radio dispatch tells us to make call outs. "All units and all areas it's time to make a call for your one thirty callouts, the Jaycee callouts, and the gym chapel. Also make a call out for your basketball teams. New York and Indiana. All units do you copy?"

"New York and Indiana basketball!" I shout from the end of a tier. "One thirty! Jaycees!" I pop the door, let a few people out, and go to the next tier. Bacle does the same. The unit comes to life. A din of chatter, laughter, and cussing fills the space. "Excuse me, excuse me" an inmate says to Bacle. "I'ma need your social today."

"No," Bacle says.

"I'ma need to write it down today."

"I said no! You're not getting it! Period!" Bacle shouts. "You ask me again, I'm gonna do paperwork."

"I-I-I got a lawsuit in progress though!"

"I don't care. You're not getting my social number. Period! There ain't but one damn Bacle here and that's me." The inmate laughs. I look at him from behind Bacle and snicker silently. No matter how many times he does this, Bacle never gets that he's just trying to rattle him.

When I open A2, an inmate with a fleur-de-lis tattoo on his neck begins to walk out. I'm tired of the way this guy's been staring at me lustfully as I walk the floor. When we let them out for chow, he and Tattoo Face sometimes stand at the back of the key together and watch me pass back and forth.

"Where you going?" I ask him.

"I'm going out on the yard," he says.

"They didn't call yard."

"Come on man. Everybody out there. I am going to basketball man!"

"No you're not," I say. "Get back." He stays in the threshold and won't let me close the door. His eyes look permanently stoned. "I'm gonna write you up if you don't step back in right now." I demand his ID.

"Man! I'm gonna buck out this bitch. Everybody out there." It's true that people are trickling out onto the yard, but they aren't supposed to be.

He steps back inside the tier. I close the door. "Give me your ID."

"Man fuck you," he says.

"All right," I say. "You want to play like that? You got it."

I walk away and let the rest out. Derik stands at the front of his tier,

C2. I know he doesn't play basketball, but I let him out without saying anything.

Minutes later, they radio for us to let inmates out to the yard. I open up A2 again and the inmate with the fleur-de-lis tattoo comes out, looking smug. "I'm still waiting for that ID," I say.

"Man I'm gonna bat you if you write me up for something!" He clenches his fists and draws back slightly. "I'll bat you in your fucking mouth!" His lips are clenched. I wait for him to strike. I'm unsure whether I should put my fists up in defense. Will that make me appear afraid?

"You're not smart talking like that," I say, and walk away.

"Know the game!" he shouts. "Know the game!"

I let people out of the next tier. Fleur-de-lis and Tattoo Face are standing together on the floor, looking angrily in my direction. For the rest of the day, I look over my shoulder and never stand with my back to other prisoners. I try to suppress the rising sense of panic inside as I wait for them to jump me. When I see Sergeant King later, I tell him what happened, hoping Fleur-de-lis will get sent away. He pulls Fleur-de-lis aside and tells him to go to his tier. He refuses.

"I was getting ready to lock his ass up, then I thought about it," Sergeant King tells me later. "To me it's a serious offense to threaten to inflict harm on a correctional officer. I was about to put his ass on the goddamn wall and get those hand restraints on him and get him on up out of here. But let's be real. We have a use-of-force down here. What kind of backup? What kind of support we got up top? I feel bad about saying that as a leader, but what's the truth? Y'all know the truth."

When I see Fleur-de-lis again, he laughs at me menacingly.

I step outside, take a deep, cool breath and look at the horizon. The church steeple is cutting through the setting sun. The light is becoming golden. Derik walks up and stands under the camera so no officer but me can see him.

"What's going on?" he says.

"Ready to go home," I say.

"You tired?"

"Yeah."

"Yeah, it be like that, brah. Get yourself some fresh air and do some number counts and go back in there."

I take a deep breath and let it out slowly. I want to resist the impulse to confide in him. I don't trust him, but I don't trust anyone here, so does it matter? Bacle is no help; when I talk to him about these problems, he just goes on a rant, either about how CCA doesn't give a shit about us or about how we should be able to take prisoners out back and beat them.

"You gonna go home soon," Derik says.

"Yep, one hour."

"See once you go to working here for a while, you gonna realize the ones talking shit just talking shit."

"I know, but I gotta react."

"You think because you got that white uniform on, you got to react. You gotta just give them a hard look and just walk off."

"Nah, it's one thing if someone's just talking shit, but if someone threatens me, I got to do something."

He laughs. "You got to do something, huh?" His presence is calm and disarming. "I tell a lot of people: Stop coming at people with that uniform. Come at a person like you would treat 'em in that world. Okay, you might lock your door on me if you see me in the parking lot and you getting out your brand-new car and I'm getting out a hoopty. That's cool. Treat me that way. Don't come with the authority role. You can treat me like, 'Okay I don't trust you. I gotta keep my door locked.' I respect that. But don't come through with that authority shit man. That shit ain't go' get you nowhere. 'Cuz I don't have to do what you say to do. That's just in your mind. You think I do. I'm a man like you. Know what I'm sayin'?"

An inmate comes up Ash walk, interrupting our conversation. "What you got going on, Big Man?" Derik asks him.

"Man, my gal *always* been by my side," Big Man says, "but when I call her it's like, 'Hold on, I got to do this right quick.'" Always busy and distracted. "You don't supposed to do that there to a nigga that's incarcerated boy."

"They got to give you your time," Derik says.

"Yeah, because I don't give a fuck if it's ten, twenty, thirty minutes. You got to give me that."

"That's why I hate when I call home," Derik says, "She be talking to the children while I'm talking to her."

"Exactly!" the other inmate shouts. "Fuck them little motherfuckers. Listen to what *I'm* saying. It's more important. Because I got a brief moment here. They might be about to lock the compound down, and kill every bitch here."

"You just need that little comfort zone," Derik says.

"That 'I-love-you!' It ain't gotta be a whole lot. That's what I told my niece and my sister and them. I said for eighteen years, if they couldn't send me no money, they could send me a piece of paper with "I love you" on it, ain't nothing else, and I will cherish that more. That's more than money to me. Fuck the money! Ain't no thing mean more than that motherfucking paper."

Big Man goes into the unit. "That's my boy right there," Derik says. "He like me. He chill, laid back, quiet, don't fuck with nobody. But you let that quietness fool you if you want to. Dudes be getting that shit fucked up. They'll see you quiet and laid back and take that shit for granted, not realizing that nigga will kill you."

He asks me for a piece of gum. We aren't allowed to give inmates anything from the outside world, but I give it to him. "COs be thinking they have reinforcements," he says. "But you got to realize something: Why the fuck you think six or seven come to wrastle one motherfucker down?

You got to think about that one minute. While you fucking, drinking, druggin', or whatever you doing, this man out here running the yard, exercising, doing shit, isolating himself all day every day. You'd be a fucking fool to run up on a motherfucker and think you could take him.

"I like to do a lot of thinking for people," he says. "Sometimes I gotta think for the COs. I see how they be violating. They come in to work, probably got something going on in that world out there or somebody on another tier done pissed them off. Before they know it, they taking their problems out on me. And I don't want their problems. Know what I'm saying? I'm trying to avoid all problems at any cost."

"Bauer!" I hear Calahan shout from inside. I ignore her.

"There be many times I gotta think for Miss Reeves,"—the chief of unit management—"I was inches from slapping the shit out of her one day. My brother had just got killed." He says he tried to talk to her about it, but she refused.

"I'm trying to eat my sandwich," he recalls her saying. "I've been dealing with inmates all day."

"I tell you what," he said to her. "I'll give you time to take a bite. By the time you get to that corner, I'm gonna make you run back down here because I'ma pick somebody and slam them on they fucking head."

"Are you threatening me?" she shouted.

"I will bat the FUCK out you," he shouted back.

"Cuff him! Cuff him! Cuff him!" she screamed.

As he tells the story, I feel a glimmer of fear. I catch a look in his eyes that makes me think he notices. "Man look here, I ain't going to wait for no five or six of y'all to get up in no line talkin' about putting them cuffs on. I'm gonna beat yo' ass."

On my way home, I stop to get gas. While I stand in line I catch myself, for a split second, casing the black men that enter the store. I drive to the supermarket and push a cart listlessly through the aisles. I buy a frozen pizza and consider buying salad, but the greens are wilted. I toss a handful of protein bars into the cart along with bread, wine, and beer. I still have two days of work before a break, so I buy a six-pack of Red Bull to get me through.

I go home, take off my boots, open a beer, put the pizza in the oven, transfer files from my camera watch and pen recorder, and turn on a camera that sits across from the kitchen table. I talk about the inmate who threatened to punch me in the face and my growing suspicion of my supervisors. "I want to know that there are people who have my back, because the people I am dealing with on the other side of the bars have a bunch of people who have their backs. If somebody decides to throw down on me, I don't want to be alone."

When I stop the recording, my apartment is quiet. I take my CCA uniform off, run a bath, and jot down the main events of the day on my laptop. I will go back to them on my days off, transcribe the recordings, and write more. In the tub, I lay back and submerge my ears. Afterward I look in the mirror and debate whether I should trim my beard or let it go wild. I sit on the couch. I used to read, but I've mostly stopped that. Instead I watch *Breaking Bad*.

I get a text from Anthony. He and Matt are shooting pool at the bar. I am tired, but I walk over anyway. Inside, a cop is standing next to the bartender, who looks nervous and makes sure to check everyone's IDs. Anthony tells me his girlfriend just had a baby, that he's going back to Afghanistan soon, and that he is going to break the jaw of the guy who is standing over by the jukebox. Apparently the man beat Anthony at pool a while ago, and he keeps giving Anthony a look. Also, he is a Yankee.

I stick around after the cop leaves and hope the guy will do something to provoke a fight, but nothing happens. There is a pot of gumbo and paper bowls sitting on a table, and the man who brought it tells us to help ourselves. It's a little cold, but it's not bad. I check the time. Five hours until I need to get ready for work. I walk home and sleep. When I wake up, I feel the exhaustion pulling at every fiber. I leave the house five minutes later than usual, grabbing two Red Bulls on my way out. As I drive down the long, dark road to Winn, a cop pulls me over. He tells me I was going sixty-four in a forty-five zone. I try talking to him like a comrade, telling him I'm heading to the prison to handle the people he's taking off the streets. He snickers and gives me a ticket for $286.

Later, at the recommendation of my barber, I wear my uniform and go to the sheriff's office and tell a sprightly, wrinkled lady in bright-red lipstick that I work at Winn Correctional. "I'll knock it down to a hundred and keep it off your insurance," she says. I reach for my debit card. She doesn't look up from her desk. "Cash or money order," she says.

| 18 |

As states phased out convict leasing in the early twentieth century, did the prisoners notice? The end of the system was hailed as a great reform, but for most convicts, life as a prisoner still meant a sentence of unpaid forced labor. Decades after convict leasing was abolished, people like Albert Race Sample, whose incarceration was described in chapter two of this book, would continue to be tortured on state-owned plantations for not picking enough cotton. Stories like his were replicated countless times on Angola in Louisiana, on Parchman in Mississippi, and other plantations throughout the South. But not all prisoners went to plantations. Some went to a new type of labor camp: the chain gang.

"The South today is enjoying an era of prosperity and expansion," wrote the director of the US Department of Agriculture's Office of Public Roads in 1910. "Its manufacturing industries are being enlarged; its railroads are being extended, and its agriculture is . . . opening up to new possibilities. . . . But in order for this growth to continue it will be necessary that the roads of the South be improved." Like factories and railroads in the past, roads were the South's new gateway to modernity. Crops had to get to cities faster and automobile use was on the rise.

When Georgia abandoned convict leasing in 1908, nearly fifty thousand felony and misdemeanor convicts were sent out to work on the state's roads. In 1912 the Georgia Senate estimated that convict labor cost less than half what free labor would cost. By 1923 the state was using 88 percent of its convicts in road camps, and it estimated the value of their work at $5 million ($73 million in 2018). A legislative committee gloated that "the magnitude of the work being done in Georgia by the convicts, and the results being accomplished, are almost beyond conception." In a single year alone, the committee claimed, convicts had "graded and made permanent" six thousand miles of road and had permanently improved another fifteen thousand miles. This was possible because, "with little or no inconvenience [the convict] accomplishes double as much in a day as a free laborer." In the eleven years from 1904 to 1915, convict labor increased the quantity of surfaced roads in Georgia from sixteen hundred miles to thirteen thousand.

The main advocates for using convict labor in road construction throughout the South was the budding "good roads movement," led by self-styled progressives who couched their approval of forced labor in the language of humanitarian reform. "A considerable amount of evidence had been collected which goes to show that this out-of-door work not only improves the physical health of the convict," read a study by the US Department of Agriculture, "but that their experiences as road builders have actually improved their general character and prepared them for better citizenship." An article in *Charities and the Commons*, a periodical that focused on issues of social workers, claimed that once prisoners understood the benefits of their improved "physical and mental condition" by doing roadwork, "the desire to escape almost entirely disappeared." North Carolina's *Orange County Observer* argued in 1909 that not only did prison labor on roads benefit the taxpayer but also it turned convicts into "bronzed, sturdy, healthy and efficient laborers." The idea of roadwork as an improvement over costly prison cells was praised by the International Prison Congress in Budapest in 1905 and at the National Prison Association meeting in Albany, New York, in 1906.

The notion that forced labor was reformatory was as old as the original Protestant penitentiaries, but like convict leasing, the chain gang was first and foremost an institution driven by financial considerations. And despite claims by good-roads advocates and the heads of penal systems to the contrary, investigations were finding that conditions in the state-operated chain gangs were hardly different from their company-run counterparts. Most people sent to chain gangs were convicted of minor crimes. In 1908, 77 percent of Georgia's misdemeanor convicts were sent to work on roads. One road camp was made up of around 150 people convicted for drunkenness, disorderly conduct, fighting, violating city ordinances, reckless driving or riding, throwing rocks, loitering, and "suspected loitering." One North Carolina judge found men at road camps being "chained with iron neck collars, poorly fed, and severely whipped by drunken guards." One county official in North Carolina told a journalist that "the mules at the camp were better housed and better treated in every way than the convicts."

In his message to the Florida legislature in 1911, Governor Gilchrist described his visit to a Georgia convict road camp where "the men sleep in a moveable car placed on four wheels, with bars, constructed very much [like] . . . a car . . . in which animals are conveyed [by] . . . the circuses showing throughout the state, with this exception: in the circus cars there are usually only one or two animals. In the convict cars, there are sometimes ten or twelve convicts. They are shackled and connected with a chain at night." On Sundays and holidays the men were often locked in the cages all day long. "On hot days . . . the sun streams down on the cage and makes an oven of the place, and the human beings in it roast." Some camps had barracks or tents rather than cages, and the men were chained inside. In 1930 a man in a Florida chain gang was burned to death and several others maimed when a guard tossed a cigarette into some dynamite near a guard house. A year later, eleven prisoners were burned to death in a similar manner in North Carolina.

As was true under convict leasing, men were still whipped, hung by cuffs, and put in sweatboxes for not working fast enough. In a Florida road camp in 1932, Arthur Maillefert, a teenage boy from New Jersey, was punished for complaining of illness when he was ordered to work. He was stripped naked and put in a forty-five-pound oak barrel with only his head and feet protruding. He was left to walk around the camp like this for forty-eight hours, being fed bread and water. He could neither sit nor lie down, and his legs were bitten and stung by the various insects that teemed in the swamps surrounding the prison. Desperate, he slipped out of the barrel and ran naked into the everglades, but was captured about an hour later by guards with bloodhounds. When he was brought back to the camp, the whipping boss beat him with a rubber hose, and then entombed the teenager in a sweatbox, fastening a heavy chain around his neck and fitting heavy stocks around his ankles. When guards opened the box in the morning, the boy was dead.

As was the case under convict leasing, white supremacy helped justify chain gangs. In 1912 a federal engineer working for the USDA wrote privately that, "Personally, I favor the employment of convicts [only] in the Southern States in the building of public roads, as in this section of the country the convicts are largely made up of negroes, who are benefitted by outdoor manual labor," and aren't embarrassed in the same way as white people by working in chains in public. Another USDA engineer wrote his superior in Washington in 1905 that he believed free labor was deficient because "a nigger is born happy, and he is going to stay that way if possible. So as soon as money is earned, it is spent in dissipation . . . and the next morning [you] find him disqualified for work. If you hire that kind of a nigger [for road work], he won't do much and you can't make him." Forced labor was the only way to bring roads to the South, he claimed, because "the convict is kept in his place, sleeping at night. . . . Nature has no mortgage on him, the only one is the shackle he wears. As long as that is on him, he must obey." Chain gangs endured in the South through the 1930s.

| 19 |

What do they see when they look at me? I begin eating protein bars a couple of times a day and go to the gym as much as possible, trying to add muscle to my slender frame. In between sets of curls or bench presses, I walk back and forth in front of the long mirror. I don't see the twist in my walk everyone talks about, but I discover that if I tighten my core, my hips move less. In my normal life, I try to diffuse any macho tendencies. Now I try to annihilate anything remotely feminine about me.

At count time, I've learned to tally bodies, not faces. If I look at faces, it means I have to keep the numbers straight while constantly calibrating sternness and friendliness in my eyes for each individual. When I go down the tier, I make a point to walk in a fast, long stride with a slight pop in my left step, trying to look tough.

Today I steel myself for A1. For some reason, they are always testing me on this tier. As I walk down one side, someone makes a comment about my "panties" as I pass. *You like that dick. You like that dick*, someone sings as I go by. I ignore it. Another comments that I look like a model.

I pretend I don't hear him. On my way back toward the front, I hear again, *You like that dick. You like that dick.*

This has been going on for weeks, but this time, something snaps. I stop count and march back to the guy calling out to me, a thirtysome-thing black man with pink sunglasses and tattoos crawling up his neck. *What did you say to me?* I shout.

I ain't said nothin'.

Why are you always saying shit like that? You are always focusing so much on me, maybe you like the dick! Bitch ass!

Say that again?

Maybe you like the dick! I shout. I am completely livid.

He doesn't know how big a mistake he just made, another inmate says as I storm out.

When we finish count, I go back to his tier. *Give me your ID*, I say to him. He refuses. *Give me your ID! NOW!* I shout at the top of my lungs. He doesn't. I get his name from another officer and write him up for making sexual comments. He says he's going to file a Prison Rape Elim-ination Act grievance on me.

I try to cool down. My heart is still hammering ten minutes later. *Are you alright, sarge?* a prisoner asks me. Slowly my rage turns to shame and I go into the bathroom and sit on the floor. Where did those words come from? I rarely ever shout. I am not homophobic. Or am I? I feel utterly defeated. I go back to A1 and call Pink Shades to the bars.

"Look. I just want you to understand I don't have a problem with any of y'all," I tell him. "I think a lot of you are in here for sentences that are too long. I'm not like these other guys, all right?"

"All right," he says.

"But, you know, when people disrespect me like that for no reason, I can't just take that, you know what I mean?"

He tries to deny taunting me—"Look, you going to have inmates talkin' crazy"—but I won't back down.

"But you don't want me talking crazy to you, right?" There are inmates staring at us in astonishment.

"I feel you. You came here and talked to me like a man. And I apologize. I ain't got nothing against any of y'all officers. You feel me? I understand that you gotta live. You got to survive. Those words hurt you. I feel you. I mean I was singing a song, but you probably took it the wrong way. It triggered something in you." He's right. Something about being here reminds me of being in junior high, getting picked on for my size and the fact that I read books, getting called a faggot.

I tear up his disciplinary report and throw it in the trash. When I walk back down the tier for the next count, no one says anything to me.

One day in Ash, a few inmates shout, "Man down! Man down!" A large man, Mason, is lying on his bed in C2, his right hand over his bare chest. His eyes are closed and his left leg is moving back and forth slowly.

"We just put him on his bed. He had fell off this side of his fucking bed just now, bro," an inmate says to me. "He's fucked up." I radio for a stretcher.

Mason starts to cry. His left hand is a fist. His back arches. "I'm scared," he mouths. Someone puts a hand on his arm for the briefest moment: "I know, son. They finna come see you now."

A stretcher finally arrives. The nurses and their orderlies move slowly. "They weren't supposed to send that man back down here," an inmate says to me. Earlier today Mason was playing basketball and fell to the ground in pain, he explains. He went to the infirmary, where they told him that he had fluid in his lungs.

Three inmates pick up Mason in his sheet and put him on the stretcher. His hands are crossed over his chest like a mummy as two prisoners wheel him away.

Within a few hours he is sent back to the tier.

A few days later I see him dragging his feet, his arms around his chest. I tell him to take my chair. He sits and hunches over, putting his head in his lap. It feels like a "throbbing pain in my chest," he says. We call for a wheelchair. "They told me I got fluid on my lungs and they won't send me to the hospital," he says. "That shit crazy."

A nurse happens to be in the unit, passing out pills. I tell her they keep sending Mason to the infirmary but won't take him to the hospital. She insists "nothing serious" is wrong with him.

"When I saw him last week, he was almost passed out," I say. "He was in a lot of pain."

She looks at me sidelong. "But the doctor still ain't going to send him to the hospital just 'cause of that."

If he were sent to the hospital, CCA would be contractually obligated to pay for his stay. For a for-profit company, this presents a dilemma. Even a short hospital stay is a major expense for an inmate who brings the company about thirty-four dollars per day. And that's aside from the cost of having two guards keep watch over him. Medical care within the prison is expensive too. CCA does not disclose its medical expenses, but in a typical prison, health care costs are the second-largest expense after staff. On average, a Louisiana prison alots 9 percent of its budget toward health care. In some states it can be much higher; health care is about 31 percent of a California prison's budget. Nearly 40 percent of Winn inmates have a chronic disease such as diabetes, heart disease, or asthma. About 6 percent have a communicable disease such as HIV or hepatitis C.

CCA finds ways to minimize its obligation to provide adequate health care. At the out-of-state prisons where California ships some of its inmates, CCA will not accept any prisoners who are over sixty-five years old, have mental health issues, or serious conditions like HIV. The company's Idaho prison contract specified that the "primary criteria" for screening incoming offenders was "no chronic mental health or health care issues." The contracts of some CCA prisons in Tennessee and Hawaii stipulate that the states will bear the cost of HIV treatment. Such exemptions allow CCA to tout its cost efficiency while taxpayers assume the medical expenses for the inmates the company won't take or treat.

At least fifteen doctors at Winn have been sued for delivering poor medical care. The prison hired several of them even after the state had disciplined them for misconduct. One, Aris Cox, was hired in the 1990s, after his license was temporarily suspended for writing prescriptions to support his tranquilizer addiction. While Mark Singleton was at Winn, the Louisiana board of medical examiners discovered that he had failed "to meet the standard of care" at his previous position in New Mexico. He was put on probation, but CCA kept him on. Winn hired Stephen Kuplesky after his license had been temporarily suspended for prescribing painkillers to a family member with no medical condition. Robert Cleveland was working at Winn when he was put on medical probation for his involvement in a kickback scheme with a wheelchair company. He was later disciplined for prescribing narcotics from his home and vehicle.*

In 2010 the company and Immigration and Customs Enforcement settled a federal lawsuit brought by the ACLU that asserted immigration detainees at a CCA-run facility in California were routinely denied prescribed medical treatment. In a rare case that made its way to trial in 2001, the company was found to have violated the Eighth and Fourteenth Amendments and ordered to pay $235,000 to an inmate whose broken jaw was left wired shut for ten weeks. (He removed the wires himself with nail clippers while guards watched.) The jury wrote they

---

* It's not clear if he was working at Winn at the time. CCA says all doctors at Winn had "appropriate credentials."

hoped the message sent by the ruling would "echo throughout the halls of your corporate offices as well as your corporate housing facilities."*

CCA has also been the subject of medical malpractice cases involving pregnant inmates. In 2014 it settled a case for $690,000 over the death of a prisoner's baby at a county jail in Chattanooga, Tennessee. When the inmate went into labor, she was put in a cell with no mattress and left there for three hours as she bled heavily onto the floor. CCA employees did not call an ambulance until approximately five hours after the prisoner asked for help. Her newborn baby died shortly thereafter. In court proceedings the warden testified that surveillance footage showed no signs of an emergency. But before the footage could be reviewed, CCA claimed it had been accidentally erased. The court sanctioned the company for destroying evidence.

CCA settled another case for $250,000 after a pregnant woman being held in a jail in Nashville complained of vaginal bleeding and severe abdominal pain. She said medical staff demanded "proof," so they put her in solitary and turned off the water so her blood loss could be "monitored." She claimed they did nothing to alleviate her pain as she endured contractions, filling the toilet with blood. The next morning, the inmate was shackled and taken to a hospital, where doctors found that she was already dilated. While prison guards watched, she gave birth and was immediately sedated. When she woke up, medical staff brought her the dead baby. She said she was not allowed to call her family and was given no information about the disposal of her son's body.

Because most inmates can't afford legal counsel, it's nearly impossible for them to prevail in court. Even so, the company settled six hundred cases in the ten years leading up to 2008. When I made public-records requests in a couple of states for a more recent accounting of lawsuits settled by CCA, the company intervened, arguing that a list of

---

* CCA appealed and settled for an undisclosed amount.

settlements involving claims of medical malpractice, wrongful deaths, assaults, and the use of force "constitutes trade secrets."

On my mandatory overtime day, I go to Rapides Regional hospital in Alexandria. "Are you weapons qualified?" my partner, who has worked here for well over a decade, asks.

"No, I'm not. We haven't taken the class yet." I never got past one session of classroom training. We never made it to the shooting range.

"You'll hold a gun anyway."

"What's that?"

"I said you'll hold a gun anyway. It ain't no big deal."

For twelve hours I sit with him at the bedside of an inmate who just had open heart surgery. I don't want to go anywhere with the revolver on my belt, but eventually I need to eat and go to the bathroom. I stand in line in the cafeteria and notice people looking at me. Am I doing something wrong? Do I look too casual? I normally try to appear disarming. Is that out of place with the firearm on my hip? Should I keep my hand near it? Where does one put one's hand? Rested on the butt? In your pocket? There is an image that should be projected to the people around you when wearing a weapon like that, but surely it's different than the one I try to project inside the prison. What if someone would try to grab the gun? The inmate we are guarding can hardly stand, so an escape attempt is remote, but what if something happened to which I was expected to respond? What if I messed it up?

My reconciliation with Pink Shades encouraged me. Every time I have a problem with a prisoner, I try the same approach and eventually we tap knuckles to show each other respect. Still, these breakthroughs are fleeting. In the moment, they feel like a glimmer of a possibility that we can appreciate each other's humanity, but I come to understand that our positions make this virtually impossible.

We can chat and laugh through the bars, but inevitably I need to flex my authority. My job will always be to deny them the most basic of human impulses—to push for more freedom. Day by day, the number of inmates who are friendly with me grows smaller. There are exceptions, like Corner Store, but were I to take away the privileges Bacle and I have granted him, I know that he, too, would become an enemy.

My priorities change. Striving to treat everyone as human takes too much energy. More and more I focus on proving I won't back down. I am vigilant; I come to work ready for people to catcall me or run up on me and threaten to punch me in the face. I show neither fear nor compunction. Sometimes prisoners call me racist, and it stings, but I try as hard as I can not to flinch, because to do so would be to show a pressure point, a button that can be pressed when they want to make me bend.

Nearly every day the unit reaches a crescendo of frustration because inmates are supposed to be going somewhere like the law library, GED classes, vocational training, or a substance abuse group, but their programs are canceled or they are let out of the unit late. Inmates tell me that at other prisons, the schedule is firm. "That door would be opening up and everybody would be on the move," an inmate who's been incarcerated throughout the state says.

Here there is no schedule. We wait for the call over the radio; then we let the inmates go. They could eat at eleven thirty a.m. They could eat at three p.m. School might happen, or maybe not. It's been years since Winn has had the staff to run the big yard. Sometimes we let the inmates onto the small yard attached to the unit. Often we don't. Canteen and law library hours are canceled regularly. There just aren't enough officers to keep everything going.

Guards bond with prisoners over their frustrations. Prisoners tell us they understand we are powerless to change these high-level management problems. Yet the two groups remain locked in battle like soldiers in a war they don't believe in.

Whenever I open a tier door, I demand that everyone show me his pass, and I use my body to stop the flood of people from pouring out. Some just push through.

I catch one. "Get back in!" I shout. "I'm writing you up right now if you don't get back in there. You hear me?"

He walks back in, staring me down. "White dude all on a nigga's trail, man," he says. I shut the door, ignoring him. "You better get the fuck from down here before I end up hurtin' one of y'all," he shouts at me. "You green as a motherfucker!"

I'm tired.

An inmate comes around the key. Bacle is following him and calls for me to stop him. I stand in the inmate's path. I know him, the one with the mini-dreadlocks. I feel threatened, frankly, whenever I see him. "This way," I say, pointing back to where he came from. He tries to walk past me. I lock eyes with him. "This way!" I command. He turns back and walks slowly away. I walk behind him. He stops, spins around, throws his hands in the air, and shouts, "Get the fuck off my trail, dog!" I know he's testing me. I open his tier door. He walks in, stands just inside, and stares me down hard. I grab the door and slam it shut—bang!—in his face.

I turn and step back into the throng of inmates milling around the floor. *Motherfucker's going to end up dead!* he shouts after me. I stop and turn around. He just stares. I grab the radio on my shoulder, and then pause. Was I ever taught what to do when something like this happens? I know how to press the button and speak into the radio, but whom do I call? I think of King, the officer who'd smashed the kid's jaw. "Sergeant King, could you come down to Ash?" I say into my shoulder.

"En route."

When he arrives, I take him into B1 tier. I find Mini-Dreads.

"He needs to get locked up," I say, looking him in the eyes.

King cuffs him. I tell him the inmate threatened my life. He needs to go to seg.

"What happened?! I ain't said nuttin'!" the inmate shouts. I walk away.

I go back to chasing the others into their tiers. "What you lock that dude up for?" an inmate asks me. "Dude was 'bout to go home," another says. "He ain't go' go home now." I walk away, unyielding. In the back of my mind, however, there is a voice: Did you see him say anything? Wasn't your back turned? Are you sure what you heard? It doesn't matter, really. He wanted to intimidate me, and it was about time I threw someone in the hole. They need to know I am not weak.

I am on a roll. I ask Bacle to come stand at the end of A1 tier while I walk down to look for an inmate who called me a "faggot-ass motherfucker" so I can write him up. He told me his bed number, and I want to make sure he didn't give me a fake one. I stand at the front of the tier and call for bed six, like I do when I'm handing out passes for individuals to attend classes or see visitors. A prisoner approaches, but it's not him. I walk through the tier, but can't recognize him. When I get back to the front, the tier is locked and Bacle is gone.

Everyone in the tier starts shouting. "Ooooh! There we go! Get him!" People run up from the back of the tier toward me. "Hey, Bacle!" I shout. "Bacle!" My voice sounds a little more panicked than I'd like.

"He ain't go' pay you no mind," one man yells at me. "See how it feels to be locked behind bars?!" another shouts. There is a cacophony. I wish I could tell them that yes actually, I do know what it's like. I wish I could tell them why I'm here. I wish I could redeem myself somewhat.

"I feel you," I say, sounding ridiculous.

"Now you see how it feels to be ignored, huh?!"

Bacle opens the door, apologetic, and I leave the tier. I give up on finding the guy who called me a faggot.

Later, as prisoners go to chow, Bacle runs past me shouting, "Code Blue outside!" I dash toward the front door, through a crowd of around fifteen inmates, shouting for them to go inside. A couple of prisoners are pinning another up against the fence, and a frail-looking white man is rolling around on the ground.

I run to him.

He rolls from side to side, whimpering and heaving in panic, grasping at small cuts and lumps on his arms. They are not deep like stab wounds; they are shallow and there are many. Under those there are a multitude of tiny scars on both arms, cut crosswise—the trademark mutilation of the sexually abused.

"Calm down man," I say, leaning over him. "We are going to take care of you. You are going to be alright. Just calm down." He keeps rolling and crying.

"He didn't get nothing he ain't deserve!" someone shouts from down the walk.

The captain and Sergeant King come and cuff the inmate pinned up against the fence. When the crowd around him clears, I am shocked. It's Brick, a charming, gray-haired inmate who passes the time with me chatting through the bars, who has commiserated with me about the difficulty of my job, who heats ramen for me when I am trying to do favors for other inmates.

As Brick is taken off the Cypress, he calls the man a "bitch." Two officers come, look down at the young man disdainfully, pull him off the ground, and take him away. Brick beat him with a lock in a sock. He was angry because the young man stayed in Cypress for seven months, partly by his own choice. He was supposed to come back to Brick. He is his punk.

There are many things about this incident that I don't know—intimacy and rape in prison are deeply complex issues. Did the young man stay in Cypress to escape Brick? Does he belong to Brick like a sex slave? Or would he say the relationship is consensual in a similar way that a battered woman might say she stays with her husband because she loves him? Did he understand that once he crossed that bridge there would be no going back?

Once a punk, always a punk. Miss Carter, the mental health director, told us she's seen just two inmates reverse their punk status in the eight years she's been here, and both cases involved stabbing a lot of people. Guards here do not turn a blind eye to overt rape, but the more subtle abuse of punks is accepted. Inmates and COs know a punk when they see one. He will do menial tasks when someone demands it. He is expected to keep his face clean-shaven at all times. He has to pee sitting down or by backing up to the urinal with his penis tucked between his legs. He must shower facing the wall.

Since 2003 the federal Prison Rape Elimination Act (PREA) has required prisons to take measures to prevent sexual assaults. At Winn this includes teaching new cadets about the law. "Why is the law so important?" our instructor Kenny asked us during training. "Liability." It was never fully clear whether the goal was to eliminate rape or to suppress homosexuality in the prison. Even consensual sex could lead to time in seg. "Don't even go there and entertain nicknames," Kenny said. "There's homosexuals down here got nicknames: Princess, Malibu, Tiki, Coco, Nicki. By calling them nicknames, that's entertainment. They think they got you goin' along with what they got goin' on. We can't stop a hundred percent of the homosexuality that goes on down there, but we try to prevent and slow it down as much as possible."

Nationwide, as many as 9 percent of male inmates report being sexually assaulted behind bars, but given the antisnitch culture of prison, the
real number might be higher. In the 2014 fiscal year Winn reported almost 550 sex offenses, a rate nearly 70 percent higher than that of Avoy-
elles Correctional Center, a publicly operated prison of comparable size
and security level. In 2012 the company turned down a proposal by a
shareholder that it regularly report its progress in preventing prison rape
to investors. Prison has a reputation as a place of homosexual predation,
but it's not that simple. Inmates like Brick rarely see themselves as gay,
and once they get out, predators typically go back to pursuing women.
Self-identified gay or transgender prisoners are, however, on the receiving end of the abuse. More than one-third of gay prisoners and nearly
two-thirds of trans inmates have reported being sexually assaulted in
male prisons.

But not all sex in prison is violent; many of the letters I read in the
mail room were full of tenderness and longing. Take, for example, this
one from a man in Angola prison, written to one of the most flamboy-
ant men in Ash unit:

> *I can't wait until we get out and meet back up. We're going
> to have so much to talk about and catch up on (smile). . . . I
> really miss you a lot and wish I were there with you. But I knew
> one day we would have to be parted for a little while. The main
> thing is we keep in touch and remain faithful to one another.
> You know I AM a faithful MAN and there will never be
> another after you. You are the only same sex person in my life.
> So you have to never worry about anyone taking your place, not
> even a female. Cause I'll let them know about you and how
> much you mean to me. I be laying on this rack thinking about all
> the good times we've had. Especially the sex those were some
> amazing times. Stuff like that we don't forget. Just sitting out*

on the yard or in the gym were good times, because I was with
you. These things meant so much to me. I know it meant a lot to
you also. You just had your own way of expressing it. . . . [You]
are a good wife. I don't give a damn what anybody said because I
saw the good in you; the true you. That's why when we had sex
I'd always look you in the eyes. To truly understand you was my
hardest goal but when I did our relationship got so good.

An hour after the young man is picked up off the floor and brought
to the infirmary, he walks into Ash unit, his arms still bleeding. It's not
clear whether Brick's absence is good or bad for him. Now he has no
protection. A couple of muscular inmates stand at the bars and look at
him lustfully, telling him to try to get placed on their tier. He says he
will. He speaks with Miss Price, and she abruptly tells me to put him on
D2 tier—Brick's dorm. "Why is she putting him back on this tier?" I
ask Bacle. Inmates have complained to me about this sort of thing—
even people who have stabbed each other are sometimes put back in the
same dorm. I open the gate and watch him walk down the tier.

A few minutes later, he asks me to let him out. I do. He talks to the
Miss Price, telling her he is in danger. People think he's a rat. Maybe
they think he snitched on Brick to get away from him. Miss Price doesn't
give it a moment of consideration and tells him to get back on the tier.
When I open the gate, a large, bearded man inside pushes him back out
onto the floor. "You was asking her to put you on another tier?" he says.
"If you think you can't live in here, you can't live in here. We don't need
that kind of shit on the tier anyway." He slams the bars behind him.

Miss Price tells the young man he has two options—go back on the
tier or go to the count room, where they will assign him to another
unit.

"Take him out," she says to me.

"You gotta go," I tell him half-heartedly.

"I don't want to go on no PC, man," he says to me. He thinks they are going to put him in protective custody.

"I don't know what to tell you," I say. I really don't.

Consider the options swirling in his mind. He could go back to his tier, where a man twice his size has made it very clear he is not welcome. There, he would risk nights as a punk without a protector. He might get robbed. He might get raped. He might get stabbed.

Then, there is the alternative, the only one that Winn, like many other prisons, offers to inmates like this: the protective custody wing in Cypress. He would be put in a cell, maybe alone, maybe with another man, for at least twenty-three hours a day. He would be branded a snitch just for going there, which means that when he eventually left, the odds of getting stabbed would be high.

He storms past me, back to the key. "I ain't going on no PC man," he shouts at Miss Price. "I just come from Cypress!"

"Let me tell you something," she shouts at him. "You getting the hell up out of here!"

He backs up. "Y'all go' have to drag me out this bitch, man. I just did extended in the blocks, man. Seven months. Real talk. Fuck all that!" He paces back and forth, working himself up. "I ain't trippin' on what y'all fixing to do to me," he says, pointing at Bacle and me. "Real talk! 'Cuz I ain't going on no PC." Miss Price screams for him to get out.

"Man, I can live on any fucking tier you put me on!" he shouts. I escort him out of the unit; he's eventually placed on another one.

During our training Kenny warned us how easy it was to be manipulated into sex by inmates. Even male guards "fall victim to bein' involved in a relationship wit' a' inmate," he said. "We got some folks come in here with relationships on the outside, and it just blows my mind how these inmates get in that ear and they wind up falling victim.

That's just the way it is. They don't call 'em cons for no reason." He warned us to be vigilant, because even in a consensual relationship, the guard could be classified as a sex offender. He told us about one captain at Winn, Charlie Roberts,* who got "involved wit' a' inmate. Havin' oral sex wit' him. So guess where he is sittin' at? A federal institution."

This story came up several times as an example of a guard who had to face the consequences of his weak will. Nothing was ever said about the inmate who gave Roberts blow jobs. When I looked at the files from Roberts's case, I learned the inmate was a transgender woman who went by the name China. She had identified as a girl from age eleven. Her father beat her repeatedly, and she told the court that by the time she turned thirteen, she had left home and begun stripping on Bourbon Street in New Orleans. In 2000 she was sentenced to four years in prison for a "crime against nature"—oral sex for pay—and sent to Winn. During her first year, she was serving a stint in seg for a dirty urine test when, she later testified, Roberts shackled her, brought her to an office, and told her to give him a blow job. If she didn't, he said he would put her in a cell with an inmate who would "handle" things. When she later told two administrators about what had happened, one allegedly told her that if she ever lied about one of his guards again, he would throw her in seg.

During the next two years, China said, she was raped several times by inmates, but she kept it to herself. "I was ridiculed and picked on by the staff, and that made it to where I couldn't go to the staff for help at all," she said in a deposition. "If an inmate did want to rape me . . . who could I turn to?" She became another inmate's punk. One day in 2003 Miss Price sent her to the count room for having an "outrageous" feminine haircut. There, an officer ordered her to take another urine test by peeing into a cup while standing. China had been through this with him before—she'd told him she couldn't pee standing up. After a long

---

* Charlie Roberts is his real name.

standoff, Roberts showed up and told her she could sit on the toilet. The other guards left. As she peed, Roberts entered the bathroom and closed the door behind him. He told her that if she didn't give him oral sex again, he would taint her urine test and send her back to Cypress.

"Stop playing," China said. Roberts slapped her in the face. She dropped to her knees and did what he asked. When she finished, he said, "Bitch, you better swallow."

"I would die before I ever fucking swallowed anything he put in my mouth," she later recalled. She held the semen in her mouth and spit it out onto her shirt. After she filed a grievance and contacted the American Civil Liberties Union, she called the FBI. An agent came to the prison, took the shirt, and interviewed Roberts. The next day CCA shipped China off to a publicly operated state prison, where she was held in a solitary cell "no bigger than a broom closet" and never let out for exercise. She was released from prison eleven months later.

"If I knew that the prison was going to shave me bald and send me to another prison and put me on maximum security lockdown," she later testified, "I would have swallowed." Even harder than the solitary was knowing that had she swallowed, she would have been able to finish her auto body class, which might have kept her from having to live on the streets and going back to sex work when she got out. "I would have swallowed, and I would have kept on swallowing until I got that piece of paper."

CCA denied all of China's allegations, but it settled the case out of court for an undisclosed amount. Roberts also denied her allegations when the FBI interviewed him, but the bureau found that the semen on her shirt was his. Roberts pleaded guilty ultimately to sexually assaulting China and making false statements to the FBI, and he was sentenced to six years in federal prison and a $5,000 fine. Roberts served his sentence and was released in 2012.

Nearly half of all allegations of sexual victimization in prisons involve staff. CCA prisons' rate of reported staff-on-inmate sexual harassment is five times higher than that of public prisons. But prisoners also sexually harass and abuse officers. A recurring issue is inmates standing at the bars and masturbating at women guards sitting in the key. I see some women's reports of sexual abuse by prisoners handled swiftly, but I hear other female guards complain that their sexual harassment charges have gone nowhere.* Once I wrote up an inmate for masturbating in front of a nurse, a violation that should have caused him to be moved to Cypress, but he wasn't. I regularly see the macho culture of prison transcend the division between guards and inmates—male officers routinely ignore the harassment of their female colleagues. "Some of them staff, they'll wear clothes so tight you can see everything they got," Kenny lectured in class. "They'll walk down there and they just struttin' they stuff. We got one, shoot, trying to sue the company 'cuz an inmate touched her on the butt. Man, you was down here every day shaking your stuff! If you do all this trying to draw attention to yourself, you go' get some, and if you ain't mindful, you'll get more than what you asked for."

---

* CCA says it "takes any allegation of sexual harassment very seriously and has strong policies and practices in place for investigating such claims."

| 20 |

N ot long ago, prisons were literally run by inmates. When convict leasing ended, Southern states tried to squeeze every dollar they could from their prisoners without the investment of private companies, so many instituted "trustee guard" systems. Typically, prisoners convicted of the most brutal acts were appointed to the job because of their willingness to assault others. If a trustee guard shot and killed an inmate assumed to be escaping, he was granted an immediate pardon. When Arkansas governor Winthrop Rockefeller visited his state's Tucker prison farm in 1967, his police escorts had to turn their guns over to the inmates. Arkansas's two prisons were both massive plantations, and they were guarded by inmates armed with whips, .38 caliber revolvers, and shotguns.

On the sixteen-thousand-acre Cummins plantation and the fifty-five-hundred-acre Tucker farm, some two thousand prisoners worked ten to fourteen hours a day, six or seven days a week, growing crops like cotton, rice, and strawberries to be shipped to Chicago and other markets. The farms brought an average of $1.4 million per year in revenue, adding hundreds of thousands of dollars in profits to the state treasury. "To make these profits, the prisoners were driven remorselessly from dawn to dusk in the fields, especially at harvest time," said a 1966 state police investigation. In the nearly sixty years since the state had abolished convict leasing, it appeared that little had changed. "They received insufficient food and clothing, and were punished for falling behind in their work by official floggings with a heavy leather strap, or by unofficial beatings with hoe handles or anything that was at hand."

The 1966 police investigation included numerous corroborated accounts and photographic evidence of whippings. Some prisoners even turned over recordings to investigators that they'd secretly made in the prison. In one, the superintendent, Jim Bruton, catches an inmate telling another that he could get a good job if he bribed the captain. Bruton orders the inmate to take his pants off. The investigation notes that in the recording, one can hear the sound of the five-foot-long leather strap against skin. "Oh Captain!" the inmate shouts. Crack! "Oh Captain!" Crack! "Oh Captain!"

"Now I forgot how many licks that is," the captain says. "One or two?"

"Three," the inmate replies. Crack!

"How many's that, four?"

"Four," the inmate replies. Crack!

"Oh Captain! Five." Crack!

"Oh Captain! Six." Crack! The captain whips the man ten times.

"You ol' son of a bitch, you're fixin' to get killed," Bruton says. He orders a guard to send the whipped man straight to the fields in the morning.

The investigators found other instruments of torture. One was a device invented by Bruton known as the "Tucker telephone," an electric generator taken from a crank-operated telephone, wired with two batteries. In the Tucker hospital, a naked inmate would be strapped to a table and electrodes would be attached to his big toe and penis. When the crank was turned, it would send electrical shock through his body. Perhaps the most egregious of abuses was the treatment of death row inmates: Some had never been out of their six-by-nine-foot cells in eight or nine years.

During the investigation, the assistant superintendent asked an investigator if he would like to have his job, telling him it included "$8,000 per year, a new car each year, a fourteen room house, a complete expense account, and all food furnished. . . . He states that a lot of gifts would be offered from business people in the farm supply trade, people in the clothing business, and other 'interested persons.'" The police investigation was published weeks before Winthrop Rockefeller became governor. At his inauguration, he called Arkansas's prison system "the worst in the nation" and promised to reform it. He immediately hired Tom Murton, a professional penologist from Arkansas, to run Tucker, the smaller of the two farms, to see whether the system could be changed.

Tom Murton's experience at Tucker is worth examining in some detail, and not just because he left behind a candid memoir. Murton was a reform-minded administrator, and his efforts to make conditions at the prison more humane were enlightened by the standards of their time. Murton challenged a for-profit model of incarceration that reached back to slavery, and it destroyed his career. His ultimate defeat would open the doors for T. Don Hutto, who would save forced plantation labor in Arkansas while making it profitable again for the state. In Arkansas, Hutto would master the skill that would later make him rich: how to adapt the prison business just enough to suit the times while making it even more profitable than it had been under the old regime. Seven years later, he'd use this skill to create CCA, bringing corporate-run prisons back to life after more than five decades of extinction.

For the fifty-one years the state had been running Tucker, Murton wrote in his memoir, the job of the superintendent was not to run the prison but to manage agricultural operations and to "see to it that the penal slaves make money for the state." When he began, there were only two other "free world" employees at Tucker, a doctor and a business manager. The other sixty-seven staff members were unpaid prisoners.

One inmate described to Murton why prisoners took the trustee guard positions. "When the press compares Tucker with German concentration camps, they aren't exaggerating," he said. "They had their capos and we have our trustees." Regular inmates, called "rank men," became accustomed to being beaten and extorted by inmate trustees, so when one was offered a job to beat other inmates, "you take it because there are two types of living conditions: you exist, or you survive. If you existed, you walked around in the barracks with an army blanket around you—no underwear, no t-shirt, no socks. A trusty had underwear because he took it away from a rank man." Trustees freely ate pork chops, steak, and hamburger and fed the rank men a soup mixture of beans and collards. According to the police investigation, rank men were typically forty to sixty pounds underweight. "A trusty was surviving; a rank man was existing. So, you became a trusty and were glad to do it. . . . The oppressed become the oppressors is what happens."

Arkansas wasn't the only state to use inmate guards. Alabama, Mississippi, and Louisiana used them on the plantation prisons until a federal court ruling banned the practice in 1971. From 1928 to 1940 there were ten thousand recorded floggings by convict guards at Louisiana's Angola prison, some with fifty lashes each. Texas continued to use "building tenders" as pseudoguards until the 1980s. When Murton arrived at Tucker, he discovered that about a dozen of the highest-level trustees there did not live in the main prison building. Instead they had built squatter shacks in other parts of the plantation, scrounging lumber and paying the electrician a couple of steaks to get the power installed. They piped in gas and bought TVs and ranges. "The squatters did not escape because they had the best of prison life," Murton wrote in his memoir. "They had power over the other inmates; the former superintendent allowed them to have women; and they were permitted to go in town to get whisky." Trustees were not paid by the state, but they had money because they exploited the rank men whenever they could. If a regular prisoner wanted a haircut, medicine, or any food better than gruel, he had to pay a trustee for it.

It was nearly impossible to survive without cash in the prison, and the only legal way for rank men to make money was to sell their blood. The prison doctor, Austin Stough, paid the inmates $5 a pint, which he then converted to plasma at a building he leased at Cummins. He sold the plasma to the Berkeley-based pharmaceutical company Cutter Laboratories for $22 a liter, making some $130,000 annually from his Arkansas contract alone. Stough operated blood centers in five prisons, located in Arkansas, Oklahoma, and Alabama. By 1964, just a year into his operations, a hepatitis epidemic broke out in all of them. More than five hundred cases of hepatitis were firmly established to have been connected to his operations, but Arkansas allowed him to keep selling blood, and Cutter Laboratories continued doing business with him.

Stough also contracted with at least thirty-seven pharmaceutical companies to test experimental drugs on inmates, who received $1 a day for taking pills. A number of the drug companies were among the three hundred largest corporations in America. To ensure that they would keep earning money, some inmates concealed the drugs' side effects. Others destroyed or sold the pills they were supposed to be testing. Once Stough's medical experiments became known to the public, several major pharmaceutical manufacturers acknowledged that his methods were extremely dangerous, but they continued their contracts with him anyway. Dr. Stough's gross income in a good year approached $1 million. The federal Institutional Review Board, created in the wake of World War II as a response to experiments by Nazi physicians, explicitly forbade medical trials on prisoners, on the grounds that prisoners can't give true consent while confined. Nevertheless, the Food and Drug Administration took no action against Stough and still considered the results of his clinical trials to be valid. Murton ended Stough's "blood sucking program" and set up a program where inmates were paid $7 for blood donations and the profits were used to fund better medical care for inmates.

As superintendent, Murton's top priority was to get rid of the trustee system and hire "free world" guards. When the trustees heard that he wanted to take away their guns, they threatened to go on strike, which would have meant there would be no one guarding the prison or driving the other inmates to pick cotton. Murton met with the trustees. "Normally, when I take over an institution, I come in and say, 'This is how it's going to be and this is the way we're going to run things,' but this is ridiculous in a situation like this because you guys have the guns and the keys and you're running things so there's no way I can take over." In the coming months Murton managed, one step at a time, to begin breaking down the power structure in the prison. He destroyed the squatter shacks, banned the whip and the Tucker telephone, ended automatic pardons for trustees who killed escapees, and took away "brozene," the prison's internal currency. He slowly began to hire paid guards to work alongside the trustees. Because there were no free world guards in Arkansas, he hired former inmates. Before Murton, the only prisoners to escape were rank men; trustees preferred to stay at the prison where they had money and power. "When I began to attack the power structure, the rank men stayed, because their lives and living conditions were improved, but the trustees began to bust out," Murton wrote. "Many of the trusties who escaped were simply unable to live in a prison society without the means of exploitation."

Five months after becoming superintendent of Tucker, Murton moved to take over Cummins, a prison plantation three times its size. On New

Year's Day, 1968, he drove into Cummins with a single assistant. "The gun on my hip was of little comfort," he wrote. "We were outnumbered and in enemy territory." To prepare for his arrival, the governor put on standby sixty state troopers, a national guard company of about two hundred soldiers, and a battalion of paratroopers from a nearby base. Inmates were prepared for his arrival. They pushed their bunks and bedding up to the front of their barracks, planning to set them on fire when he arrived. Murton negotiated with the trustees, promising not to take their guns away any time soon, and they backed down.

As he had at Tucker, Murton began to break down the trustees' power at Cummins bit by bit. But there were consequences. "The success of reform meant the death knell of profitable exploitation," Murton wrote. Before Murton, the entire prison system had only thirty-five paid employees. But as he phased out the trustee system, the size of the free world staff tripled. And as he reined in trustees' ability to brutalize the rank men, crop production declined. Arkansas penitentiary reports show that, the year before Murton took them over, Arkansas prisons were showing a profit of nearly $300,000. While Murton was in charge, however, the prisons operated at a loss of nearly $550,000. Legislatures began to complain about Murton on the floor of the state's House of Representatives. "They have refused to make crops," state representative L. L. Bryan said. "They have refused to let their inmates do what they call stoop labor because it's beneath their dignity." Under Murton, Tucker produced thirty-seven bushels of rice per acre while neighboring farms produced 105.

In March 1968, Murton was fired. He recalled that, in a private meeting, the chairman of the Board of Corrections told him that, although he was impressed with Murton's reforms, he could not tolerate a situation in which the prisons do not turn a profit. The man who took his place, Bob Sarver, was determined to get crop production back on track, but he faced obstacles. The prison population, and its labor force, was declining. To drive up production, women were made to labor in the fields for the first time. Prisoners were pulled from educational classes begun by Murton to work in the fields. Inmates who resisted were chained to a fence for several days at a time. In October 1968, 120 men refused to work, protesting working conditions, poor food, and medical services. Murton had changed state policy on whipping, so to force inmates back to work, Sarver's officers pumped rounds of birdshot at close range into the crowd of striking inmates. A group of inmates sued Sarver over prison conditions, and in 1970 the US Supreme Court ruled in their favor, making Arkansas the first state to have its entire prison system declared cruel and unusual.

Sarver needed to be replaced. Few were qualified to run a prison plantation as large as Cummins. The only ones that rivaled it in size were Parchman in Mississippi, Angola in Louisiana, and Ramsey in Texas, where future CCA cofounder Terrell Don Hutto was warden. Arkansas Governor Dale Bumpers was particularly impressed with the way Hutto ran Ramsey, so in May 1971, he called Hutto to ask if he'd be interested in running Arkansas's prison system. Hutto said yes.

| 21 |

Ash unit smells like feces. On D2, liquid shit is oozing out of the shower drain, running down the tier. "It's been here over twelve hours," one inmate says.

"Man, we got worms and everything on the floor. Real talk."

"This is a health and safety violation!"

"Man this is cruel and unusual punishment!"

We let inmates out to go to the small yard. As they flow out of the tiers, I see a large group run to A1 tier. Bacle pushes the tier door shut and calls a Code Blue over the radio. Inside the tier two prisoners are grappling, their bodies pressed up against the bars. Each is gripping a shank in one hand while holding the other's arm to keep him from swinging. Drops of blood splatter on the floor. The surrounding scene is oddly calm. Inmates stand around and watch, not saying anything.

"Break it up," Bacle says half-heartedly. "Break it up."

The two combatants are speaking to each other quietly, almost in a whisper.

"Come on," one says. "Come on with it big dog."

"I'ma do you like you did me."

They grapple some more.

"Break it up!" Bacle yells.

"Come on!" I shout, feeling utterly impotent.

Bacle, Miss Price, a CCA employee from out of town, and I stand just two feet from them, separated by the bars, and watch the two try to press their knives into each other.

One man breaks his hand free, swings it up, and jams his shank into the side of the other man's neck. My breath stops for a moment, and I utter a gagging sound. "It ain't sharp enough big dog," says the guy who was just stabbed. "Let me show you where the sharp one is."

Bacle reaches through the bars and grabs the stabber by the hood of his sweatshirt as the other inmate struggles to break loose. For first the first time, the other prisoners make noise. "You're gonna get him killed!" one shouts at Bacle. Bacle lets go and the two men tumble across the floor, landing in a heap by the toilet, and now blocked from our view by a short wall. They keep scuffling. An arm swings up and jabs down. One inmate walks over to the urinal located two feet away from them and pees as they keep stabbing.

The fight lasts nearly four minutes, until a SORT member comes in with a can of pepper spray. "Don't fucking move," he barks. "Everybody lay the fuck down." He sprays the men as they try to stab each other. One, who's had a bit of his ear sliced off, is taken to the hospital. The other goes to seg.

The other prisoners are impatient for us to wrap up the stabbing business so we can let them outside. It's unusually warm. We let about 150 prisoners out onto the yard, and I stand on the walk, taking in the sun. I watch a white man with a sheet around his waist run as fast as he can as another white man struggles to hold him back. Nearby a fat, white, shirtless prisoner punches the air and kicks another white guy's hands. Another white inmate in a muscle shirt walks toward me. "My

Caucasians are getting ready over here," he says as if to no one in particular. He leans against the fence and asks how I'm doing.

"I'm all right," I say. "How are you?"

"This little camp here is the wildest camp I been through," he says. "There's no structure here. There's nothing." He says he's in for attempted murder. He knocked out a man who touched his girlfriend during Mardi Gras and then kicked him in the head with his cowboy boot. He's been to prison a few times, doing stints in the Texas State Penitentiary and Angola.

A white inmate walks past. "Why aren't you out here punching on somebody?" asks the man in the muscle shirt. The passerby shrugs him off. Muscle Shirt looks across the yard. With the exception of his small group practicing their kicks, most people are black. "They got me locked up with barbarians," he says to me. "You ever see somebody try to stab me, just watch. I like doing that shit. I ain't no average white boy. I ain't got these bolts on my chest for nothing." He pulls his shirt back, revealing two faded Nazi SS bolts under some scars. He says a black prisoner stabbed him. "I had to bite his face off. What you gonna do? You need to get in as close as you can and"—he makes a chomping sound while holding the air in a bear hug—"try to hurt him or kill him. That's what they need. They need some of these dudes to start dying."

I go back inside. The smell of pepper spray is fading, but the smell of shit isn't. It's not until the afternoon that someone comes in to fix the toilets and finds a shank stuck in the plumbing.

Later I recount to a sergeant the way one of the inmates was poking the knife into the other guy's neck. "Did you learn something from that?" he asks me.

"Not really."

The inmate could have slit the other guy's throat if he wanted to, he says. But he didn't. "Both of 'em scared. That's the reason for havin' them shanks in the first place, 'cuz they are scared."

. . .

At the end of my shift I stride briskly down the dark walk. I am relieved
to be going home, but I'm afraid in a way I didn't used to be. The longer
I work here, the more people have grudges against me. As I head down
the walk, inmates are coming and going from various parts of the prison,
and I can't see any other guards around. I don't have a radio—I am required to give it to the officer who relieves me. I've seen the surveillance
footage, and I doubt it would be clear enough to identify anyone who
might jump me in this darkness.

The gate before the exit is locked, and I am routed through the visitation area. There, twenty or so officers from my shift are sitting at
tables, frowning. Two inmates are serving pizza. We've been trapped in
a company meeting. Assistant Warden Parker is there. The chief of security. HR. I grab some pizza and a raffle ticket and sit down, frustrated.

"How many people here have less than a year in?" Parker asks. I raise
my hand. "You've probably seen a lot of bad days, okay? We're gonna
change that. And it takes all of us working together. It really, really does.
As long as we stay as a decent team and we remember that the bad guys
are the ones who stay here twenty-four seven and don't get to leave."

On the wall is a painting of a black kid and a white kid lying on their
stomachs on a grassy hillside, looking at a rainbow. There is another of
an American flag with a lion and a tiger tearing through it and an
American eagle flying overhead. "The CCA Way" is written above it.

"The company took a look at things and they realized that we need
to do a little bit better for our staff here at Winn. I'm not going to say
that we've waved a magic wand and everybody's walking out of here,
gonna go buy new cars, but the hourly wage of a correctional officer is
going to go up to ten dollars an hour. So congratulations to everybody
sitting inside this room." He starts clapping and a few people join in

unenthusiastically. "This is going to be one of those proud moments," he says.

"Does anybody know what the ACA is?" Parker asks. "Have you been hearing about 'We got ACA coming up. Ooooh! ACA's coming.' We gotta panic! Hit the panic button!"

"The American Correctional Association," someone volunteers.

"Okay, why do we care about ACA?" Parker asks.

"We need our jobs. We need to pass."

"That's a theme that goes with it. Years and years and years ago, I think it was 1870, there was a governor upset with what he thought was cruel and unusual punishment," he lectures. "So he started drafting up a little group of people that would go around and they would check on prisons and prison conditions to ensure that the people who were confined were not being treated cruelly. After time they started developing a sophisticated auditing process. So, a third-party person who has no dog in the fight, so to speak, comes in and they take a look at how are we treating our inmates. And they give us a stamp of, 'You're treating them with proper care.'

"That way when we go to court and the inmate says, 'Oh, they made me eat Pizza Hut pizza! That's cruel and unusual punishment! It should have been Domino's!'—when it goes to court, we pull up our ACA files and say, 'Hey, look, here's how we prepare the food in our kitchen. We prepare the food in our kitchen under these standards.'"

ACA is a trade association, but it's also the closest thing we have to a national regulatory body for prisons. More than nine hundred public and private correctional facilities and detention centers are accredited under its standards. Winn was first prison to be accredited in Louisiana.

I've been, twice, to ACA's semiannual convention and was kicked out of one by armed guards after tweeting from its workshops. Lecture topics included sex between COs and inmates and how to deal with the challenge of drug-dealing staff. A class on handling the media recommended that spokespeople avoid answering the calls of particularly tough reporters, and that whenever possible, they should cite ongoing lawsuits to avoid discussing difficult topics. The lecturer also recommended releasing information on Friday nights, to bury it. Topics like suicide and transgender inmates were discussed in terms of financial liability. One company offered a Harley-Davidson to anyone who could hang him- or herself from their suicide-proof vent grills.

Business dominates ACA's conventions. Major prison companies throw parties with free food and drink. In the massive expo halls, where everything from drone detection devices to shank-proof e-cigarettes is on display, CCA's booth is always front and center. CCA and ACA share a long history. Shortly after T. Don Hutto cofounded CCA, he became the president of ACA. Hutto then spent several years as the head of ACA, pushing for privatization. CCA later hired Hardy Rauch, the former director of accreditation of ACA. When CCA went public in 1986, its initial public offering stated "the Company can reduce its exposure to civil rights claims by having the Company's facilities satisfy ACA standards." In 2017 Mississippi prison commissioner and ACA president Chris Epps was sentenced to nearly twenty years in federal prison for taking more than $1 million in bribes and kickbacks in exchange for steering $800 million worth of contracts to private prison companies.

"Where do you think is one of the number one areas that we get hit on as a confinement business?" Parker asks us. "Medical! Inmates have this thing that if they have a sniffle they are supposed to be flown to a specialist somewhere and be treated for that sniffle." ACA accreditation can go a long way in defending against medical lawsuits, Parker says. His tone becomes incredulous. "Believe it or not, we are required by law to take care of them.

"Now do you think an inmate will have an opportunity to say you were treating them with cruel and unusual punishment? Trust me! If it hasn't happened yet, get ready for the ride. It's a fun ride! I was a correctional officer being sued. I was a lieutenant being sued. I was a chief being sued and I was an assistant warden sued by inmates for cruel and unusual punishment, and one of the best things that came along was"—he makes a popping sound with his lips—"ACA accreditation. Therefore"—he clicks his tongue—"how can it be cruel or unusual?"

During the next few weeks, inmates paint every unit in preparation for the ACA audit. The maintenance man is run ragged as he tries to fix the busted vents, plumbing, and cell and tier doors.* In anticipation of the audit, I read the ACA standards. How will the auditors deal with the fact that the cells in segregation are more than twenty feet smaller than required? Or that inmates only get ten minutes to eat, not the mandated twenty? There are many other ACA standards and recommendations Winn does not meet: We rarely have the required number of positions staffed; guards' pay is not comparable to the pay of state corrections officers; guards rarely use the metal detectors at the entrances to the housing units; prisoners often don't get one hour of daily access to exercise space; suicide watch meals are below caloric requirements; and there aren't enough toilets in the dorms.

Then again, Winn passed its last ACA audit, in 2012, with 99 percent, the same score it received in its previous audit three years earlier. Auditors noted that "offenders feel Winn Correctional Center is a safe place to do time" and that "staff morale is good" and they "view their jobs as a good career." In fact, CCA's average score across all its accredited prisons is also 99 percent.

A few years ago a riot erupted in a low-security CCA prison in Mississippi over inadequate health care and poor food. A guard was beaten

---

* "We didn't own the facility," CCA's spokesman told me, noting that major maintenance issues at Winn were the DOC's responsibility. CCA's contract states that it was responsible for routine and preventive maintenance.

to death. Four years after the riot, the federal Bureau of Prisons found that little had changed: The prison was understaffed, the staff were inexperienced, and very few spoke Spanish, despite the fact that most of the inmates were from Mexico. The ACA audit during that time gave the prison a perfect score.

On the morning of Winn's audit, we wake everyone up, and tell them to make their beds and take the pictures of women off of their lockers. Two well-dressed white men in suits enter the unit and do a slow lap around the floor. The only questions they ask Bacle and me are what our names are and how we are doing. They do not examine our logbook, nor do they check our entries against the camera footage. If they did, they would find that some of the cameras don't work. They do not check the doors. If they did, they would see they need to be yanked open by hand because most of the switches don't work. They don't check the fire alarm, which automatically closes smoke doors over the tiers, some of which must be jimmied back open by two guards. They do not ask to go on a tier. They do not interview any inmates. They do a single loop and they leave.

In the morning meeting, the captain is exasperated. There was a stabbing yesterday in Ash, and a few days before, an inmate got stabbed in Elm more than thirty times. But that's not his main concern. "Last night we found a lock blade—a knife—that came off the street," he says. Several guards gasp. Someone is giving actual knives to prisoners? "Everybody you work with, you can't trust. It's sad, but that's just the nature of the beast. I'm telling you: Somebody is going to get hurt because a lot of us are being very selfish. These guys are in here for a reason." He assumes it was a female guard who brought it in. "When these guys leave they are going to go out and find another woman. I have been here long enough to see it. They play you long enough while they in here, because they want what they want. Soon as they hit the street, they forget about you. So long sucker, in other words. When they get busted, they gonna rat you out. Bottom line. Let me tell you something: Eventually, you *will* get caught. Sometimes we are dealing with more than inmates. We are dealing with us."

We all leave the meeting solemnly. "A *real* knife," Sergeant King says to me. "Come on guys. If he or she brought a knife in here, why didn't they bring him a pistol? Try to break him out? Kill one of us?"

Calahan didn't show up for work today, so when we get to the unit, Childs leaves his post on the gate to work the key. He's been here more than twenty years. This violence doesn't seem to faze him. Inside the key he smokes a cigarette and ashes it into a can. He says he's mastered a technique to position his face and blow smoke in a way that the camera doesn't pick up.

"You're writing somebody up already?" he says to Bacle, who is hunched over, scribbling on pink paper. It's about seven in the morning. "Oh you're an asshole."

"Thank you. You're welcome," Bacle says.

"And he probably ain't done nothing," Childs says.

"Hey," Bacle says. "I told him to hurry up and get out of the shower and all he had were smart-ass remarks."

"Look, it's *his* dick. He can wash it as fast and hard as he wants to. He was probably lusting after you and your sexy body."

"Shit. If he poked me with that thing I'd shit all over it."

Bacle tells Childs he's cutting back to part time in thirteen months, once his Social Security kicks in. Childs insists that once he sees that part-time check, he'll be back to full time. That's what Childs did. He's been working here since the prison opened and still makes nine dollars an hour. He can't afford to retire. "You're not upper-class white folks," Childs says to Bacle. "You're still lower class. It's just that your head is above poverty. The rest of you is below it."

"Well once Social Security kicks in, part time should be enough," Bacle says.

"Wrong!" Childs says. "Wrong!"

Once, Childs threatened to quit if they didn't stop making him work in Cypress. He had high blood pressure, and the stress was putting him at risk. "I've had piss, shit, everything throwed at me back there." They gave him a new post for a while, but a new administration put him back. Last year, he says the nurse told the captain that with his blood pressure problems, and at his age, they shouldn't make him work in seg. "The captain said, 'Ah, he can handle it.' A week later I had a heart attack. He still puts me back there on suicide watch." He pauses. "It's been a pretty good job. You don't get rich and you barely survive." He takes a sip of coffee.

The day progresses slowly. Corner Store sits in my chair next to the key and uses Bacle's chair as a desk. A twenty-year-old inmate serving a forty-year sentence hopes to have his book published. Because prisoners don't have access to copy machines, he gets Corner Store to copy it by hand so he can mail it out.

I wander around the unit and see Derik standing at the bars of C2. I am relieved to see him. The other day I heard the coach radio the assistant supervisor about some confrontation with Derik. I thought he might have been sent to Cypress. I open the door and let him out without saying anything. After some time passes, I go out onto Ash walk. He is out there, alone, and takes his position under the camera.

"You need that fresh air," he says.

I sigh. "This shit wears you out," I say.

"It wears *you* out? I live in there. Motherfuckers playing in there all day, don't shut the fuck up. You trying to read and a thousand motherfuckers talking and shit. That shit builds a lot of anger in me. You got to think for fifteen hundred inmates all the time." He steps front to back as he talks. His eyes are constantly scanning our surroundings.

"Then you got a free man coming out of that world and you got to think for him because he don't know what he's doing. He doesn't want to compromise. That's why I flashed out on coach over there. Coach was talking all that motherfucking shit. He can't talk to me like that. I'll choke his stupid ass out. This jail is fucked up, brah. The people in this motherfucker fucked up, and the officers running it fucked up. *You* fucked up."

I feel a pang. "You think I'm fucked up?"

He says it scares him the way I lock eyes with him when I'm doing count or see him on the floor. "I be thinking that you must see something different in me than the other inmates and you want to know more. Like you probably studyin' me to see what's going on. Like I'm the type of person you could let your guard down. I know it's not all one hundred percent a good thing. You interested, but you don't know what you interested in." I laugh. Will I ever tell him?

"Why you hate cops so much?" I ask.

"For one thing, cops crooked." He says that once a cop stopped him on the street, patted him down, took $1,500 cash from him, and told him he could come retrieve it at the station. When he did, he found that the officer only recorded $900. "You just ripped off my bread like I'm your bitch-ass nigga," he told the cop.

"You got some good cops," he says. "I done been around some good motherfuckers. At the same time you got some that are cocky, conceited, arrogant. They just feel like, Fuck it, I rule the world. And they really do rule the world. They killing and getting away with that shit. They getting away with that shit left and right, left and right, left and right. Even the president's not even bucking."

"This cop you killed," I say. "You ever think about him? You ever think about his family?"

"I don't give a fuck." He laughs. "Dealing with the fact that I had to raise my children from jail, I'd probably do it different. I'd change it.

But I can't." About the cop himself, "I don't give a fuck one way or another. I don't feel it. To me killing is like a football game. It come and go. There was pain for the moment, then it's gone. If I could have killed your ass in here and got away with it, you best believe one motherfucking thing—your ass woulda been outta there."

I look at my watch. "I better get back in there or they're gonna ask me what I'm doing." I go inside. If anyone deserves to be in prison, I think, Derik does.

The day drags on and I become consumed with my minor battles. One inmate fakes a medical emergency so he can get off the tier and deliver a pair of pants to someone on another tier. Tattoo Face flips out when I try to put him in his tier. "I got a hundred years and I just got here!" he shouts, the implication being that he has nothing to lose, so back off. I find out later that the man who was stabbed the other day in Elm was his brother. I try to cut him slack. Then there is Gray Beanie. He used to crack jokes with me, lightening the mood while I was trying to get everyone in their tiers. Then one day he called me to the bars while he was in the shower. "If I ask you a question, are you gonna write me up?" he asked. I told him no, and he asked if I was gay. Before I answered, he got an erection. I told him I wasn't and walked away. Since then, his jokes have gotten louder and more confrontational.

As people mill around the floor during midday chow, an inmate is doing push-ups outside of his tier.

"Get it in," I say jokingly.

"Get it in?" Gray Beanie says. "That's how you talk?"

"You're obsessed," I spit.

"Obsessed with *you*," he says.

By six o'clock I am exasperated. Inmates are coming back from chow, and there are dozens of people who won't go in their tiers. I can't go home until they are all locked away. I walk from one tier to the next, unlocking the doors for people who are waiting. I open C2. Gray

Beanie, standing in front of the tier, doesn't enter. I tell him to go in. He walks off. I follow him, ignoring all the other inmates asking me to open their doors. "Give me your ID," I say.

"I don't have no ID," he says. The floor is full of inmates. I tell him to give me his name and DOC number. He tells it to me and leaves. I check the bed book and don't find it—the name and DOC number are fakes. Fuming, I march into his tier, looking for him in each bed, searching the TV room. He isn't here. I hand my key and radio to the night shift officer and walk out of Ash unit. People are still coming in from chow. It's dark and I see an inmate on the walk who I recently wrote up. "It's just you and me now Minnesota," he says and runs up on me. I jump back. "Hahaha! Don't get scared."

The next morning Gray Beanie is still on my mind. It's becoming harder for me to let go of the previous day's gripes. When it's time to let inmates out for the small yard, he begins walking out of his tier.

"You're not coming out without no ID," I say.

"I don't have no ID."

"Then you're not coming out."

"Man, you starting the same stuff from yesterday man."

"It's not finished. You lied. You didn't give me your name."

"I did give you my name! Bed eleven man. Gordon St. John. I don't have no ID!"

"I'ma go check it. You got to wait." I check the bed book, verify his name—it's the same last name he told me yesterday, different first name. I let him out. "Faggot-ass motherfucker," he says.

I write him up and put yesterday's date on it. One for aggravated disobedience. Another for lying about his name and DOC number: theft by fraud. Another dated today for calling me a faggot: defiance. I want to bury him.

I go stand on Ash walk and eat my apple. It's cold.

Gray Beanie approaches from the yard on the other side of the fence. "I apologize," he says.

"I don't want to talk to you," I say.

"I'm coming to apologize! Now we could settle this like men or both of us gonna get a write-up 'cuz you took something from your job yesterday and carried it on to another day. I got a rule book in the dorm." He says he knows I am writing up something and putting yesterday's date on it, which is against the rules. I deny it.

"Well I just know that you asked me for sexual favors and I'ma write that up," he says and walks away.

"Shit!" I say dismissively.

He stops. "So you know how to play the game. I'ma play the game too. And I got three witnesses." He continues walking. "I know what I'm doin'."

A couple of hours later, after everyone is back in, an inmate tells me the yard orderly needs some bags. I grab a couple and go outside. Derik is in the yard, alone. I hand two bags through the fence. "Here you go." We are the only two out here.

He tells me Gray Beanie is his friend, and he heard about what happened between us.

"Hey man, spare him, bro," he says. "For me."

"Nah man."

"Spare him brah, 'cuz—"

"He's playing so many fucking games, I don't fuck around with that."

"Listen man, he's never gonna fuck with you no more," he says. His offer is tempting. This is why it's good having a cop killer on my side. He can make things happen that I can't. But who is in control here? I let him off of his tier whenever he asks. Bacle has noticed me letting him walk out of the unit to go to the yard, alone. I tell Bacle he's a yard orderly, even though I know he's not. I'm not completely sure anymore why I do this. At first I thought Derik would take me deeper into the story, perhaps show me something that others wouldn't. I've been waiting for him to proposition me to bring in drugs or phones, but he's too smart for that—he's waiting for me to take the step. I appreciated how frank he was, but some of his stories have been gnawing at me. I'm beginning to wonder what is true—Did he really kill a cop, or is that a story he made up to intimidate me? Our conversations all head toward one purpose—him trying to bring me close to make me think I can trust him, while planting a seed of fear about what could happen if I ever acted against his will. It's starting to work.

"Sorry man," I say. "Can't do it."

"Listen, I know he done bad. I'm telling you that the dude yesterday was under a lot of pressure." He tells me to look him in the eyes. For a second I do, then I look away. "I'm the type of person that if I can't help you then I'm gonna try to hurt you, it's just as simple as that."

A Code Red is called over the radio.

I come in the next day for mandatory CPR training. The instructor is visiting from North Fork Correctional, a CCA prison located in Sayre, Oklahoma. He teaches us how to pin an inmate's arm against his own body with our foot when we perform CPR, so that if the inmate is faking, he can't punch you with that hand. Then you check the inmate's pulse on the side closest to your body, so if he dies, it doesn't look like you are choking him on the camera.

Sergeant King says he's afraid to do CPR on an inmate, because if the inmate dies, he might be sued. He pumps a dummy's chest. Prisoners just have it too good in here, King announces to the room.

Some of them *want* to stay in prison, Miss Crowley replies. She is responsible for discharging inmates. Everyone, sitting on blue mats on the floor, is immediately engaged by this topic. "Why should I go home right now?" Miss Crowley says, mimicking a prisoner. "I'm getting free meals. I'm getting a free bed." She counts her points on her fingers. "Free cable. Free whatever I want. Why would I go to the street and have to work for it?"

"Do you know how much laser eye surgery costs?" King says.

"Thank you," Miss Crowley says.

"Five dollars," the instructor says. "All they pay is five bucks."

"Like I said, they have more rights than we do," Miss Crowley says.

"It's easier to commit a crime than to work for a living," King says.

The Code Red yesterday was caused by King. He had suddenly decided to enforce the dress code in Elm when inmates went to chow. Everyone had to be carrying his ID and wearing his blue armband that designated him as an inmate of Elm. He wouldn't allow anyone out with modifications to their prison uniforms. Amid the frustration of King's sudden strictness, an inmate had grabbed mop buckets and began throwing them on the floor. King says the prisoner seemed high, wigging out in the way people do after smoking mojo, or synthetic marijuana. "I wasn't really worried about nothing," King boasts. "I can handle my business." When King tried to make him stop, the inmate grabbed him.

"Let me tell you, it's an extreme challenge to stay down there on that floor in Elm for twelve hours," King says. "I'm not kidding you man. An *extreme* challenge. And look: It's not the inmates. My extreme challenge is controlling my anger and exercising patience. The inmate don't be my problem. My problem is myself. Once he put his hands on me, it was over. I was in self-preservation mode."

The CPR instructor looks King straight in the eyes and says, "You were fearing for your life."

"I was in self-preservation mode, but uh—" King says.

"When you write that report, you were fearing for your life. Remember that."

| 22 |

When Hutto moved to Arkansas to run its prison system in 1971, he didn't want to live near headquarters in Little Rock, where commissioners typically lived. He wanted to live on the plantation. One of his first initiatives as commissioner was to kick the Cummins superintendent out of the main house and move his family in. It was a comfortable home, containing some artifacts left by previous men who had lived there. In the bedroom where Hutto slept, a buzzer had been installed by a former superintendent. When pressed, it rang in the women's reformatory, located just fifty yards from the house, where around forty female inmates lived. The superintendent would use it when his wife was away, buzzing it to summon his favorite female convict.

After Hutto settled in, he began a prison rodeo. In August 1972, some thirty-five hundred free world people bought tickets to watch inmates compete for small cash prizes. Prisoners with little experience, wearing cartoonish uniforms with black and white stripes, rode broncos. In one inmate's riding debut, he was kicked in the stomach and had to be carried off in a stretcher. About twenty prisoners piled on top of a greased pig, trying to capture it to win a ten dollar prize. A crowd favorite was an event called "Hard Money," in which inmates attempted to grab a tobacco pouch containing seventy-five dollars that was tied between the horns of an enraged bull as he ran around the ring. Describing the rodeo to a reporter, Hutto said, "Our objective here is to return each inmate to society better equipped to handle his responsibilities and this can be a start in that direction."

Hutto's mandate was to implement the US Supreme Court ruling that Arkansas improve its prison conditions, including getting rid of convict guards, but he quickly came under pressure from legislators to make the prisons profitable again. Murton's reforms made the state lose its prison profits; Cummins and Tucker had been in the red for several years. Initially Hutto demurred, saying it would be very difficult to run a good prison for monetary gain. "A good prison is very profitable to society," he said. If a prison could successfully hold a prisoner in custody and reform him enough to prevent him from committing crimes after release, then as far as he was concerned that prison was on a "profitable basis." Nevertheless, he revamped the farming operation, converting it from a "manual, inefficient, marginal operation to a highly productive mechanized one." He curbed the raising of food crops in favor of high-volume cash crops like cotton, rice, and soybeans. During Hutto's first year in Arkansas, farm operations totaled nearly $1.8 million in revenue, half a million more than the year before, and more than they were making before Murton's time.

Hutto began his own empire in Arkansas, hiring many of his staff members from Ramsey. Nearly half of the high-level positions in Cummins and Tucker were filled by Texans who brought with them their own methods of forcing inmates to work. In a federal hearing on prison conditions under Hutto, an inmate testified that he had been stripped and left naked in an unlit "quiet cell" for twenty-eight days for refusing fieldwork. Guards blasted air-conditioning into his cell, without giving him a blanket, and fed him only bread, water, and "grue," leading him to lose thirty pounds. When he later refused to go to the fields again, guards beat him with blackjacks and put him back in the quiet cell.

Inmates also testified that failure to pick one's quota of cotton was grounds for a punishment called "Texas TV." An inmate would be forced to stand with his forehead against the wall and his toes several feet away from the wall with his hands behind his back. He would be left there for up to six hours, sometimes naked, and often without food. "They get you up in the morning and give you two pieces of bread with syrup and tell you to pick cotton all day and when you don't pick enough they stick you on that wall so you don't get any supper or clean clothes," one inmate testified. "Then the next morning, it's the same thing. How are you gonna have a good attitude when it doesn't do no good?" Other inmates testified that, as punishment, they were cuffed behind their backs, put on the hood of a truck, and driven at high speeds through the plantation, sometimes falling off. Despite the hearing's findings, Governor Dale Bumpers was satisfied with Hutto, telling reporters it appeared the inmates worked harder for him than they did for his predecessor.

Hutto's prisons attracted more attention when a seventeen-year-old boy died at Cummins. The boy was there as part of a "one day wonder" program, in which juvenile offenders were given a taste of prison life after committing minor offenses. Under Hutto, guards would shoot at the juveniles' feet as they entered the prison, chase them with cars, and order them to keep up with the fastest cotton pickers. After going through this treatment, seventeen-year-old Willie Stewart died, possibly from a heart attack, prompting an FBI investigation.

The governor and the press frequently praised Hutto, but by October 1974, more than three years after he came to Arkansas, an appeals court ruled that the state was still failing to "provide constitutional and, in some respects, even a humane environment" at Cummins and Tucker.

The judge called conditions under Hutto "sub-human," condemning the "use of various forms of torture," total lack of rehabilitative programs, overcrowding, racial discrimination, abuse of solitary confinement, continuing use of trusty guards, and lack of adequate medical care, including "basic emergency services." After the ruling, about two hundred inmates refused to work until guards in riot gear forced them to the fields. The prison system may have harmed Arkansas's reputation, but in another sense, it was doing better than ever. The year of the appeals court ruling, prison farming operations made nearly $700,000 in net gains. Hutto had made prison farms profitable again.

He would be the last. After Hutto, Cummins would forever operate at a loss. The same would be true for other prison plantations. Angola in Louisiana, Parchman in Mississippi, and many in Texas are still run as prison farms, but lawsuits changed how these prisons could be run and today they cost money, rather than add to state coffers. Not until Hutto introduced a new model with CCA would prisons be profitable again. Lucky for Hutto, when he left Arkansas to run Virginia's prison system in 1976, the landscape of American prisons began going through another dramatic shift. Prison populations began to climb. In the decade after Hutto left Arkansas, the national prison population would more than double, rising from 263,000 to 547,000 prisoners. It would continue to skyrocket until peaking at 1.6 million inmates in state and federal prisons in 2009. Rather than make a profit, prisons would come to cost state and federal governments nationwide $80 billion a year.

Hutto and his new business partners found a way to capitalize on overcrowding. Did Hutto know that when prison populations boomed in the past, states relieved their financial burdens by privatizing? Did he know the history of American prisons and see an opportunity to replicate the past to his benefit? Or was he just another businessman, taken by the ebbs and flows of profit and punishment that have existed since this country's foundation? There were so many questions I wanted to ask him.

I sent him an email. "I would guess that you are aware of me and my article on Winn Correctional for *Mother Jones* magazine. I am working on a deeper history of private prisons and I would very much like to interview you for it." To my surprise, he wrote back the same day—"Of course!"—and asked when I would like to meet in Nashville. We made a date, I bought my plane ticket, and I scoured news archives for everything I could learn about his past. Then he emailed again: "I am sorry, but I will be unable to meet with you. Thank you." I wondered if he had guessed at my growing list of questions: What was the nature of his relationship with his "houseboys" in Texas and Arkansas? How did it feel to preside over black men picking cotton from dawn to dusk? Maybe he had an inkling that I wanted to know how, in a single mind, the thinking evolved from running an operation in Texas that so blatantly resembled slavery to a slick corporation that would make billions by warehousing people.

I emailed him again and again. "Is it an issue of timing?" "Could we touch base by phone about this?"

He did not respond.

| 23 |

can't find Derik. Normally when I do count in C2, he is there on his bed. Our eyes usually meet for the briefest moment as if to say good morning. Today his rack is empty. While I'm doing paperwork in the key, I ask a case manager what happened to him. I try to make the question sound casual, like an afterthought. *Locked his ass up*, he says, leaning back on his chair.

What did he do? I ask. His eyes widen and he looks at me.

Acted a fool.

But like, what did he do? He sits upright in his chair as though astonished by the question.

He. Acted. A. Fool.

Derik is gone and soon Corner Store will be gone too. After nearly two decades, he is about to be free. He has just six weeks to go before he qualifies for early release with the "good time" he's earned. How does someone reenter the world after two decades behind bars, with no friends on the outside and no money to his name? His first step, he says, will be to stay in a shelter until he can get on his feet. He doesn't know where he will go yet. He tells me he doesn't want to count the days. "It stresses me out. Anxiety sets in. Your mind goes, working and thinking about stuff. How am I going to do this? How am I going to do that? It causes a panic attack. When I walk, I walk."

But fantasies creep into his mind. "I'ma get me a big bottle of Kaopectate, a big German chocolate cake, five gallon thing of milk," he says. "Just get out the way, that's all I'ma tell you." We are outside, talking through the fence; he's on the small yard and I'm on the Ash walk. "After that, I want me a seafood platter, a real seafood platter about the size of the kitchen table, just for me and Mom. It's all about Mom when I go home."

He puts his hand on the fence and leans in. "What I'm sayin' is this here, man: I just wanna go have fun, boy. And fun does not mean me-gettin'-in-trouble fun. Fun means just enjoying life. I wanna be able to take my mothafuckin' shoes off and socks off and walk in the sand. I wanna be able to just go outside in my shorts and just my house slippers and stand in the rain and just—" he spreads his arms, points his face to the sky, and opens his mouth. "Them thangs I miss. You can't do that in here. Alls I'm sayin' is this here: When I get out, I don't want to have to poke my chest out any longer. It hurts to poke my chest out. It's a weight on my shoulders I've been toting for the last twentysomethin' years, and I'm ready to drop that weight because the load is heavy."

I'm starting to be asked to train new cadets. Today I am paired with a short white man in his forties with peppered black hair. He says he worked as a security contractor in Iraq and Afghanistan for Triple Canopy and Blackwater. He is hoping to go back to Afghanistan soon. "I had terrorists who blew up schools and shit that I had to take care of. It wasn't all PC like it is here." Prisoners here, he says, get treated with kid gloves. "They got rights and all this crap. Fuck that."

I show him how to open the doors and do callouts, and I tell him we are going to begin letting people out for chow soon. "What do you mean?" he says, suddenly looking frightened. "You are just going to open the doors and let them out? I can't believe that!" He doesn't think they should go out at all. "Fuck 'em. Not unless you have absolutely an emergency. Or you're on a work plan or some shit like that. I'd make prison so bad that you would never want to come back. When I was growing up, my mom used to live in Mississippi. They had all the work gangs and they were all in orange and all chained up. Chain gangs and shit like that. That's how it should be. Make it so bad, you'd never want to come back."

"It's pretty bad in here," I tell him. "People get stabbed here all the time." At least seven inmates have been shanked in the last six weeks. As people come in from chow, I hear on the radio, "Code Blue in Elm! Code Blue in Elm!" A CO is frantically calling for a stretcher. Several inmates are stabbing each other; they can't count how many.

"Everyone on the tier!" Bacle shouts to the prisoners milling about.

"Fuck all that," one says. "We'll have another Code motherfucking Blue." Bacle blows his whistle. We get everyone in and I head out onto the Ash walk to see what is happening.

A minute later, a bleeding man is wheeled by on a work cart, and I return inside. Several people were injured, and I hear one was stabbed about thirty times. Miraculously no one dies.

Three days later I see two inmates stab each other in Ash. A week after that, another inmate is stabbed and beaten by multiple people in Elm. People say he was cut more than forty times. During this time, Miss Price quits after nearly twenty-five years of service. She says she's tired of this work. We will go without a unit manager in Ash for weeks. Not long after she leaves, someone is beaten unconscious and stabbed through the cheek in Birch, and another inmate is stabbed in Cypress.

It is difficult to imagine how someone gets stabbed in segregation.

How do shanks get in? How do inmates get to each other? The morning after the stabbing in Cypress, I hear Assistant Warden Parker call over the radio for maintenance to come and fix the cell doors there. A month ago, he told us that inmates in the unit could pull some cell doors off their tracks and open them without keys. A month before that, Mr. Tucker, the SORT commander, told us something similar. Apparently this problem still hasn't been fixed.

Miss Calahan tells me they had the same problem in the unit before I started. She points at D1 tier and says that for two months, she and Bacle told the higher-ups to fix the door. At least one inmate filed a grievance about it. "I popped it several times using my foot," Bacle says. He even showed the warden how it was done. Then, one evening, two inmates shook the tier door open from the outside, apparently unnoticed by the floor officers. One was carrying an eight-inch knife, the other an ice pick. According to a legal complaint, the two inmates found another inmate who lived on the tier and stabbed him twelve times in the head, mouth, eye, and body. One of the attackers warned that he would kill anyone who alerted the guards, so the victim lay bleeding, waiting for a CO to come through for the mandatory half-hour security check. Unsurprisingly, no one did. He bled for an hour and a half until a guard came by for count. He spent nine days in the infirmary. "Child, next day they was out here fixing that door!" Miss Calahan says.

Bacle says he wishes an investigative reporter would come and look into this place. He complains about how, in other prisons, inmates get new charges for stabbing someone. Here they are put in seg, but they rarely get shipped to another prison with tighter security. "CCA wants that fucking dollar!" Bacle says through clenched teeth. "That's the reason why we play hell on getting a damn raise, because all they want is that dollar in their pocket."

High levels of violence have been documented at several CCA prisons. In an Ohio prison, inmate-on-inmate assault nearly tripled and inmate-on-staff assault quadrupled after CCA took over. When CCA asked the state to raise its per diem rate in Kentucky, the state refused because the company's prison was twice as violent as its state-run counterpart and because a suicidal employee smuggled in a gun and shot herself in the warden's office. A 2016 federal government study found that private prisons reported 28 percent more inmate-on-inmate assaults than public prisons did, and that inmates in private prisons had nearly twice as many weapons.

But are any of these numbers accurate? If I were not working at Winn and were reporting on the prison through more traditional means, I would never know how violent it is. While I work here, I keep track of every stabbing that I see or hear about from supervisors or eyewitnesses. During the first two months of this year, at least twelve people are shanked. The company is required to report all serious assaults to the DOC. But DOC records show that for the first ten months of 2015, CCA reported only five stabbings.*

Reported or not, by my seventh week as a guard the violence is getting out of control. The stabbings begin to happen so frequently that on February 16, 2016, the prison goes on indefinite lockdown. No inmates leave their tiers. The walk is empty. Crows gather and puddles of water form on the rec yards. More black-clad men are sent in by corporate, and they march around the prison in military formation. Some wear face masks.

The new SORT team, composed of officers from around the country, shakes down the prison bit by bit. The wardens from the DOC continue to wander around, and CCA also sends in wardens of its own from

---

* CCA says it reports all assaults and that the DOC may have classified incidents differently.

out of state. Tension is high. No inmates except kitchen workers can leave the tiers. Passing out food trays becomes a daily battle. Prisoners rush the food cart and take everything.

"CCA is not qualified to run this place," an inmate shouts to me a day into the lockdown. "You always got to shut the place down. You can't function. You can't run school or nothing because you got everybody on lockdown."

Another inmate cuts in. "Since I been here, there's been nothing but stabbings," he says. "It don't happen like this at other prisons because they got power. They got control. Ain't no control here, so it's gonna always be something happening. You got to start from the top to the bottom, you feel me? If [the warden] really want to control this prison—goddamn!—why ain't you go' call and get some workers? But you know what it's all about? It's about the money. 'Let them kill theyselves.' They don't give a fuck."

One day a former public-jail warden visits Ash unit. "I don't know what's going on down here, but it's not good," he says to me. "There's something fucked up, I can tell you that."

I ask if Winn seems different from publicly operated prisons. "Oh, hell yeah," he says. "Too lax." If this were his prison, he says, there would be four officers on the floor, not two. At his public facility, officers begin at $12.50 an hour. When they go to police academy, they get another $500 a month. Every time they pass a quarterly fitness test, they get $300. The initial training is ninety days. I tell him it was thirty days here. "This is a joke," he says. "I been doing this for sixteen years. This is a free jail to me. Too much shit going on down here. Not no consequences." He says CCA could lose its contract.

One day SORT comes to Ash. One masked officer keeps watch over everyone with a PepperBall gun. Other SORT members stand around, eating Twinkies and Oatmeal Creme Pies and drinking Mountain Dew. The inmates are sent to the gym and SORT tears up the tiers, throwing things out, slicing up mattresses. They find mojo, cell phones, heart-shaped pills, and white powder.

"Anyone know what cocaine looks like?" a clean-cut SORT officer says sarcastically, his eyebrows raised. He and another SORT member joke about stealing it. "We never found it! Hahaha!"

Bacle tries to stop them from taking inmates' coffee or destroying their matchstick crafts. Their overzealousness riles him. "Some people here think just because they're locked up they're a bunch of shitheads. I look at it, they fucked up and they're doing their damn time."

When SORT is finished, the inmates are brought back to their tiers. Many of their mattresses are useless, cut open and emptied of their stuffing. When the commander sees that some are coming to the bars to complain about things that went missing, the SORT commander orders his men to enter the tier. "Get on your bunks!" one shouts. "We will use force!" They file in, an officer stopping in front of each bunk. A man with a PepperBall gun stands at the end as does another wearing a black mask over his face and carrying a grenade launcher with less-lethal buckshot in it. The commander walks up and down the tier. "If you feel that something was taken from you, you need to fill out a lost property claim and go through the proper channels. My guys are not here to take your stuff. You cannot be standing at the bars complaining. Understood?"

Later, an inmate is standing at the bars, digging through a garbage can. Two SORT officers cuff him up and pull him out. The commander stands him against the wall. "What did we tell you about coming to the bars?" he says. The inmate says he was looking for his ID in the trash. "Why don't you put your forehead against the wall," the commander says. The inmate does. "Now. If your forehead comes off the wall again we will put you on the ground. Is that clear?"

"Yessir."

"We don't work here. Not regularly. Things are going to change around here. It's probably going to be a bit of a painful process, but we are going to make it better. In order for us to do that, we gotta regain control, do you agree with that?"

"Yessir."

"I don't want to have to make an example of you. Fair enough?"

"Yessir."

"I'm not going to have no issues again am I?"

"No sir."

As soon as SORT leaves, inmates scream over one another to tell me what was taken, cursing me for not standing up for them.

During the lockdown Corner Store asks me to let him out of his tier. With the canteen closed, his services are badly needed. Everyone's commissary is getting low; many inmates are in search of cigarettes. They ask me to ferry things from one tier to the next, but I refuse, mostly because I know that once I do, the requests will never stop. I don't let Corner Store out. I tell him it's too risky with all these eyes around. For days, he just lies on his bed, staring at the ceiling.

His release date is five days away, but he still doesn't know where he's going when he gets out. "Isn't it Tuesday you are getting out?"

"Supposedly," he says. Louisiana law doesn't allow early release unless the inmate has an address to go to. New parolees have to stay in the state, and his mother doesn't live in Louisiana. With no one outside to assist him, he has to rely on CCA to make arrangements with a shelter. The prison's coach was trying to help, but Corner Store says he got "roadblocked" by the administration.

"So they just keep you here?" I say, incredulous.

"Yeah, basically. I'm not even angry, man. I just know my day is coming. I've waited years for this. I'm not mad."

I ask Corner Store's case manager what is happening with him. "He might be supposed to be getting out," he says, but "as long as he don't have that [address], his feet will not hit outside that gate. It ain't nothin' I can do for him."

"They don't want nobody to leave," Corner Store tells me. "The longer they keep you, the more money they make. You understand that?"

One of the SORT members tells me they'll be at Winn for months. Yesterday, they found fifty-one shanks in Elm, roughly one for every seven men. During the first four months of this year, CCA reported finding nearly two hundred weapons at Winn. That made it the state's most heavily armed prison, with more than five times more confiscated weapons per inmate than GEO Group's similarly sized Allen Correctional Center, and twenty-three times more than Angola. "They getting ready to start a war," one officer says in a morning meeting.

Sergeant King stops by Ash. As he makes to leave, people begin shouting from their tiers. "What's up with the fuckin' store?" Because of the lockdown, it's been three weeks since anyone here went to canteen. Inmates are up at the bars, looking angry. "You 'bout to start a whole riot," one says to King.

Bacle seems nervous. "If they start throwing shit, you step right up here where they can't gitcha," he tells me, pointing toward the entrance. Less than a week ago, inmates rioted in a privately operated immigrant detention center in Texas. I saw prisoners here watching it on the news.

I walk over to one of the tiers.

"There ain't go' be no count or no nothing!" one shouts at me. "Ain't no COs coming in this bitch until we go to canteen."

"That's what's up. We all standing behind that."

"We gonna put this bitch on the channel eight news."

"Y'all risking your fucking life around here playing these fucking games!"

"Fuck the count! Bring the warden down here."

King comes over to one of the tiers. "Y'all gotta give me an opportunity. Before y'all start bucking. Before y'all start refusing. Because here's what's going to happen: They're gonna bring the SORT force down here."

"We don't give a fuck!"

"I ain't got no fucking soap! No nothing! No deodorant! No fucking cigarettes! This place is shit!"

I don't want to give the impression we are afraid, so I walk the floor. Everyone, everywhere, is pissed. I feel an explosion coming and I want to flee. "I'm surprised ain't nobody got you yet," a white inmate with a shaved head says to me, his eyes cold and focused. "They go' get you."

Someone calls King a "house nigger" and he pretends not to hear. He calls Bacle and me to the door. "Listen, it's a lot of tension down here," he says.

"No shit," Bacle says.

"They found seventy-five shanks in two days. These sonsabitches is dangerous, y'all. I don't want y'all goin' in them tiers. I don't want y'all lettin' nobody out. As of right now, if this shit don't get handled, y'all going to have a fuckin' riot on y'all hands. All the black suits ain't going to do nothin' but PepperBall and gas all of they asses." He leaves.

A while later a CCA warden from Tennessee comes and talks to the inmates. "You know why it's like this?" an inmate asks him. "All these dudes are running around stabbing each other and ain't nothing happening to them. Plain and simple. They're punishing everybody else who's not doing nothing, and they aren't punish the dudes that's actually stabbing each other. Go give 'em street charges and shit, man!"

"We didn't even do nothing, man!"

"I understand that," the warden says. "Y'all saying that y'all are being mistreated. I got plenty of people here. If we want to act like refugees and animals, then we can do it that way." The prisoners don't back down. A couple of hours later, SORT comes and escorts the inmates to the canteen.

Bacle tells me Walmart is raising its wages to ten dollars an hour now, same as us. Might be something to think about.

The lockdown lasts a total of eleven days. When it ends, Corner Store stands at the bars, waiting for me to let him out to work the floor. I ignore him. He pleads, but I am unbending. I have become convinced that he thinks he has influence over me, though I can't articulate why. I become suspicious of his friendliness and wonder if he is manipulating me. I begin to talk to him like every other inmate and he looks at me with confusion. When he lingers too long as I hold the gate open for chow, I slam it shut and let him stew. He calls my name as I walk away.

I feel a twinge of guilt, but it lasts only momentarily. His release date comes and goes, but he doesn't leave. When I do count, I see him lying on his bunk. Eventually he stops making eye contact as I pass.

An inmate orderly corners me. "Listen, what's the problem?" he says, leaning against his broom.

"What problem?" I say curtly.

"Listen, be cool. Be cool. We talking. Relax. Why you so aggressive when I talk to you? You're too snappy."

"I'm not aggressive, man!"

"No, no, no. There's been a drastic change in you. What the fuck went wrong?"

I tell him we are under pressure from management to tighten up. This is true, but there is more. I see conspiracies brewing. Things I used to view as harmless transgressions I now view as personal attacks. When a physically disabled man doesn't leave the shower in time for count, I am certain he is testing me, trying to break me down, to dominate me. The same is true when I see prisoners lying under their blankets during the daytime or standing at the bars. I don't care about the rules per se; many of them seem arbitrary. But I become obsessed with the notion that people are breaking them in front of me to whittle away at my will.

One day the key officer tells me to go to the captain's office. I am nervous; this has never happened before. He is sitting alone at his desk.

"I think you are a very strong officer," he says. I relax—it's my employee evaluation. "I think you are a very detailed officer. You got a knack for this. You got a' 'it' factor for this. It's just who you are as a person. So, like you went down there to Ash and you just took the bull by the horns and just ran with it. It seems like them guys are starting to understand now—this is how this unit is go' run. This is how CO Bauer go' run it."

The computer screen in front of him reads, "He is an outstanding officer. He has a take-charge attitude. He is dependable and stern. He would be an excellent candidate for promotion."

"That's how we feel about you. I just think that you need to stay consistent with what you are doing. Don't break."

Despite myself, I crack a smile.

Even after the lockdown ends, SORT does not leave. They patrol the walk, frisking random inmates, and shake down tiers relentlessly. One morning I spot white buses parked outside the prison as I pull in for work. At the morning meeting there are about fifteen wardens and COs from public prisons across the state. The Winn warden steps up to the podium. "Our friends here from the Louisiana Department of Corrections have come to help us out," he says. This is the moment everyone has feared. Is it taking over? Will we lose our jobs?

A warden and a couple of officers from Angola follow Bacle and me to Ash. One tells us they are taking inmates who are too friendly with staff and shipping them to other prisons. I am surprised to see them tell the Ash floor orderly, the most trusted inmate here, to pack his things. As he digs through his locker, a small bundle of drugs drops onto the floor. "What is this?" the Angola officer asks him.

"I don't know what that is," the orderly says in the same perfectly innocent tone that I've always heard from him. "I just found it there on the floor." I've never suspected this man, even for a second. The cuffs they put around his wrists seem tiny and fragile on his massive arms.

"Very influential," one of the officers says. "They think he has had a lot to do with what's been going on around here. He has too much influence over the inmates and the free folks." He says they've also been administering lie detector tests to officers. Several have already refused to take it and walked off the job. I get nervous and go into the bathroom and flip through my notebook. I rip out notes from the morning meeting and notes on a comment I hear a coworker make that her sexual harassment complaint hasn't been answered in nine months. I throw them all in the toilet and hold the handle down for a good ten seconds.

Now all that is left in the notebook are little jottings of inmates' transgressions:

> 6:10 I'll slap the fuck out you. Pussy ass. I'll beat your
> fucking ass. Stole tray.
> 4:04 Bed 29 wouldn't leave shower. D2
> C1 24 refused to leave. "I'll jack off on you. I'll knock your
> ass out. Write it up!"
> 11:02 C1 bed 8 "CO my dick hard as a motherfucker."
> 10:57 Marshall didn't sit on bunk during count time.
> "Make a nigga put hands on u."
> 8:17 D2-8 "You want that dick. That's what you want."
> 5:45 on D2 "It's about time I put another one of you on my
> belt."

One inmate tells an Angola officer he wants an ARP form to file a complaint on me because I've been unfair to him. Three officers get up, stand around him, and tell him to take off all his clothes. The inmate strips, they search the garments, and tell him to go get on his bed. "I don't want to hear all that bullshit he talks," one of the officers says to me. "They try to use that ARP to intimidate you. I don't care nothing about no ARP." I tell him about how Gray Beanie threatened to write me up for a PREA violation.

"We all been through that, man," he says. "I even had to go to investigation to take a swab 'cuz a dude had said I came in and knocked him out and then I raped him. They had to get a court order and all this stuff to do a swab on me. All it was was we shook him down and he didn't want to be shaken down and then we did what we call house arrest down on the cell block. We take everything they can't have in seg but we keep him in the same cell. He didn't like that so he [made up the accusation]. But that's another game that the higher-ups gave them to play. They got a' ARP system. They got PREA. They got one-eight-hundred Crime Stoppers. They got all this stuff to fight security with. And they put us through all this stuff. I wasn't worried because I already knew it was a lie, but some people can't handle it."

"It's a mental game," I say.

"That's right. And let me tell you something else to be careful of. Be careful of the cans and bottles that y'all bring. Take 'em back home with you. Get 'em out of here, because they'll . . . go digging in the trash can and get your DNA. Then they'll say, Well, how did they get your DNA? Then you got to explain that you threw a plastic spoon in the trash can and they got it. We encounter so many penitentiary games, man."

Later, Ash's new corrections counselor brings one of the Angola officers to a tier. With the officer at her side, she tells the inmate he should have pulled his hands out of his pants when she ordered him to.

"If you are sitting there with your hands in your pants, I am going to have to assume—"

The officer looks at her. "Assume? Let me tell you something. Calm down. Even if you don't see him, he's got to be doing a stroking motion." The officer makes as if he's stroking a giant dick. "He's got to be *doing* something." They let the inmate go.

When it's count time, the COs from Angola blow a whistle and bark for everyone to sit up straight on their bunks. Bacle and I have never done this. They tell us that if we get used to counting people sleeping under their blankets, we might eventually count someone who is dead. All the inmates sit up without hesitation. As long as the DOC officers are here, everything is quiet and smooth. They make inmates walk through the metal detector as they enter the unit, while Bacle and I put them in their tiers.

With DOC here, I feel less worried about getting attacked, and some inmates tell me things are better for them too. Others say that as soon as the DOC is gone, things will go back to the way they were. "It's like Mommy and Daddy back home," one prisoner says. "But when they go back on vacation, the kids is back out. They got to raise the pay for y'all. If they don't do that, this bitch ain't never gonna change. I don't care what you do, who you put here, nothing. If you don't raise the pay, it's not go' be right, because it's go' be certain things that just ain't worth it. DOC gets paid good money so it's worth all the shit they do. But you want me to do the same thing they do and they get seven, eight dollars more than me? No!"

While DOC is here, Winn becomes the front line between elite troops of two different prison systems: the State of Louisiana's and the Corrections Corporation of America's. When SORT comes to Ash, the DOC officers watch them closely and treat them as incompetent, overconfident jarheads in battle dress. They scoff when SORT walks around with large cans of pepper spray while there are no gas masks in the unit.

But to SORT, many of whom are former military, the DOC officers are a bunch of hicks. Louisiana is merely one node in SORT's national mission to keep CCA prisons under control. Its job is like no other in American prisons. In a country where each state operates its own virtually autonomous prison system, there is no public equivalent to CCA's national SORT team.

The Winn COs are deferential to both the SORT members and DOC officers, but in private they describe them as elitist pricks. It feels like incompetence has been replaced with overzealousness. The DOC officers chide us for letting inmates smoke inside, and when they spot someone smoking on camera, they find him and strip-search him in front of everyone. When I sit on a chair to take a break, an Angola officer, staring at the monitor inside the key, tells me to go into a TV room in one of the tiers. There is an inmate in there whose pants are sagging. He orders me to tell the man to pull them up.

As inmates come in after evening chow, I spot one named Wilson outside the bars of another tier. I tell him to go to his tier. "I need to get my T-shirt," he says. The inmate he is talking to pulls his shirt off and hands it to him. The two shake hands and I see a small crumpled note pass between their hands. Wilson tries to walk out the front of the unit. I shout after him.

He says he needs to deliver the shirt to someone outside.

"No," I say. "Come on!" He walks to his tier and I open the gate.

"They ain't gonna give you no extra money for this," he says.

"Give me that note," I bark. "Give me that thing in your hand." He walks away and puts something in the front of his pants.

"Wilson! You want me to strip-search you? Come on!"

"I ain't got no note man." As he walks, something falls out of his pant leg. I pick up a tiny ball of green herbs wrapped in cellophane that smells like incense. The inmate's face is full of guilt. He says nothing. I put it in my pocket, walk out of the tier, and feel something heavy and dark pour over me. *What am I doing?*

Bacle sees me walk off the tier with something in my hand. "What is that?" he asks.

"Mojo," I say.

A new set of officers from Angola show up and pull Wilson and the inmate he was talking to out of their tiers. SORT comes and cuff them. I've had many problems with Wilson in the last couple of months, but they all seem minor compared to what I'm doing now: sending someone off to the dungeon for drugs.

Before I go home, I go to the count room to fill out an incident report. As I am writing the chief of unit management, Miss Reeves, enters. The captain, sitting at his desk, opens a drawer and pulls out a large bag full of tobacco pouches he confiscated from an inmate. They whisper to each other and the captain glances nervously toward the other office, where some DOC wardens are talking. "I'll try to stash it somewhere," the captain says to Miss Reeves. He tells her to send Unit Manager Taylor in. When Taylor enters, the captain shows him about twenty tobacco pouches. "That's for me?" Taylor asks.

"Yeah."

"All this you took?"

"This is it. We didn't do no write-ups on it."

"You giving this to me? Some of it?"

"All of it."

I hand the captain my report and leave. On my way out I meet Miss Carter, the social worker. We stand around, me rocking back on my heels, she looking off toward the sky as we wait for an officer to open the gate for us.

"How do you like it so far?" she asks.

"It's okay," I say. "It can be exciting."

An officer unlocks the gate. "It gets in your blood, doesn't it?" Miss Carter asks. "Someone asked me if we were pretty picky about who we hire. I said, Well, I'd love to tell you yes, but we take 'em six-legged and lazy. We take whatever we can get!" she says with a laugh. "But then we come across a few good people like yourself. That's not the norm."

Outside there is a chorus of frogs and crickets. The air is sweet and balmy. As I do every night when I get off work, I take a breath and try to remember who I am. Miss Carter is right. It is getting in my blood. The boundary between pleasure and anger is blurring. To shout makes me feel alive. I take pleasure in saying no to prisoners. I like to hear them complain about my write-ups. I like to ignore them when they ask me to cut them a break. When they hang their clothes to dry in the TV room, an unauthorized area, I confiscate the laundry and feel a thrill when they shout from down the tier as I take it away. During the lockdown, when Ash threatened to riot, I hoped the SORT team would come in and gas the whole unit. Everyone would be coughing and gasping, including me, and it would be good because it would be action. All that matters anymore is action.

The road is open during my drive home; the forest flicks past in the edge of my headlights. Who am I becoming? How could I, someone who spent twenty-six months in segregation, cause someone to be put in isolation for drugs? *For drugs.* I think of the men in Cypress, grabbing hold of the bars in the front of their cells, shaking them in panic and rage. I think of the clamor, the constant, desperate shouting. I think of lying on the floor of my own cell, watching the miniature ocean waves I made by sloshing water back and forth in a bottle; marveling at ants; calculating the mean, median, and mode of the tick marks on the wall; talking to myself without realizing it.

Iran's Evin prison and Winn are so different that it's never made sense to compare them, but as I drive, my mind runs through the details of each: Isolations cannot really be compared, because the difference between one person's mental stability and another's insanity is found in tiny details. I had a mattress in Evin. In Cypress they have thin pieces of foam. I didn't have to breathe pepper spray regularly, but they do. The concrete open-air cell I exercised in was much larger than the outdoor cage the Winn inmates go to for an hour a day. I couldn't write letters, but they can. I could only talk to nearby prisoners in secret, but they can shout to each other without being punished. And unlike Evin, Cypress inmates have to shit in front of their cellmates, if they have any, and in view of the guards.

When I get home, I draw a bath. I pour a glass of wine, then another, and another. I try to empty my mind. Inside me there is a prison guard and a former prisoner and they are fighting with each other, and I want them to stop.

I decide I need to end this. Four months is enough. I'm going to quit.

When I come back after my days off, the DOC officers are gone. Assistant Warden Parker is jubilant—CCA has hung on to the prison. "The great state of Louisiana came in with both guns a-blazing," he tells us during a morning meeting. "They were ready to tear Winn apart." In interviews with staff, the DOC learned that staff members had been "bringing in mountains and mountains of mojo"—synthetic marijuana—and having sex with inmates. "One person actually said that they trusted the inmates more than they trusted me, the warden. One staff member said, 'The inmate made me feel pretty. Why wouldn't I love him? Why wouldn't I bring him things he needs because you all won't let him have it?'"

Guards shake their heads. A few days ago I saw Miss Sterling, one of my co-cadets from training, being escorted out of the prison by SORT members for smuggling in contraband and writing love letters to an inmate. Willis, the former inmate turned guard, was fired after he left the prison recently and a bunch of cell phones were found at his post.

How, exactly, should I leave? Should I just turn my key in during a quiet moment in Ash and walk out the front door, ignoring anyone who calls after me? Should I shake Bacle's hand before I go, say goodbye to some of the inmates? Should I give Corner Store my number and tell him to call when he's out? When I leave, I'll get into my truck and rip through the dirt roads in the woods, mud spraying, music blaring.

Parker schools us on the lessons he learned from the DOC wardens. They said everyone here, including him, lacked a sense of ownership. From now on there will be no more leeway. When we open a tier door for chow, we should give the inmates a minute and thirty seconds, he says. Then, "Shabam! Shut!" If they get angry about missing dinner, they might stand at the bars and complaining. We should tell them to back away and if they don't, that's officially noncompliance. "Hmmm. All we got to do is call who? Pa-pow! We put the black ninjas in there and let them have at it. We will bring the gates of hell down on that place." Maybe I should go to Parker's office and give my resignation directly to him, tell him some of the things I've observed in the prison, tell him about the complaints of the prisoners and guards.

I go to Ash, and later in the morning, I clench up when my old instructor Kenny enters the unit and approaches me. Ash has been without a unit manager since Miss Price quit weeks ago, and Kenny was just appointed to take over. There would be a particular satisfaction in telling him—he who suspected me early on—that I quit. "The warden told me to find somebody that's knowledgeable and ready for leadership," he says to me, smiling slightly. "Out of all y'all's crew down here, I'm gonna handpick you. If you are interested in moving on up, I'm go' make it happen." He says I can be a sergeant, lieutenant, corrections counselor, whatever I'm interested in. It hasn't been four months since I got here and began training.

"Get prepared over the next week," he says. "I'm going to start working with you. I'm going to train you for the next level."

I sit. Maybe I could become a sergeant and walk freely around the prison without a regular post. What new doors would a position like that open? I've come this far; maybe I should hang on for a while. I'll call Mr. Tucker, too, and tell him I'd like to join the SORT team. I want to see its training center in the Midwest. I'll take the promotion, go through SORT training, and then I'll go.

Days pass. I email my editor and say the job is "almost unbearable." She responds and says "maybe it's time to wrap." I don't reply. The days slide back into their old routine. With the DOC officers gone, the order they imposed vanishes. The only difference is that prisoners resist more than usual. In anticipation of my promotion, I walk up and down the tiers at count time, barking at inmates to sit up on their bunks like the DOC officers did. If they are asleep, I kick their beds. I don't lose my temper anymore. I just write inmates up all day long. One paper after another, I stack them, sometimes more than twenty-five disciplinaries in a day. If they don't sit up during count: aggravated disobedience. If they cuss me out: defiance. Being in the shower after I holler to get ready for count: unauthorized area. I cut makeshift clotheslines off bunks on which inmates hang their clothes to dry. Clotheslines are prohibited.

Getting off from work has become less and less of a relief. Things between my wife, Sarah, and I have been difficult. It's been feeling like I battle prisoners all day, and when I get off, the battle continues with her over the phone. It's become routine: I call, we talk, we fight, we hang up. She encouraged me to do this project, but she's feeling like I've gone too far. She says I'm changing. All I talk about with her is the prison, and the way I talk about it makes her uncomfortable: I used to focus on the problems of the system. Now I mostly talk about my problems with inmates, the latest stabbing, or my frustrations with my prison colleagues. She feels like I am angry all the time, and that I don't see what I am becoming. She resents that I have no time or energy to return her support.

She comes from California to visit in the middle of March. When she is physically present, our tensions ease. Our worlds don't feel so far apart. But she tells me there is always agitation in my face, and that I'm developing small tics. My breathing isn't normal. I toss and groan in my sleep. Sometimes I feel that she came here to convince me to leave. She keeps asking me when I will quit. I tell her I'm thinking about it. Other times, I just change the subject.

Late one night, Sarah wakes me. James West, my *Mother Jones* colleague who recently came to Louisiana to shoot video for my story, has not returned from trying to get a nighttime shot of Winn. Something is wrong. We decide to call his phone. Sheriff Cranford Jordan of Winn parish answers. James, he says, will be in jail for a while. I feel the blood drain from my face, and then I wonder: *Will he come for me?* Sarah and I scramble to pack up everything that has anything to do with my reporting and check into a hotel at two a.m.

James had parked his rental car on the roadside near the prison around seven forty-five p.m. Located across the road from the prison, he attached a small GoPro camera to a sign to shoot some time-lapse footage of the place. He then walked through a wide, unfenced field and into the forest to search for a place to get a shot of the prison with his telephoto lens. As he fumbled in the dark, his foot plunged deep into mud, so he pulled his iPhone from his pocket and used its light to navigate through the muck. A few minutes later, searchlights beamed in his direction from the prison located some one thousand feet away. He ducked and froze, and when the light was gone, he made back toward the car. The beam swept the trees again, and when he got back to the road, a prison patrol van pulled up 150 feet behind him.

James waved. Hello? Hello? No one answered and the vehicle did not approach. He got into his car, and as he was driving away, he remembered the GoPro. In its memory card, there was the footage of an interview he shot of me. If the guards found it, my cover would be blown. He pulled off the road in a dark place and waited for forty minutes to pass. Then he went back. When he came out of the dark forest into the prison clearing, he saw blue and red lights. Several police cars and prison vehicles were blocking the road outside of Winn. He approached them and they told him to get out of the car.

Three sheriff's deputies and five or six SORT members surrounded him. James handed them his Australian driver's license, and they asked what he was doing in the woods earlier. Panicked, he told them he'd stopped only to take a piss on the side of the road. The SORT members began pulling things from his car and putting them on the street. His bags were full of camera equipment. Okay, he said, he's a photographer and he's been taking pictures of the local area.

As they rummaged through his belongings, James asked them to stop. They didn't. He told them he thought the search was illegal. They continued. *You are lucky you didn't get shot out there!* one deputy said. *We don't know who you are. You could be a terrorist.* Two deputies turned on their body cameras, capturing the following:*

"What kind of pictures you got there?" asks a paunchy deputy with a white mustache named Kelly Fannin, pointing to James's camera on the ground.

"They're my pictures, sir," James says, his voice tinged with fear.

Fannin demands to see the camera's memory card.

"No, sir, I'm not going to show you that," James says. He knows they need a search warrant first.

"I will take everything you got!" Fannin says. James grabs the camera off of the ground.

---

* I later obtain the body camera footage, which recorded the action and dialogue that follows.

"Whoa, come here!" Fannin shouts and grabs James by the arm.

"You can't take my camera. I know that." Another deputy snatches it from James's grip.

"Do you want me to charge you for going on that property? And put you in jail tonight and show you what a jail is?"

"No sir, I do not want that."

A SORT officer pulls a drone in a box out of the car. We had thought about trying to get an aerial shot of the prison, but the drone didn't work, so James had been intending to return it to Amazon.

"Go ahead and turn and put your hands behind your back," one of the deputies says.

"I'm cooperating."

"No you ain't!" The officer cuffs him, reads him his rights, puts him in the back of a police car next to a caged German shepherd, and slams the door. They leave their body cameras rolling:

"We'll just book him for trespassing," one deputy says. "I know what it was: He was out there looking for kangaroos!"

"I like your style, sir," a SORT member says to Fannin. "It's that I-don't-fuck-around style." Fannin chuckles. One of the SORT members scrolls through the pictures on James's camera while the deputies look on. "Apparently they got different laws over there in New South Wales, Australia," a deputy says. "Welcome to the Free State of Winn!" Everyone laughs.

They drove James to the jail in Winnfield, where they made him strip and show his asshole. They put him in cuffs and leg shackles.

At five in the morning, I wake up in the hotel and call in sick.

After James wakes up, an inmate shouts to him from a nearby cell. *Hey girl! Hey girl! You ever slept with a man? Do you want to?* This goes on for hours. *No one's letting us rape this girl's hole.*

He asks the sheriff if he can call his parents. *Tell them we didn't shoot you at dawn!* the sheriff says.

I drive an hour away to find a FedEx so I can ship all of my notes and recordings out of the state. I speak to *Mother Jones*'s lawyer, who is trying to get bail set so James can be released, and trying to prevent the sheriff from getting a warrant to look at his camera.

Three men take James, in leg-irons, into a room where he is interrogated by two state police officers, a local deputy, and a homeland security agent. *Write all the exposés on CCA you like*, one says. *We have nothing to do with them. They have given us trouble in the past.*

I don't care if that guy works in the prison, a state trooper adds. James thinks he is referring to me. By evening, a $10,000 bond is posted, and James is released. *Send me a copy of the article when it's done*, one of the cops tells him. When the jailer lets him out, he says, *I'm so sorry you had to see that and be inside. Some of these places I wouldn't put my dog in.*

Sarah and I pick up James at a gas station in Winnfield and drive to our hotel out of town. The next morning I call in sick again, and the captain tells me I better have a note from my doctor when I return. I go downstairs and get coffee in the hotel lobby, and I see a SORT member standing outside in black uniform, flexicuffs hanging from his belt. Are they looking for me? Sarah, James, and I exit through a side door, and as I pull my truck out, I see another man I am sure I recognize from the prison. We go back to my apartment, hurriedly throw everything into plastic bags, and load it all into my truck. We drive past the prison, James jumps out and grabs the GoPro, still attached to the sign, and we drive across the border to Texas. Oil derricks bob and bushes quiver in the wind as the sun comes down over the plains. Road-worn men drink their coffee in truck stop diners. Sarah and James are relieved and elated. I feel, oddly, sad.

In Dallas we sit in a booth and drink a beer, and the tension in my chest begins to loosen. I begin to notice smiles around me, and for the first time in months, I'm not nervous about tomorrow. I savor the night of drinking and dancing and laughing. In my hotel the next morning, I shave off my goatee and I see the person underneath.

I call HR at Winn. "This is CO Bauer. I'm calling because I've decided to resign."

"Oh! Mr. Bauer, I hate to hear that!" the HR woman says. "I hate to lose you. Your evaluation looked good, and it looked like you were willing to hang in there and hopefully promote. Well, I hate it, Mr. Bauer. I truly do. In the future, if you decide to change your mind, you know the process."

EPILOGUE

When Bacle pulled into Winn's front gate after I left town, the guard told him Assistant Warden Parker wanted to see him. *What the hell did I do?* he thought. In his office, Parker asked Bacle what he knew about me. "He was a good partner," Bacle told him. "I enjoyed working with the dude. He has no problem writing 'em up." He asked what was wrong, but Parker wouldn't say.

On his way out, Bacle asked the officer at the front gate, "What's going on with Bauer?"

"You ain't heard?" the officer said. "He was an undercover reporter!"

Bacle recounted this to me on the phone ten months later. "Oh, I laughed," he said. "I don't know if you remember, but I told you once that it would be nice to have an investigative reporter out there."

Word about me got out quick. The day after I quit, the Winnfield newspaper reported that I had been working at the prison. National media picked up the story, and CCA issued a statement saying my approach "raises serious questions about his journalistic standards." A couple of guards I worked with reached out to me right away. Miss

Calahan, who'd quit before me because she thought the job was getting too dangerous, wrote to me on Facebook: "Hey boy you got they ass lol." Another sent me an email: "Wow, Bauer! I'm honored. I don't even know what to say."

I attempted to contact everyone who is mentioned in this book to ask them about their experiences at Winn. Some refused outright. Others didn't respond to my phone calls and letters, and a few I could not track down. A surprising number, however, were eager to talk. Corner Store insisted he and other inmates knew something was up all along. "I just don't know no CO to pull out his notepad every five minutes," he told me. "Everybody's like, 'Oh man, I knew it, I knew it, I knew it.'" Collinsworth said that when he found out I was a reporter, he "thought it was cool." Christian, the CO with the deformed ear and the German shepherd, thought "pretty much what most people thought: Can't wait to read the story!"

Some people whom I never would have expected to spoke to me. One was Miss Lawson, who'd been the assistant chief of security. "They were scared to death of who you were," she told me. "After they found out you were a reporter, it was like, 'Oh my God. Oh my God.'" The DOC quickly required the staff to undergo fresh background checks. CCA's corporate office sent people to Winn to open an "extensive" investigation on me. They gathered "everything that had your name on it," Miss Lawson said. Ironically the investigation narrowed in on the item that, in my mind, had symbolized my transformation from an observer into a real prison guard: the cell phone I had confiscated in Ash. "I got called like four or five times for that one phone from corporate," Miss Lawson said. "It was like they were insinuating that you brought the phone in or there was some information in the phone. I'm like, 'No, he found it in a water fountain.'"

After I'd filled out the paperwork about the phone and handed it off to Miss Price, it had disappeared somewhere in the chain of command.

The mystery of the missing cell phone grew into a broader probe, in which Christian and Miss Lawson were fired for allegedly selling phones to inmates. Both deny it, and CCA did not pursue legal action against them, but Miss Lawson moved out of the state shortly afterward.

Miss Lawson also told me that Assistant Warden Parker texted her a photo of me, asking if she knew who I was. After she identified me, Miss Lawson says, Parker told her to delete the photo and "forget I sent it to you." She kept it, however, and emailed it to me. The image was a shot of a laptop screen on which a video of me was playing. I recognized the footage immediately: James had filmed it on the afternoon before he was arrested. When James was detained, he was careful to protect his camera and the footage on it, even as he was surrounded by SORT officers from the prison and Winn Parish deputies. The sheriff never obtained a search warrant for his belongings, but someone went ahead and searched them anyway. Apparently when they saw the footage of me talking about working in the prison, they took a picture of it and sent it to the warden. Geolocation data on the photo Miss Lawson sent me showed that the picture was taken in the sheriff's office.*

In April 2015, about two weeks after I left Winn, CCA notified the DOC that it planned to void its contract for the prison, which had been set to expire in 2020. According to documents that the DOC later sent me, in late 2014, while I was in training, the department had reviewed CCA's compliance with its contract and asked it to make immediate changes at Winn. Several security issues were identified, including broken doors and cameras and unused metal detectors. The DOC also asked CCA to increase inmate recreation and activities, improve training, hire more guards, hire more medical and mental health employees, and address a "total lack of maintenance." Another concern raised by

---

* The Winn Parish sheriff says he was "not aware" of anyone searching James's things.

the DOC, CCA's chief corrections officer acknowledged, was a bonus paid to Winn's warden that resulted in a "neglect of basic needs." The DOC also noted that CCA had charged inmates for state-supplied toilet paper and toothpaste and made them pay to clip their nails. In a message to its shareholders, the company gave no hint of any problems at Winn; it only said the prison wasn't making enough money.

LaSalle Corrections, a Louisiana-based company, took over Winn Correctional Center six months after I left. By the following summer, Louisiana slashed its prison budget, dropping Winn's per diem rate to twenty-four dollars per inmate per day, ten dollars less than it had been making under CCA. As a result, LaSalle cut medical services, keeping only one part-time doctor who spent around twenty hours per week serving 1,400 inmates. Psychological services and several educational programs were also dropped.

Some guards stayed on when LaSalle took over, but many left. Some who had been fired by CCA, like Christian, were rehired by LaSalle. Bacle got a job at a lumber mill, where one of his coworkers was a prisoner we used to guard in Ash. Miss Calahan became a CO at a local jail. One went on to army basic training. Another took a security guard job in Texas. Others are still unemployed. Assistant Warden Parker took a similar position at another CCA prison. Some Winn prisoners have been transferred across the state and others have been released. I still don't know what most of them were in for, but I was shocked to find out that Corner Store was in for armed robbery and forcible rape.

Five months after I left Winn, *Mother Jones* received a letter in which CCA threatened to sue should we publish the article. The letter came not from CCA's in-house counsel, but from a law firm that *Mother Jones* was very familiar with. The firm had also been representing a billionaire political donor, Frank VanderSloot, in a lawsuit aimed at punishing

Mother Jones for reporting on his anti-LGBT activities. When Vander-Sloot lost, he pledged $1 million to support others who might want to sue us.

CCA's letter dropped hints that the company had been monitoring my recent communications with inmates and was keeping an eye on my social media presence. CCA's counsel claimed I was bound by the company's code of conduct, which states, "All employees must safeguard the company's trade secrets and confidential information." Since guards are not privy to confidential business information, the implication is that the regular goings-on I experienced and observed inside Winn are "trade secrets."

In hopes of minimizing any damage my story might inflict on the company, CCA hired Hillenby, a PR firm that specializes in countering investigative reporters. The firm claims on its website to have success-fully curtailed the publication of investigative reports "with every na-tional television network, investigative cable news programs and several other print, digital and broadcast outlets, including hardline activist media." It says it helps companies to "incorporate certain language" into their correspondence with investigative reporters to "introduce the concept of legal risk."

CCA never sued me or *Mother Jones*, but after my article was pub-lished, the company sent around a memo to reporters titled, "Get the Facts on the *Mother Jones* Report." It labeled me an "activist reporter" who sought to "force onto *Mother Jones* readers a rehashed and predeter-mined premise instead of a factual and informed story." The document focused largely on the fact that I sought employment as a prison guard rather than simply interviewing CCA personnel about their company. It accused me of having "jeopardized the safety and security" of the prison and its employees by writing about the things I had witnessed and experienced there rather than reporting them to my supervising officer. The memo also criticized me for neglecting to speak "to a person supportive of our company and the solutions we provide." It didn't mention that the company had declined my requests for an in-person interview after I left Winn. Even its spokesperson had refused to speak to me. CCA did eventually reply to the more than 150 questions I sent. In the memo the company later sent to reporters, it accused me of being "reckless" for not providing all of the "clarifying information" it had requested for some of my questions. It did not mention that the clarifying information it was requesting involved the names of corrections officers and inmates, people whose identities I felt a responsibility to protect. In one letter to me, CCA's spokesman scolded me thirteen times for my "fundamental misunderstanding" of the company's business and "corrections in general." He also suggested that my methods were "better suited for celebrity and entertainment reporting."

In March 2016 Corner Store walked free. He stayed in prison a full year after he became eligible for release, while CCA was supposed to help him find a place to go. A lawyer eventually tracked down his father's address and arranged for him to stay there. He rode a Greyhound bus to Baton Rouge, and his mother drove from Texas to see him. He got his seafood platter and he walked in the rain. He got a job detailing cars. Sometimes he would hop on a bus, any bus, and ride the entire route just to see the city.

Two weeks after he got out, James and I visited him at his house on a quiet street near the airport. His father invited us in.

"You all taking [him] somewhere?" his father asked us as we sat on the couch waiting for Corner Store to get ready.

"Yeah, we were going to see if he wants to go anywhere," I say.

"You all ain't come here to arrest him?" Corner Store came out of his room and walked directly outside. He told us to get straight in the car—no talking in the street. He was tense.

"Hey, this no names involved, huh?"

"What are you worried about?" I asked.

"Let's just say something happens and I go back."

"Who would you be worried about?"

"The free people."

"Do you think you might go back?"

"Anything is possible," he said. The smallest parole violation could land him back in prison. "If they were ever to see me again, they wouldn't have too much of a liking for me. They feel like you shouldn't even be talking about this."

When we picked up Corner Store the next day, he told me he hasn't seen the Mississippi yet. He used to fish in it, growing up. We headed to the river. After we sat and talked awhile, he stopped scoping out everyone who passed by and stared out at the glistening surface. A tugboat chugged past. He walked down to the bank, scooped up some water, brought it to his nose, and breathed in deep.

A year later Corner Store was arrested for offering to perform oral sex on a ten-year-old girl and bribing her to keep it a secret. He's now back in prison.

Fourteen months after I left Winn, *Mother Jones* published my article. Inmates and staff of CCA prisons around the country sent me letters and emails describing similar problems in their facilities. Only one message was critical. It was from Christian's wife. She was angry that I wrote about Christian collecting prepaid debit cards called Green Dots and insisted I made it up. She said she had worked there several times since she was nineteen years old and that my portrayal of Winn was a "misconception." Why would I interview a former inmate, for example? "You were afraid because you weren't made for that life," she wrote.

"Others are." She said she was grateful I didn't like the job, because now I won't have a reason to return to Winnfield. "Enjoy your life."

A former facility investigator from a CCA prison sent me an email. She had worked in the prison system for fourteen years, "and the five years I spent working for CCA were by far the most detrimental to my— well, to my *everything*," she wrote. "The impacts of working for that company and in that particular setting broke me and changed me in ways I don't think I have discovered even now. Reading your article . . . I wept, chuckled a little, healed a lot, and felt a very strong connection to your 'author's voice.' . . . As I'm sure you can imagine, I have some pretty terrifying stories that I sometimes think need to be told. I also sometimes think they need to be buried and never thought about again."

It wasn't just her relationship to prisoners and the psychology of power that she was grappling with; she was struggling with the fact that she dedicated years of her life to protecting the company. A part of her job was to gather evidence CCA could use to defend itself whenever someone at the prison sued them. Whenever a serious incident involving guards occurred in her prison—a use of force, for example, or a sexual assault allegation—she and other high-ranking staff members gathered in the warden's office to watch the surveillance footage. "If the video looks good on the part of the company, then everyone rushed around to make sure we have this burned on a disk," she told me over the phone. If it didn't, they typically left it to be automatically erased. She said that during the five years she was there, only one case entered a courtroom. Many were settled. "The idea is, What is the smallest amount of money we could give to make the problem go away.

"I think this kind of work has an expiration date for everyone," she said. "I became an entirely different person at home." One day a new inmate was admitted to her prison and housed in the medical wing. He had been shot by a cop and, after a period in the hospital, was still recovering from his gunshot wound. Shortly after he arrived, he was found dead in his cell. Rigor mortis had set in, suggesting that he'd been dead for at least eight hours. During her investigation, she spoke to other inmates who were in the unit, and they told her the inmate had been calling for help all night long, but no one came. She asked them to write statements and took the reports to the warden's office.

"I thought you might want to read these," she said to him.

"Why would I want to read inmates' statements?" she recalls him saying.

"I think they have some things to say that are important."

"You can throw those in the trash on your way out."

She brought the dead prisoner's belongings outside and gave them to his mother, who was in her car. His three children were crying in the back seat. "And you're telling me, screw what happened and what these forty-five witnesses say happened?" A month later she quit.

"The part I struggle with is, is that the dehumanization of one man, or is that the company? Is that a systemic issue in this company, or is it bad apples who are in charge? I don't know the answer, but I know that reading your article, so much matched and so much clicked. Maybe this is a systemic corporate greed issue."

Perhaps the most surprising email I received was from the Department of Justice's inspector general's office, asking whether I'd discuss with them the things I'd seen at Winn. When I spoke with the senior counsel to the inspector general, he told me that what DOJ staff read in my article was similar to what they'd seen in federal private prisons. An assistant inspector general asked if I would come to Washington, DC, to speak to his office. "Quite simply, we found your undercover story of CCA and the Winn Correctional Center immensely interesting and overwhelming germane to our mission," he wrote. I agreed to come. A week later the DOJ inspector general released a damning report on the safety, security, and oversight of private prisons. It found that private prisons are more violent than publicly operated prisons, don't provide the same level of correctional programs, and "do not save substantially on costs."

A week after that, the federal government announced that it would stop contracting with private prisons. The decision applied only to federal prisons and not state prisons like Winn, but it meant that thirteen facilities, housing more than twenty-two thousand inmates, would no longer be privatized. Department of Justice contracts represented just 11 percent of CCA's revenue, but the federal directive caused the stock prices of CCA and the GEO Group to fall by nearly half. Weeks later CCA announced that it planned to lay off fifty-five full-time corporate positions to save money.

In May 2017 I visit CCA's corporate headquarters in Nashville, a nondescript four-story building with green-tinted windows. Not a single logo or sign bears the company's name. About twenty protesters are standing outside, holding signs that say "People Not Profit" and "Invest in People Not Prisons." When I drive up to the empty parking lot, a pair of security guards with wraparound shades stops me. I tell them I'm a shareholder, here to attend the annual shareholder's meeting, and hand them my ticket to enter. It's been more than two years since I left my job at Winn. Not a single person in this building has agreed to speak to me. So I purchased a single share for $34, which allows me to come here and see them in person.

After I pull into the lot, a car enters that is driven by a thin, elderly man. I barely recognize the once portly Texan. It's the company's cofounder T. Don Hutto. When he gets out of his car, I approach him. *Hi Don, Shane Bauer.*

Oh hi!

Do you know who I am? I ask. He says yes, but then looks confused. *I emailed you about meeting*, I say. *I'd still like to get a chance to talk to you about founding CCA.*

Oh, I don't think I can remember much from those days, he says. *Well it's nice to meet you!* He enters the building.

In the lobby there are a number of smiling, attentive people. A lady checks my ID and points me to a man gripping a handheld metal detector. He scans me to make sure I don't have a cell phone or any recording devices. I don't. A woman at a desk asks me to sign in and write down how many shares I own. She points me to the elevator, where a smiling woman is waiting inside to escort me. I enter, and a familiar-looking man follows. The door closes and he stands in front of me, staring blankly ahead, his fingers interlaced in front of him. *Have we met before?* I ask.

He doesn't turn his head, but looks at me sideways and grins. *Yes we have*, he says. I remember. He came to Winn. Bacle and I didn't know who he was back then, only that he was from corporate because he wore khakis and a polo shirt. He looks uncomfortable. The elevator door opens.

Another smiling woman is waiting for us outside the elevator and motions toward the meeting room. I walk down the hall, where more women wearing lanyards stand in front of the glass offices, ensuring that no one will stray. The man from the elevator follows. When I sit down in the meeting room, he stands at a slight distance behind me. Whenever I look in his direction, he is watching.

T. Don Hutto sits in the front row. When people enter, they go directly to him, shaking his hand reverently.

Sir, good to see you, one man says.

Still alive! Hutto says.

As people filter in, backs are slapped, hands are shaken firmly. It's like a class reunion: *Mitch! Mark!* Despite the fact that their company had been plunged into a crisis since the last shareholder meeting a year ago, everything is looking up. The election of Donald Trump changed everything. The day Trump won, CCA's stock soared 50 percent, jumping more than that of any other company in the stock market.

Investors perhaps speculated that Trump's promises to crack down on immigration would translate into the creation of more detention centers, contracts for which would likely go to CCA and GEO Group. Immigrant detention, after all, is the frontier of private prison growth. During the last decade, the portion of immigrant detention beds contracted out to private prison companies has gone up from 25 percent to 65 percent. Nine of the ten largest immigrant detention centers today are privately operated. Immigration and Customs Enforcement (ICE) contracts make up 28 percent of CCA's revenue. The deals can be massive: In 2014 the federal government granted CCA a four-year billion-dollar no-bid contract to run a detention center in Texas that houses 2,400 women and children, most of whom are from Central America. In the last year of Obama's presidency, ICE placed more than 350,000 immigrants in detention facilities, a number that is expected to grow under Trump.

If investors thought Trump would be good for private prisons, they were right. A month after his inauguration, Attorney General Jeff Sessions reversed the Obama-era decision to stop using private prisons. CCA's stock is now stronger than it was a year ago.

Some thirty people take seats, almost all of them old white men. There are three black people in the room, one of whom is Thurgood Marshall Jr., the son of the great civil rights lawyer who won *Brown v. Board of Education* and went on to become the first African American Supreme Court justice. Marshall Jr. has been on CCA's board since 2002. The shareholder booklet I was handed when I entered says one of the reasons the company appointed him was "his contribution to the Board's cultural diversity." I emailed him months ago, asking for an interview, but he declined. How does the son of a great civil rights lawyer end up on the board of a private prison company? According to the shareholder booklet, he is paid an $80,000 "retainer" plus $120,000 in stocks every year. The same amount is paid to board member Charles Overby, former CEO of the Freedom Forum, a foundation that promotes press freedoms. Same goes for board member C. Michael Jacobi, the chairman of gunmaker Sturm, Ruger & Co. The only individual shareholders in the room who don't work for the company are me and four anti-private prison activists. Like me, most of them own only a single share. Ninety-four percent of CCA's shares are owned by banks and mutual funds. Most of the remaining shares are owned by board members and executive officers.

The chairman of the board, wearing a crisp suit with a little American flag pin, approaches the podium. His name is Mark Emkes and he's the former CEO of Bridgestone, the world's largest tire and rubber company. Two large screens at the front of the room display the company's new name: CoreCivic. Two months after the Department of Justice decision, CCA announced it was rebranding. It now calls itself a "government solutions" company, though its business is the same. *Today is a unique meeting*, Emkes says. *It is our first time holding a meeting as CoreCivic. Since rebranding, we've received overwhelming support from the public and government.* A couple of weeks ago, a DOJ audit of CoreCivic's Leavenworth prison in Kansas and found it severely understaffed and overcrowded. He doesn't mention that.

He plays a video. The soundtrack is soothing yet motivational. A bird flies through palm trees. A black man and a white man shake hands. "Working side-by-side with government, we serve people," says a woman's voice. "We serve ideals. We serve the public good." There are lots of images of inmates smiling, laughing, shaking hands. "We are CoreCivic. We are innovating and transforming, while remaining true to everything we've built. All of this we do, guided by a single purpose: to better the public good."

Emkes reads through some bureaucratic matters for stockholder votes, all of which are read and approved in less than ten minutes. Then his tone becomes empathic. *I want to take a moment to recognize the incredible work being done to help people successfully return to their communities*, he says. He plays another video featuring a vocational program in which "as many as thirty-five inmates" print books in Braille. It describes CoreCivic's commitment to giving people job training that will help them succeed once they are released. *At the end of the day, I know I have accomplished something*, the instructor says. *I know I have made a difference.*

I think that deserves applause, Emkes says when the video ends, prompting a round of claps. *Programs like this help CoreCivic reduce recidivism*, he says. The video said that 95 percent of Braille books are made in prisons. If this is the case, it is difficult to understand how such a skill is useful to people who aren't locked up.

Damon Hininger, the fiftysomething CEO with a shiny head, stands next to Chairman Emkes. Emkes asks if any shareholders have a question.

One of the activist shareholders, Alex Friedman, stands and asks about the suicide of Damien Coestly, which I wrote about for *Mother Jones*. Damien, he reminds everyone, weighed seventy-one pounds when he died. *At the time of his death, due to his extreme weight loss, he looked like he'd been housed at Auschwitz*, he says. Someone sniffles. The faces in the room are utterly devoid of emotion. Friedman asks what CoreCivic is doing to prevent suicides. Harley Lappin, the chief corrections officer, stands. Before joining CCA, Lappin was the director of the federal Bureau of Prisons, a position he left after being arrested for drunk driving. *We always regret when we lose a life*, he says. *Suicide prevention is a high priority. We work with medical and mental health staff to develop new techniques.*

But I asked what has CoreCivic done differently to prevent situations like this, Alex says.

I think I could provide, Lappin stutters. *I'll look into—We are continuously trying to improve in this area and I can find more on that for you.* He sits.

Another activist asks whether the company will agree not to attempt to block a bill pending in Congress that would make private prisons open to the same public records laws as their public counterparts. *Openness and transparency is very strong in our facilities*, Hininger says. *If it weren't, our partners wouldn't work with us.* He calls on another executive to respond. The man stands, buttoning the top button of his suit jacket, and faces the woman who asked the question. *We're always working with our partners to establish protocols on public information*, he says. *I'll look into it.* He sits.

There are no questions from any regular shareholders. Nothing from any analysts.

I stand. Hininger has refused to talk to me, his company has threatened to sue me, and he hired a PR firm to try to discredit me. But as I look him in the eyes, he betrays not a single sign that my presence means anything to him.

I mention multiple government reports that have found CCA prisons to be more dangerous and more understaffed than public prisons. I reference a recent prison riot over inadequate medical care and the Idaho prison that was so violent and understaffed that the state didn't renew CCA's contract. I touch on things I saw at Winn: the violence, the understaffing, the use of force, all of which were more extreme than at publicly run prisons. I tell him that after my article was published, staff from CCA prisons around the country complained of similar issues. *Why do these issues arise over and over again in your facilities?* I ask. I also tell him it's commonly understood that increases in staff pay would raise staffing levels, cut down on contraband, and boost morale and security. *How do you justify paying a fast-food wage to people who risk their lives on a daily basis?*

I know these questions will go nowhere because, ultimately, they are about whether private prisons should exist at all. Conditions in for-profit prisons have been worse than the already dismal conditions in public prisons since penitentiaries were first privatized more than 150 years ago. But is serious reform of private prisons even possible? Programs, medical care, mental health services, security, fair wages—all of these cost money. As it is, private prisons are barely cheaper than their public counterparts. If CCA raised guards' wages, hired enough staff, and provided adequate services, it would lose its profit margin. If, on the other hand, states raised their rates to cover the cost of reforms, they would no longer be saving money, which means there would be no reason for them to rely on private companies to run their prisons.

Hininger's expression does not change. In no way does he acknowledge who I am. *Incident reports last year from our media relations folks have been exhaustive*, he says, *so I have nothing to add there. What I will say is the biggest judge is our partner. In the last five years we've had north of a ninety percent contract renewal rate. If we weren't enjoying high rates of security, adequate staffing levels, low recidivism, we wouldn't have those renewal rates. I am extremely proud of what we do at our facilities. We have a wonderful track record.*

I sit.

Chairman Emkes takes the podium. *I'd like to take a moment to thank the management and staff at our prisons because what you do is important to the offenders in our care*, he says. *There are critics everywhere, in every industry. We even had critics when I was at Bridgestone!* He laughs, as though such a thing is absurd. The criticism he's referring to, I later learn, was Bridgestone's use of child labor in its Liberian rubber plantations. *Don't lose sight of what you do*, Emkes continues. *Auditors exist in every industry. They only look at the negative. They don't look at all the good we do. Don't lose sight of the incredible good you do for offenders in our care.*

How many times have such meetings been held throughout American history? How many times have men, be they private prison executives or convict lessees, gotten together to perform this ritual? They sit in company headquarters or legislative offices, far from their prisons or labor camps, and craft stories that soothe their consciences. They convince themselves, with remarkable ease, that they are in the business of punishment because it makes the world better, not because it makes them rich.

The meeting ends. Hininger, Hutto, Marshall, and the entire board leave the room immediately. I follow them out, but they go into a break room and close the door. I go outside, hoping to catch some on their way out. No one comes except a man whose job appears to be to watch me.

ACKNOWLEDGMENTS

So many people have helped me with this project in ways big and small. First I want to thank the people I worked with at Winn and the prisoners who dealt with me every day. Special thanks to the Winn staff and inmates who spoke to me after I stopped working there, especially Dave Bacle, Jennifer Calahan, and the assistant chief of security, "Miss Lawson." Thanks to Wendy Porter for speaking to me about her son Damien's tragic death and for being gracious enough to let me dig through his paperwork. Gratitude to Anna Lellelid at the Louisiana Community Law Office for assisting me in my reporting on individuals held at Winn.

This book could not have happened without the financial, editorial, and legal support of *Mother Jones*. In particular, I'd like to thank Clara Jeffery and Monika Bauerlein not only for supporting this project so fully, but also for helping to make me the journalist that I am. Thanks to my *Mother Jones* editor Dave Gilson for helping me hone the magazine story that led to this book. Thanks to Becca Andrews, Gregory Barber, Brandon Ellington Patterson, and Madison Pauly for doing additional research and fact-checking. Thanks to James Chadwick, Guylyn Cummins, David Snyder, and

Robin Regnier at Sheppard Mullin for their tireless work on the legal front. Really, the entire staff at *Mother Jones* played a role in this project in some way. The names are too many to list here, but I cannot express enough gratitude.

So many through the years have done impressive research on American prisons, and some of their names can be found in the bibliography of this book. I am deeply indebted to Alex Friedman of *Prison Legal News* for his years of dogged reporting on CCA and the research he so generously shared with me. Same goes for Christopher Petrella, who walked me through the ins and outs of private prison contracts. Many archivists have gone beyond the call of duty to help me locate primary materials. Many thanks to the staff at the Texas State Library Archives, the Arkansas State Library, the State Archives of North Carolina, the Alabama Public Library Archives, the State Library of Louisiana, the Louisiana State Archive, the Louisiana State University Libraries, Cammie G. Henry Research Center at Northwestern State University of Louisiana, and Cane River Creole National Historical Park. Thanks to Marriane Fisher-Giorlando, Guy Lancaster, Colin Woodward, and Bruce Jackson for dedicating their time to helping me find primary sources. My sincere gratitude to my research assistant Vinay Basti who put in countless hours of historical research for this book.

Thanks to Blue Mountain Center, the MacDowell Colony, and the Carey Institute for Global Good for giving me the support, community, and solitude needed to write this book. Also a bow to all the writers in residence I met at these places, who talked through my project with me.

Thanks to my agent, Bill Clegg, for seeing the potential in this project and delivering me into the hands of Scott Moyers at Penguin Press, who not only was a superb editor but also encouraged my vision of this book as it morphed and grew.

Many thanks to those who gave me feedback and guidance, including Liam O'Donoghue, Shon Meckfessel, David Kambhu, Ted Conover, and Adam Hochschild. Thanks to Loubna Mrie for help with photo editing.

Thanks to my friends and family who supported me in the decision to go undercover in a prison while the memory of my incarceration in Iran was still fresh.

Thanks to my mom for teaching me at a young age that racism should not exist, and to my dad for showing me that storytelling is an essential part of life. Finally, thanks to Sarah Shourd, who took much of this journey with me and whose support I will forever be grateful for.

Once you've been in prison, prison stays in you. Thanks to the countless people who have been with me through the bumps of this long road. You are too many to name.

PHOTO CREDIT

1 Page TK

NOTES

INTRODUCTION

000 **130,000 of our nation's 1.5 million:** Ann E. Carson, *Prisoners in 2016*, US Department of Justice, Bureau of Justice Statistics, January 2018, www.bjs .gov/content/pub/pdf/p16.pdf.

000 **When our friend Josh Fattal came:** The experience of our imprisonment in Iran was detailed in the following book: Shane Bauer, Joshua Fattal, and Sarah Shourd, *A Sliver of Light: Three Americans Imprisoned in Iran* (New York: Houghton Mifflin Harcourt, 2014).

000 **Nearly 4,000 prisoners were serving:** Shane Bauer, "Solitary in Iran Nearly Broke Me. Then I Went Inside America's Prisons," *Mother Jones*, November/December, 2012, https://www.motherjones.com/politics/2012/10/solitary-confinement-shane-bauer/.

000 **The United States imprisons a higher:** Roy Walmsley, *World Prison Population List (tenth edition)*, University of Essex, International Centre for Prison Studies (2013), www.apcca.org/uploads/10th_Edition_2013.pdf.

000 **In 2017 we have 2.2 million people in prisons:** The Sentencing Project, *Fact Sheet: Trends in US Corrections*.

000 **We now have almost 5 percent:** According to the US Census Bureau's population clock (www.census.gov/popclock), as of January 5, 2018, the United

States had approximately 3.27 million of the world's 7.4 billion people. According to the International Centre for Prison Studies' most recent World Population List, the United States has 2.24 million of the world's 10.2 million prisoners. Walmsley, *World Prison Population List.*

000 **The reasons for our overinflated:** The causes of mass incarceration and the reasons for its persistence are highly debated and beyond the scope of this book. For contemporary readings on the topic, see Michelle Alexander, *The New Jim Crow: Mass Incarceration in the Age of Colorblindness* (New York: The New Press, 2010); John F. Pfaff, *Locked In: The True Causes of Mass Incarceration and How to Achieve Real Reform* (New York: Basic Books, 2017); Marie Gottschalk, *Caught: The Prison State and the Lockdown of American Politics* (Princeton, NJ: Princeton University Press, 2016); James Forman Jr., *Locking Up Our Own: Crime and Punishment in Black America* (New York: Farrar, Straus and Giroux, 2017); Chris Hayes, *A Colony in a Nation* (New York: W. W. Norton, 2017); Naomi Murakawa, *The First Civil Right: How Liberals Built Prison America* (Oxford, UK: Oxford University Press, 2014).

000 **Their reporting was rich in details:** Brooke Kroeger, *Undercover Reporting: The Truth about Deception* (Evanston, IL: Northwestern University Press, 2012), 20.

000 **In 1887 Nellie Bly:** Nellie Bly, *Ten Days in a Mad-House* (Rockville, MD: Wildside Press, 2012).

000 **In 1892 *San Francisco Examiner* reporter:** Kroeger, *Undercover Reporting*, 37.

000 **In 1959 John Howard Griffin:** John Howard Griffin, *Black Like Me* (New York: New American Library, 2003).

000 *In 1977 the Chicago Sun-Times:* The articles ran as a 25-part series in the *Chicago Sun-Times* from January 5, 1978 to January 26, 1978, http://dlib.nyu.edu/undercover/mirage-pamela-zekman-zay-n-smith-chicago-sun-times.

000 **Barbara Ehrenreich took low-wage jobs:** Barbara Ehrenreich, *Nickel and Dimed: On (Not) Getting By in America* (New York: Picador, 2011).

000 **And Ted Conover, covering one of:** Ted Conover, *Newjack: Guarding Sing Sing* (New York: Vintage Books, 2001).

000 **When ABC News busted Food Lion:** Clara Jeffery, "Muckraking in the Modern Era: Why We Sent a Reporter to Work as a Private Prison Guard," *Mother Jones*, July/August, 2016, Editor's Note, www.motherjones.com/politics/2016/06/cca-private-prisons-investigative-journalism-editors-note/.

CHAPTER ONE

000 **About 38 percent of households here:** "Winnfield, Louisiana," http://www
.city-data.com/city/Winnfield-Louisiana.html.

000 **the last sheriff was locked up:** The Associated Press, "Former Winn Parish
Sheriff Convicted in Drug Case," *Times-Picayune* (New Orleans, LA),
February 25, 2012, www.nola.com/crime/index.ssf/2012/02/former_winn
_parish_sheriff_con.html.

000 **In 2018 he makes $4 million:** Hininger's salary was cited in a booklet dis-
tributed at the company's 2017 annual shareholder meeting, obtained by
the author.

000 **In the video, Hutto and Beasley tell:** "Corrections Corporation of America's
Founders Tom Beasley and Don Hutto," posted by *The Nation*, uploaded
February 27, 2013, featuring discussions by CCA's founders, video, 2:47,
https://youtu.be/DAvdMe4KdGU.

CHAPTER TWO

000 **Black men were lined up:** Except where otherwise noted, all details and
quotes related to the story of Albert Race Sample come from his memoir:
Albert Race Sample, *Racehoss: Big Emma's Boy* (Fort Worth, TX: Eakin
Press, 1984). For clarity and consistency, I've changed Sample's style of
dialect transcription in the quotes. Sample's descriptions of the Ramsey
plantation are corroborated by photographs in Bruce Jackson's *Inside the
Wire: Photographs from Texas and Arkansas Prisons* (Austin: University of
Texas Press, 2013). Jackson photographed the plantation and interviewed
inmates there shortly after Sample was there.

000 **"Old master don't you whip me":** This song and many others sung by pris-
oners at the Ramsey plantation are documented in Bruce Jackson's *Wake
Up Dead Man: Afro-American Worksongs from Texas Prisons* (Cambridge:
Harvard University Press, 1972), 130.

000 **Grab too much:** Harry Bates Brown, *Cotton: History, Species, Varieties,
Morphology, Breeding, Culture, Diseases, Marketing, and Uses* (New York:
McGraw-Hill, 1927), 324-25; Edward E. Baptist, *The Half Has Never Been
Told: Slavery and the Making of American Capitalism* (New York: Basic
Books, 2014), 124.

000 **Sample had been convicted:** Carol Sample, "Albert Race Sample," email message to author, November 13, 2017.

000 **From the time Sample arrived:** *Annual Report 1965*, State of Texas Department of Corrections.

000 **Nationwide, it cost states $3.50:** Jack McKee, *Annual Report 1963*, State of Texas Department of Corrections.

000 **As long as men were:** Matthew J. Mancini, *One Dies, Get Another* (Columbia: University of South Carolina Press, 1996), 167–82; Donald R. Walker, *Penology for Profit: A History of the Texas Prison System, 1867–1912* (College Station, TX: Texas A&M University Press, 1988), 52; Robert Perkinson, *Texas Tough: The Rise of America's Prison Empire* (New York: Picador, 2010), 83–130.

000 **So the state bought thirteen plantations:** Ben M. Crouch and James W. Marquart, *An Appeal to Justice: Litigated Reform of Texas Prisons* (Austin: University of Texas Press, 1989), 13.

000 **In 1913 it began running them:** It wasn't until the 1980s that Texas located a prison beyond former slave country. Robert Perkinson, *Texas Tough*, 57.

000 **An enslaved person in an antebellum:** Robert William Fogel, *Without Consent or Contract: The Rise and Fall of American Slavery* (New York: W. W. Norton, 1989), 78–79. When slavery ended and planters were forced to resort to free laborers, cotton productivity fell overall. Jon R. Moen, "Changes in the Productivity of Southern Agriculture between 1860 and 1880," in *Without Consent or Contract: The Rise and Fall of American Slavery, Markets and Production: Technical Papers, Volume I*, eds. Robert W. Fogel and Stanley L. Engerman (New York: W. W. Norton, 1992), 320–50; Baptist, *The Half*, 410.

000 **Texas prison farms into the 1960s:** The Texas Department of Corrections *Annual Report 1963* states that on Texas prison farms, production averaged one bale per acre "well above the yield for the area in which the Department farms are located."

000 **Texas allowed whipping in its prisons:** Perkinson, *Texas Tough*, 226.

000 **Arkansas prisons used the lash:** Arkansas prisons whipped inmates with a leather strap five feet long, five inches wide, and three-eighths-of-an-inch thick until the superintendent of prisons, Tom Murton, banned the practice in 1967. Tom Murton and Joe Hyams, *Accomplices to the Crime: The Arkansas Prison Scandal* (London: Michael Joseph, 1969).

000 **Before running prisons, he had been:** Tucker Steinmetz, "Quiet Prison Chief 'Intrigued' by Arkansas," *Arkansas Democrat*, May 20, 1971; "Hutto Was a Minister," *Arkansas Democrat*, April 16, 1973.

000 **Ramsey was as large as Manhattan:** According to the Texas Department of Corrections *1965 Annual Report*, Sample's plantation Retrieve was 7,000 acres and Ramsey was 15,000 acres.

000 **Policy of empowering certain inmates:** Crouch and Marquart, *Appeal to Justice*, 85–116; Perkinson, *Texas Tough*, 242–46.

000 **The houseboys were prisoners:** Bruce Jackson in conversation with the author, January 2017. Jackson went to Ramsey several times from 1964 to 1968 to record convict work songs for his book *Wake Up Dead Man* and to photograph the prison farm for his book *Inside the Wire*. During Jackson's time at Ramsey, he spent a considerable amount of it with Hutto. Perkinson, *Texas Tough*, 238, 249.

000 **Personnel at the Texas Department of Corrections:** Texas Department of Corrections, Memorandum No. 14–65, attachment No. 1.

000 **Houseboys were prohibited from washing:** Ibid.

CHAPTER FOUR

000 **Between 1980 and 1990:** Donna Selman and Paul Leighton, *Punishment for Sale: Private Prisons, Big Business, and the Incarceration Binge* (New York: Rowman & Littlefield, 2010), 42–43.

000 **During the ten-year peak:** Selman and Leighton, *Punishment for Sale*, 42–43, 53.

000 **"a heck of a venture":** Selman and Leighton, *Punishment for Sale*, 56.

000 **In return, the state would pay:** Selman and Leighton, *Punishment for Sale*, 61–62.

000 **Because the company would run:** Bill Lohmann, "Private Company Wants to Run Tennessee Prisons," *Times-Picayune* (New Orleans, La.), September 29, 1985.

000 **"You just sell it like you":** Erik Larson, "Captive Company," *Inc.*, June 1, 1988, www.inc.com/magazine/19880601/803.html.

000 Early investors included Sodexho-Marriott: Lohmann, "Private Company."

000 In 2017 the company runs more than 80: CoreCivic Inc., SEC Filing *Form 10-K Annual Report* (FY 2016), February 23, 2017, www.last10k.com/sec -filings/cxw/0001193125-17-053982.htm#fullReport.

000 Altogether, CCA houses some eighty thousand: CCA says it has a design capacity of about 89,700 beds, approximately 8,300 of which are vacant. CoreCivic Inc, *10-K Annual Report* (FY 2016).

000 Its main competitor, the GEO Group: Geo Group Inc., SEC Filing *Form 10-K Annual Report* (FY 2016), February 24, 2017, www.last10k.com/sec -filings/geo/0001193125-17-056831.htm#tx320699_25.

000 CCA receives about $34: CCA's 2010 contract with the Louisiana Department of Corrections specifies a per diem rate of $31.51, with an annual increase based on the consumer price index for all urban consumers for the previous year. *Management Services Agreement between State of Louisiana Department of Public Safety and Corrections, Corrections Services and Corrections Corporation of America*, contract #692239, acquired by the author through a public records request with the Louisiana DOC.

000 In comparison, the average daily cost per inmate: State of Louisiana, Division of Administration, *Fiscal Year 2016–2017 Executive Budget Supporting Document*, February 13, 2016, www.doa.la.gov/Pages/opb/pub/FY17 /FY17ExecBudget.aspx.

000 CCA will report $1.8 billion: Corrections Corp of America, SEC Filing *Form 10-K Annual Report* (FY 2015), February 25, 2016, www.last10k .com/sec-filings/cxw/0001193125-16-477634.htm#tx121974_40.

000 Roughly two-thirds of private prison contracts: In the Public Interest, *Criminal: How Lockup Quotas and "Low-Crime Taxes" Guarantee Profits for Private Prison Corporations*, September 19, 2013, www.inthepublicinterest.org/crim inal-how-lockup-quotas-and-low-crime-taxes-guarantee-profits-for -private-prison-corporations/.

000 Under CCA's contract, Winn was guaranteed: *Management Services Agreement between State of Louisiana Department of Public Safety and Corrections*.

000 One study estimated that private prisons: Brad W. Lundahl et al., "Prison Privatization: A Meta-analysis of Cost and Quality of Confinement

Indicators," *Research on Social Work Practice* 19, no. 4 (April 8, 2009): 383–94, doi.org/10.1177/1049731509331946.

000 **Private prisons could save states:** Simon Hakim and Erwin A. Blackstone, "Cost Analysis of Public and Contractor-Operated Prisons" (working paper, Center for Competitive Government, Temple University, Philadelphia, PA, April, 2013), Cost-Analysis-of-Public-and-Contractor-Operated -Prisons-FINAL3.

000 **Private prisons "do not save":** Deputy Attorney General Sally Q. Yates, memorandum to the acting director of the Federal Bureau of Prisons, "Reducing Our Use of Private Prisons," August 18, 2016, www.justice.gov/archives /opa/file/886311/download.

000 **What savings do exist are achieved:** James Austin and Gary Coventry, *Emerging Issues on Privatized Prisons*, US Department of Justice, Bureau of Justice Assistance (February 2001), 9, www.ncjrs.gov/pdffiles1/bja/181249.pdf.

000 **Wages and benefits account:** CoreCivic Inc, *10-K Annual Report* (FY 2016), 58.

000 **The cost per prisoner at Winn:** State of Louisiana, Division of Administration, *Fiscal Year 2016–2017 Executive Budget Supporting Document*, February 13, 2016, www.doa.la.gov/Pages/opb/pub/FY17/FY17ExecBudget.aspx.

CHAPTER FIVE

000 **He tells me he is suing CCA:** Scott v. Corr. Corp., No. 1:14-cv-00956 (W.D. La., May 7, 2014), https://casetext.com/case/scott-v-corr-corp.

000 **Into these accounts the prisoners with jobs:** *DPS&C Corrections Services Incentive Pay Report for Winn Correctional*, July 2, 2015, acquired by the author through a public records request with the Louisiana Department of Corrections.

CHAPTER SIX

000 **In 1718 Britain passed the Transportation Act:** A. Roger Ekirch, *Bound for America: The Transportation of British Convicts to the Colonies, 1718–1775* (Oxford, UK: Clarendon Press, 1987), 1.

000 **Crimes as minor as poaching fish:** Scott Christianson, *Liberty for Some: 500 Years of Imprisonment in America* (Boston: Northeastern University Press, 1998), 20; Ekirch, *Bound for America*, 59.

000 **The convicts were chained below ship:** Ekirch, *Bound for America*, 75, 99; Christianson, *Liberty for Some*, 23.

000 **Just a few companies dominated:** Ekirch, *Bound for America*, 73, 97.

000 **the merchants auctioned their human cargo:** Christianson, *Liberty for Some*, 23; Ekirch, *Bound for America*, 146; Rebecca M. McLennan, *The Crisis of Imprisonment: Protest, Politics, and the Making of the American Penal State, 1776–1941* (Cambridge UK: Cambridge University Press, 2008), 30.

000 **Planters often preferred convicts to slaves:** Ekirch, *Bound for America*, 124; Christianson, *Liberty for Some*, 37.

000 **Part of Britain's interest in convict:** CITE TRANSPORTATION ACT. James Davie Butler, "British Convicts Shipped to American Colonies," *The American Historical Review* 2, no. 1 (October 1896): 12–33, doi.org /10.1086/ahr/2.1.12; The Statutes at Large from the Magna Charta, to the End of the Eleventh Parliament of Great Britain, Cap XI, 506–11, https:// archive.org/stream/statutesatlarge54britgoog#page/n505/mode/2up.

000 **The government could increase or decrease:** Christianson, *Liberty for Some*, 23.

000 **Between 1718 and 1775:** Ekirch, *Bound for America*, 1–2.

000 **Approximately one-quarter of all British:** Ekirch, *Bound for America*, 27.

000 **Thomas Jefferson had suggested:** Christianson, *Liberty for Some*, 101.

000 **Ten years after the Revolution, Pennsylvania:** Harry Elmer Barnes, "Historical Origin of the Prison System in America," *Journal of Criminal Law and Criminology* 12, no. 1 (May 1921 to February 1922): 46, http:// lawsdocbox.com/Politics/68475122-Historial-origin-of-the-prison -system-in-america.html.

000 **Benjamin Rush argued that:** McLennan, *Crisis of Imprisonment*, 33–36.

000 **In 1795 Pennsylvania renovated:** Gustave de Beaumont and Alexis de Tocqueville, *On the Penitentiary System in the United States and Its Application in France* (Carbondale: Southern Illinois University Press, 1964), 2; Negley K. Teeters, *The Cradle of the Penitentiary* (Philadelphia: Temple University Press, 1955), 17–22.

000 The Walnut Street Penitentiary aimed: LeRoy B. DePuy, "The Walnut Street Prison: *Pennsylvania's First Penitentiary*," *Pennsylvania History: A Journal of Mid-Atlantic Studies* 18, no. 2 (April 1951): 134, 137–42, www .jstor.org/stable/27769197.

000 By 1800, ten other states: Christianson, *Liberty for Some*, 101.

000 At a moment when indentured servitude: McLennan, *Crisis of Imprisonment*, 41; Christianson, *Liberty for Some*, 104.

000 When in 1797 Pennsylvania expanded: Teeters, *The Cradle of the Penitentiary*, 86.

000 They were not generating the revenue: Beaumont and Tocqueville, *Penitentiary System*, appendix 19.

000 Calvanists called for a return to: McLennan, *Crisis of Imprisonment*, 51.

000 In 1817 a New York banker: Christianson, *Liberty for Some*, 111.

000 Fifteen years after slavery was abolished: Beaumont and Tocqueville, *Penitentiary System*, 254.

000 Auburn's captain promised to turn inmates: McLennan, *Crisis of Imprisonment*, 54–60; Christianson, *Liberty for Some*, 112.

000 "it effects the immediate submission of": Beaumont and Tocqueville, *Penitentiary System*, 41.

000 "[T]he silence within these vast walls": Beaumont and Tocqueville, *Penitentiary System*, 32.

000 For a day's labor, contractors paid: Beaumont and Tocqueville, *Penitentiary System*, 164.

000 By 1831 Auburn was making: Beaumont and Tocqueville, *Penitentiary System*, 280.

000 States could take out loans: Beaumont and Tocqueville, *Penitentiary System*, 79, 281.

000 For the first three years after: Beaumont and Tocqueville, *Penitentiary System*, 108.

000 Some reported profits as high as: McLannan, *Crisis of Imprisonment*, 68

000 In the 25 years after Auburn opened: McLennan, *Crisis of Imprisonment*, 63.

000 For the first time in the history: Barnes, "Historical Origin of the Prison System in America," 36; McLennan, *Crisis of Imprisonment*, 63.

000 **"The contractor, regarding the convict":** Beaumont and Tocqueville, *Penitentiary System*, 35.

CHAPTER SEVEN

000 **Winn inmates charged with serious rule:** This statistic was posted on the Louisiana Department of Corrections website.(The page has since been taken down.)

000 **In 2008 Kelsey Benoit was rushed:** Kelsey Benoit v. La. Dept. of Public Safety and Corrections, No. 577-052 (19th Cir. E.D. La. March 16, 2009).

000 **It's been nearly three years:** "Two Accused in Vehicle Burglaries," *Houma (La.) Today*, January 6, 2012, www.houmatoday.com/article/DA/20120106 /News/608096992/HC/; Edgar, "Escaped Convict Captured after High Speed Chase," *Winn Parish (La.) Enterprise*, December 17, 2014, www .winnparishenterprise.com/articles/2014/12/17/escaped-convict-captured -after-highspeed-chase.

CHAPTER EIGHT

000 **A steamship moved slowly up:** Samuel L. Clemens describes what that stretch of the Mississippi looked like at the time in Mark Twain, *Life on the Mississippi, Volume II* (Leipzig, Germany: Bernhard Tauchnitz, 1883), https://babel .hathitrust.org/cgi/pt?id=coo.31924021962695;view=1up;seq=74;size=125.

000 **In the coverage of his trial:** "Incidents in the Life of David Hines," *Charleston (SC) Courier*, June 16, 1840.

000 **He'd posed as women's lovers:** Except where otherwise noted, the details of Dr. Hines's account came from David Theo Hines, *The Life and Adventures of Dr. David T. Hines: A Narrative of Thrilling Interest and Most Stirring Scenes of His Eventful Life* (Charleston, SC: J. B. Nixon, 1852).

000 **On the few occasions when penitentiaries:** Edward L. Ayers, *Vengeance and Justice: Crime and Punishment in the Nineteenth-Century American South* (New York: Oxford University Press, 1984), 49.

000 **"[U]nder the Penitentiary system":** Ayers, *Vengeance and Justice*, 48.

000 **"How is this pretended humanity":** Ayers, *Vengeance and Justice*, 46.

000 "The community should never derive benefit": Ayers, *Vengeance and Justice*, 69.

000 Leading abolitionists like William Lloyd Garrison: Mark T. Carleton, *Politics and Punishment: The History of the Louisiana State Penal System* (Baton Rouge: Louisiana State University Press, 1971), 5; Marie Gottschalk, *The Prison and the Gallows: The Politics of Mass Incarceration in America* (Cambridge, UK: Cambridge University Press, 2006), 48.

000 Planters could bring their unruly human: Christina Pruett Hermann, "Specters of Freedom: Forced Labor, Social Struggle, and the Louisiana State Penitentiary System, 1835–1935" (PhD diss., Michigan State University, 2015), 127–28.

000 "with hogs, in the midst of": Gustave de Beaumont and Alexis de Tocqueville, *Penitentiary System in the United States and Its Application in France*, trans. Francis Lieber (Philadelphia: Carey, Lea & Blanchard, 1833), 13.

000 Governor Andre B. Roman promised: Beaumont and Tocqueville, *Penitentiary System*, footnote, 13.

000 Legislators were hard to sway: Hermann, "Specters of Freedom," 149.

000 Armed guards walked on top: Hermann, "Specters of Freedom," 17, 111.

000 An officer put him in: US General Services Administration, *Hard Labor: History and Archaeology at the Old Louisiana State Penitentiary, Baton Rouge, Louisiana* (Fort Worth, TX: The Administration, 1991), 3, https://babel.hathitrust.org/cgi/pt?id=purl.32754070336056;view=1up;seq=9.

000 "The first thing that strikes one": "The State Penitentiary," *Times-Picayune* (New Orleans, LA), October 2, 1844.

000 In 1839 two convicts: "Revolt at the Louisiana Penitentiary," *Baltimore Sun*, May 15, 1839.

000 the *Charleston Courier* featured the Louisiana: "Penitentiary," *Charleston (SD) Courier*, January 16, 1841.

000 The United States was growing more: Alasdair Roberts, *America's First Great Depression: Economic Crisis and Political Disorder after the Panic of 1837* (Ithaca, NY: Cornell University Press, 2012), 29.

000 New Orleans had the densest concentration: Baptist, *The Half*, 254–55; Sidney Blumenthal, *A Self-Made Man: The Political Life of Abraham Lincoln, Vol. I, 1809–1849* (New York: Simon & Schuster, 2017), 159–60.

000 "A man could borrow money from": Harold Sinclair, *The Port of New Orleans, The Seaport Series* (Garden City, NY: Doubleday, Doran & Company, 1942), 173.

000 Between 1830 and 1836 the value: Susan B. Carter et al., eds., *Historical Statistics of the United States: Earliest Times to the Present* (New York: Cambridge University Press, 2006), Table Bb212; Roberts, *America's First Great Depression*, 29; Baptist, *The Half*, 174.

000 "expensive luxury": Carleton, *Politics and Punishment*, 9.

000 From 1830 to 1844, the penitentiary: Carleton, *Politics and Punishment*, 9.

000 The company was responsible for: Carleton, *Politics and Punishment*, 10.

000 By 1850 Louisiana would require: Carleton, *Politics and Punishment*, 10–11.

000 The lessees were allowed to use inmates: Hermann, "Specters of Freedom," 109–10.

000 "These men laid aside all objects": Hines, The Life and Adventures of Dr. David T. Hines, 152–53.

000 "the manufacture of cotton goods is": *Report of the Board of Control of the Louisiana State Penitentiary* (Baton Rouge: *Daily Advocate*, 1858).

000 A year after the penitentiary was: Hermann, "Specters of Freedom," 103.

000 But the lessees mainly focused on: State of Louisiana, *Acts Passed at the First Session of the Seventeenth Legislature of the State of Louisiana* (New Orleans: Magne & Weisse, State Printers, 1845), 43, in Hermann, "Specters of Freedom," 103.

000 The lessees criticized the courts: State of New York, "Louisiana Penitentiary for 1845," in *Documents of the Assembly of the State of New York* (Albany: E. Croswell, Printer to the State, 1847), 347, in Hermann, "Specters of Freedom," 103.

000 Six years after their complaint: Hermann, "Specters of Freedom," 111.

000 "The successful introduction of cotton manufacture": *Times-Picayune* (New Orleans, LA), May 12, 1859.

000 "If a profit of several thousand": Perkinson, *Texas Tough*, 74.

000 The head of a Texas jail: Perkinson, *Texas Tough*, 78.

000 "the transportation of articles made": Walker, *Penology for Profit*, 14.

000 Dr. Hines, meanwhile, was pardoned: "Another Talented Swindler," *Times-Picayune* (New Orleans, LA), April 7, 1852.

000 By 1857, five years after Hines was released: *Report of the Board of Control of the Louisiana Penitentiary*, (Baton Rouge: *Daily Advocate*, 1858).

CHAPTER NINE

000 The company that markets the test: "True Colors International," accessed January 15, 2018, http://truecolorsintl.com/wp-content/uploads/2013/05/Research-Validity-and-Reliability-I.pdf.

000 "We all want to believe in": Philip G. Zimbardo, *The Lucifer Effect: Understanding How Good People Turn Evil* (New York: Random House Trade Paperbacks, 2008), 180.

000 should understand evil, as Zimbardo suggested: Zimbardo, *Lucifer Effect*, 211.

CHAPTER TEN

000 One named Azaline tried to poison: Hermann, "Specters of Freedom", 123–24, 140, 144.

000 The proceeds were used to fund: Material on the sales of children of enslaved women at the Louisiana State Penitentiary comes from Brett J. Derbes, "'Secret Horrors': Enslaved Women and Children in the Louisiana State Penitentiary, 1833–1862," *The Journal of African American History* 98, no. 2 (Spring 2013): 277–90, doi:10.5323/jafriamerhist.98.2.0277.

000 penitentiary became a Confederate war machine: Brett J. Derbes, "Prison Productions: Textiles and Other Military Supplies from State Penitentiaries in the Trans-Mississippi Theater during the American Civil War," (master's thesis, University of North Texas, 2011), 16, digital.library.unt.edu/ark:/67531/metadc84198.

000 In April 1962, Union ships rained: John D. Winters, *The Civil War in Louisiana* (Baton Rouge: Louisiana State University Press, 1963) 96–97; Leon F. Litwack, *Been in the Storm So Long: The Aftermath of Slavery* (New York: Vintage Books, 1980), 32.

000 Union General Benjamin Butler: Benjamin F. Butler and Jessie Ames Marshall, *Private and Official Correspondence of Gen. Benjamin F. Butler during*

the Period of the Civil War, Volume II (Norwood, MA: Plimpton Press, 1917), 209.

000 **To keep the factory going, General Butler:** Butler and Marshall, *Correspondence of Gen. Benjamin F. Butler*, 9.

000 **In August 1862, the citizens of:** Winters, *Civil War in Louisiana*, 121.

000 **General Butler decided to withdraw:** Butler and Marshall, *Correspondence of Gen. Benjamin F. Butler*, 193.

000 **To prevent the Confederacy from taking:** Winters, *Civil War in Louisiana*, 123.

000 **seven of the eight wealthiest states:** Baptist, *The Half*, 350.

CHAPTER ELEVEN

000 **I find a list of books not allowed:** Louisiana Department of Public Safety and Corrections, *Department Regulation No. C-02-009, Field Operations Security, Offender Mail and Publications, Updated 04 August 2014.*

000 **In Texas, Adolf Hitler's** *Mein Kampf*: Michael Schaub, "Texas Prisons Ban Books by Langston Hughes and Bob Dole—but 'Mein Kampf' Is OK," *Los Angeles Times*, September 27, 2016, www.latimes.com/books/jacket copy/la-et-jc-texas-prisons-books-20160927-snap-story.html.

000 **According to a lawsuit:** Campbell Robertson, "Alabama Inmate Sues to Read Southern History Book," *New York Times*, September 26, 2011, www.nytimes.com/2011/09/27/us/alabama-inmate-sues-to-read-southern-history-book.html.

000 **I reported on one California inmate:** Shane Bauer, "Solitary in Iran Nearly Broke Me. Then I Went Inside America's Prisons," *Mother Jones*, November/December, 2012

000 **one-third of prison guards suffer:** Michael D. Denhof and Catarina G. Spinaris, *Depression, PTSD, and Comorbidity in United States Corrections Professionals: Prevalence and Impact on Health and Functioning* (Florence, CO: Desert Waters Correctional Outreach, 2013), http://desertwaters.com/wp-content/uploads/2013/09/Comorbidity_Study_09-03-131.pdf. Studies suggest that PTSD affects 2 percent to 17 percent of Iraq War veterans; Lisa K. Richardson, B. Christopher Frueh, and Ronald Acierno, "Prevalence Estimates of Combat-Related PTSD: A Critical Review," *Australian & New*

Zealand Journal of Psychiatry 44, no. 1 (January 2010): 4–19, http://journals .sagepub.com/doi/abs/10.3109/00048670903393597; Terri Tanielian and Lisa H. Jaycox, eds., *Invisible Wounds of War: Psychological and Cognitive Injuries, Their Consequences, and Services to Assist Recovery* (Santa Monica: Rand Corporation, 2008), www.rand.org/pubs/monographs/MG720.html.

000 **COs commit suicide two and a:** Brevard County Sheriff's Office, *Florida Mortality Study: Florida Law Enforcement and Corrections Officers Compared to Florida General Population*, October 17, 2011, www.floridastatefop.org/pdf _files/floridamortalitystudy.pdf.

CHAPTER TWELVE

000 **Before the war, it produced thirty-one hundred:** Baptist, *The Half,* 360.

000 **seven out of ten prisoners:** "Annual Report of the Board of Control of the Louisiana State Penitentiary: January 1987," in *Documents of the Second Session of the Second Legislature of the State of Louisiana* (New Orleans: J. O. Nixon, State Prisoner, 1867), 60.

000 **producing more than twelve thousand bales:** Mancini, *One Dies, Get Another,* 132; David M. Oshinsky, *Worse than Slavery: Parchman Farm and the Ordeal of Jim Crow Justice* (New York: Free Press Paperbacks, 1996), 34–37.

000 **Georgia, whose penitentiary had been destroyed:** Mancini, *One Dies, Get Another,* 82.

000 **Alabama had leased its convicts to:** Mancini, *One Dies, Get Another,* 101; J. Thorsten Sellin, *Slavery and the Penal System* (New York: Elsevier Scientific, 1976), 150–54.

000 **A company called Huger and Jones:** State of Louisiana, Executive Department, *Annual Message of Governor H. C. Warmoth to the General Assembly of Louisiana,* January 4, 1869 (New Orleans: A.L. Lee, State Printer), 9; Carleton, *Politics and Punishment,* 16–17.

000 **"the heaviest lot of machinery ever":** "James, Buckner & Co.," *Daily Advocate* (Baton Rouge, La.), August 23, 1869; "James, Buckner & Co Factories," *Daily Advocate* (Baton Rouge, LA), December 3, 1869.

000 **imported one hundred fifty Chinese laborers:** *Tri-Weekly Advocate* (Baton Rouge, La.), March 27, 1871; "Cotton Manufacturing in Louisiana," *Macon (GA) Weekly Telegraph,* April 25, 1871; Lucy M Cohen, *Chinese in the*

Post-Civil War South: A People without a History (Baton Rouge: Louisiana State University Press, 1984), 93–94.

000 **He discovered that he could make:** *New Orleans Republican*, February 2, 1873.

000 **A convict doing levee and railroad work:** US Department of Labor, Bureau of Labor Statistics, *Second Annual Report of the Commissioner of Labor, Second Edition* (Washington, DC: Government Printing Office, 1887), 200–2.

000 **In 1875 the Reconstruction legislature forbade:** Mancini, *One Dies, Get Another*, 146; Hermann, "Specters of Freedom, 238.

000 **In 1872 Mississippi transferred:** Mancini, *One Dies, Get Another*, 133–34; Oshinsky, *Worse than Slavery*, 43.

000 **Another lessee was Colonel James Monroe:** Oshinsky, *Worse than Slavery*, 64–67; Mancini, *One Dies, Get Another*, 83–84.

000 **"You had better send me some":** Oshinsky, *Worse than Slavery*, 67.

000 **Georgia, Mississippi, Arkansas, North Carolina:** Ayers, *Vengeance and Justice*, 196.

000 **By 1886 the US commissioner:** Carroll Davidson Wright, *Second Annual Report of the Commissioner of Labor, 1886, Convict Labor* (Washington, DC: Government Printing Office, 1887).

000 **"springs primarily from the idea":** George Washington Cable, *The Silent South* (Montclair, NJ: Patterson Smith, 1969), 126, 128.

000 **By 1890 some twenty-seven thousand convicts:** Wright, *Report of the Commissioner of Labor*, 23.

000 **the number of state convicts quadrupled:** Mancini, *One Dies, Get Another*, 120; Vernon Lane Wharton, *The Negro in Mississippi* (New York: Harper Torchbooks, 1947), 237–38; Daniel Novak, *The Wheel of Servitude: Black Forced Labor After Slavery* (Lexington: University Press of Kentucky, 1978), 32.

000 **Abe McDowell of Wilcox County:** *Third Biennial Report of the Inspectors of Convicts to the Governor, from October 1, 1888 to September 30, 1890 (Montgomery: Brown Printing, 1890)*, 3.

000 **In North Carolina most of the:** Frenise A. Logan, *Negro in North Carolina 1876–1894* (Chapel Hill: University of North Carolina Press, 1964), 191–92. In 1876 there were 676 black prisoners in North Carolina. By 1890 the number had risen to 1,623.

000 the number of black prisoners increased: Logan, *Negro in North Carolina*, 191–92.

000 A legislative committee discovered in 1884: Paul B. Foreman and Julien R. Tatum, "A Short History of Mississippi's State Penal Systems," *Mississippi Law Journal* 10 (April 1938): 260, in Sellin, *Slavery and the Penal System*, 148.

000 When a grand jury inspected: Wharton, *Negro in Mississippi*, 241.

000 One Mississippi report claimed its convicts: Ayers, *Vengeance and Justice*, 193.

000 The most detailed account: Details of J. C. Powell's experiences and the camps he oversaw were drawn from his memoir, The *American Siberia* (Chicago: H. J. Smith & Co, 1891).

000 Mississippi's official Punishment Record Ledger: Malcolm C. Moss, *State Penal Administration in Alabama*, Bureau of Public Administration (Tuscaloosa: University of Alabama, 1942), 18, cited in Sellin, *Slavery and the Penal System*, 153.

000 "very elegant toilets and cordial hospitality": "Society," *Times-Picayune* (New Orleans, La.), January 6, 1884.

000 On the plantation the family kept: "Convict Camp Horrors," *Times-Picayune* (New Orleans, La.), September 11, 1888.

000 "We had plenty of servants": Quote and material Cecile James Shilstone, *My Plantation Days: The Memoirs of Cecile James Shilstone 1887–1979*, in possession of author.

000 dawn to dusk work regimen, whippings: "Convict Camp Horrors."

000 While the field workers ate: "Convict Camp Horrors" and Shilstone, *My Plantation Days*.

000 When the estate was passed on: Carleton, *Politics and Punishment*, 76.

000 "more humane to punish with death": "Penitentiary," *Times-Picayune* (New Orleans, La.), June 30, 1884.

000 the death rate of six prisons: Wharton, *Negro in Mississippi*, 241.

000 In the deadliest year of Louisiana's lease: Hermann, "Specters of Freedom," 252–53.

000 Between 1870 and 1901, some three thousand: Carleton, *Politics and Punishment*, 46.

000 annual convict death rates ranged: C. Vann Woodward, *Origins of the New South, 1877–1913* (Baton Rouge: Louisiana State University Press, 1951),

214; *Soviet Studies* scholar S. G. Wheatcroft puts the peak death rate in Soviet labor camps at 230 per 1,000 from 1942 to 1943 in "More Light on the Scale of Repression and Excess Mortality in the Soviet Union in the 1930s," *Soviet Studies* 42, no. 2 (April 1990): 356, www.jstor.org/stable /152086; Anne Applebaum cites official NKVD (the interior ministry of the Soviet Union) records to show the annual death rates of the gulags, the peak being 24.9 percent in 1942: *Gulag: A History* (New York: Doubleday, 2003), 578–86.

000 **the death rate of convicts leased:** Novak, *The Wheel of Servitude*, 33.

000 **In 1870 Alabama prison officials reported:** Oshinsky, *Worse than Slavery*, 79 and Robert David Ward and William Warren Rogers, *Convicts, Coal, and the Banner Mine Tragedy* (Tuscaloosa: University of Alabama Press, 1987), 30.

000 **"Before the war, we owned the":** Hastings H. Hart, "Prison Conditions in the South," in *Proceedings of the National Prison Association (1919):* 200, in Mancini, *One Dies, Get Another,* 3.

CHAPTER FOURTEEN

000 **There was probably no lessee that:** For more reading on TCI's use of convict labor, see Douglas A. Blackmon, *Slavery by Another Name: The Re-Enslavement of Black Americans from the Civil War to World War II* (New York: Doubleday, 2008); Mancini, *One Dies, Get Another,* 105–14, 159–66; Ethel Armes, *The Story of Coal and Iron in Alabama* (New York: Arno Press, 1973), 420–60; Ward and Rogers, *Convicts, Coal, and the Banner Mine Tragedy,* 26–50; Carl Vernon Harris, *Political Power in Birmingham: 1871–1921* (Knoxville: University of Tennessee Press, 1977), 202–7.

000 **In Alabama alone, some fifteen thousand:** Harris, *Political Power,* 203.

000 **In 1889, 18 percent of Alabama's:** *Third Biennial Report of the Inspector of Convicts,* 49.

000 **In one instance, 123 men:** Ward and Rogers, *Convicts, Coal, and the Banner Mine Tragedy.*

000 **convicts set fire to the mine:** *Third Biennial Report of the Inspector of Convicts,* 14–15.

000 Dysentery frequently swept through TCI's labor: *Third Biennial Report of the Inspector of Convicts*, 46–52.

000 When a prisoner died: Blackmon, *Slavery by Another Name*, 2.

000 "[I]t is a water that no population": Blackmon, *Slavery by Another Name*, 44–45.

000 "debased moral condition of the negro": Blackmon, *Slavery by Another Name*, 26.

000 Between 1880 and 1904, Alabama's profits: Ronald Lewis, *Black Coal Miners in America: Race, Class, and Community Conflict, 1780–1980* (Lexington: The University Press of Kentucky, 1987), 26.

000 In the twenty-two years leading: *Alabama Official and Statistical Register, 1913* (Montgomery: Brown Printing 1913), 315.

000 More than one-quarter of miners: *Report of the Special Committee to Investigate the Convict System, 1897* (Montgomery: n.p., n.d.), 22, in Ward and Rogers, *Banner Mine Tragedy*, 42; Oshinsky, *Worse than Slavery*, 76.

000 The person to thank for bringing: Karin A. Shapiro, *A New South Rebellion: The Battle against Convict Labor in the Tennessee Coalfields, 1871–1896* (Chapel Hill: University of North Carolina Press, 1998), 21–22; Mancini, *One Dies, Get Another*, 155–56; Blackmon, *Slavery by Another Name*, 55.

000 "outpost for Pennsylvania tramps": Shapiro, *New South Rebellion*, 22.

000 For $150,000 the state granted: Mancini, *One Dies, Get Another*, 154; Oshinsky, *Worse than Slavery*, 57–58.

000 In 1874 Tennessee leased 123: Fletcher Melvin Green, "Some Aspects of the Convict Lease System in the Southern States," in *Essays in Southern History*, ed. Fletcher Melvin Green (Westport, CT: Greenwood Press, 1976), 120.

000 collecting their urine and selling it: Oshinsky, *Worse than Slavery*, 57–58.

000 Colyar's TCI took over the Tennessee: Woodward, *Origins of the New South*, 232–33.

000 "One of the chief reasons": "C. Colyar Talks," *The Tennessean (Nashville)*, August 23, 1892.

000 From the beginning of convict leasing: Shapiro, *New South Rebellion*, 52.

000 For a "first class man": W. D. Lee, "The Lease System of Alabama," in *Proceedings of the Annual Congress of the National Prison Association of the*

United States (Pittsburgh: Shaw Brothers,1890), 113; Sellin, *Slavery and the Penal System*, 150.

000 Compared to free laborers: Mancini, *One Dies, Get Another*, 105.

000 An Alabama government inspection showed: *Third Biennial Report of the Inspector of Convicts*, 46.

000 "Nearly all the whipping was done": *Third Biennial Report of the Inspector of Convicts*, 106–07.

000 "Convict labor [is] more reliable": Wright, *Report of the Commissioner of Labor*.

000 "It is almost impossible to reach": Lee, "The Lease System of Alabama," 120–21.

000 In Tennessee, the state was: The events of the Coal Creek War were sourced from Shapiro, *New South Rebellion*; Neal Shirley and Saralee Stafford, *Dixie Be Damned: 300 Years of Insurrection in the American South* (Oakland, CA: AK Press, 2015), 121–46; Pete Daniel, "The Tennessee Convict War," *Tennessee Historical Quarterly* 34, no. 3 (Fall 1975): 273–92, www.jstor.org/stable /i40097530; Lewis, *Black Coal Miners in America*, 23–25; Woodward, *Origins of the New South*, 232–34; and Mancini, *One Dies, Get Another*, 163–65.

000 "That was a strong argument among": Quote and militia figure from P. D. Sims, "The Lease System in Tennessee and Other Southern States," in *Proceedings of the Annual Congress of the National Prison Association of the United States* (Chicago: Knight, Leonard & Co Printers, 1893), 128, https:// archive.org/details/proceedingsofa1893ameruoft.

000 The merger, brokered by J. P. Morgan: Blackmon, *Slavery by Another Name*, 295.

000 "Think of that!": Ida M. Tarbell, *The Life of Elbert H. Gary: The Story of Steel* (New York: D. Appleton & Company, 1925), 310–11.

000 "Are there convicts on that site?": Blackmon, *Slavery by Another Name*, 390–91.

CHAPTER FIFTEEN

000 During the next four months: Louisiana Department of Corrections, public records request, information from calendar year 2010 to April 30, 2015, requested by author on March 2, 2015.

000 When he died, he weighed 71: Damien committed suicide on June 12, 2015, after I'd left Winn. This is one of the few scenes in this book that appears

out of order. The events of his suicide were reconstructed from interviews with prisoners and the assistant chief of security, who investigated the suicide. Johnny's experience is based on letter correspondences I had with him after Damien's suicide. Details about Damien's cause of death and weight come from hospital records provided to me by Wendy Porter. Information about Damien before his death comes from prison records provided by Porter and attorney Anna Lellelid or from interviews with his family.

000 **CCA never reported Damien's suicide:** Ken Pastorick, Communications Director, Louisiana Department of Safety and Corrections, "media request," email, January 19, 2018.

CHAPTER SIXTEEN

000 **Things began to change in Texas:** Mancini, *One Dies, Get Another,* 175, and Theresa R. Jach, "Reform versus Reality in the Progressive Era Texas Prison," *The Journal of the Gilded Age and Progressive Era* 4, no. 1 (January 2005): 55, doi.org/10.1017/S1537781400003650.

000 **Convicts he didn't use:** Mancini, *One Dies, Get Another,* 177–78.

000 **To avoid the scandal of committing:** Jach, "Reform versus Reality," 5; Perkinson 123–24.

000 **The strategy backfired:** Thomas J. Goree, "Some Features of Prison Control in the South," in *Proceedings of the Annual Congress of the National Prison Association of the United States, Held at Austin, Texas, December 2–6, 1897* (Pittsburg: Shaw Brothers, 1898), 143, https://archive.org/stream/proceedi ngsofa1897ameruoft#page/n7/mode/2up; Perkinson, *Texas Tough,* 124–25; Jach, "Reform versus Reality," 57; Mancini, *One Dies, Get Another,* 179.

000 **In the first year, the state:** Goree, "Features of Prison Control," 135.

000 **The government farm was earning $501.39:** Texas State Penitentiary Board, *Biennial Report* (1890), 24–25, in Perkinson, *Texas Tough,* 125.

000 **The 1908 crop alone would pay:** Mancini, *One Dies, Get Another,* 180.

000 **By 1928 the state of Texas:** Lach, "Reform versus Reality," 57.

000 **To avoid work, prisoners amputated:** Perkinson, *Texas Tough,* 215–17.

000 **From 1932 to 1951:** Crouch and Marquart, *Appeal to Justice,* 23.

000 **In the late 1880s and 1890s:** Jane Zimmerman, "The Penal Reform Movement in the South during the Progressive Era, 1890–1917," *The Journal of*

Southern History 17, no. 4 (November 1951): 464–66, www.jstor.org/stable /2954512.

000 "not only handling a large prison" Carleton, *Politics and Punishment*, 94.

000 Because multiple companies were now bidding: Mancini discusses the importance of economic factors in ending convict leasing in the final chapter of his book *One Dies, Get Another*, 215–32.

000 Companies made higher and higher bids: Mancini, *One Dies, Get Another*, 181; Walker, *Penology for Profit*, 93–95.

000 In both Georgia and Texas: Mancini, *One Dies, Get Another*, 98, 182, 224–27.

000 "abolishing the lease system under any": Calvin R. Ledbetter Jr., "The Long Struggle to End Convict Leasing in Arkansas," *The Arkansas Historical Quarterly* 52, no. 1 (Spring 1993): 17, www.jstor.org/stable/40030832.

000 Donaghey realized that the system: Ledbetter, "The Long Struggle," 12, 24; Mancini, *One Dies, Get Another*, 129–30.

000 A man named James Kimble Vardaman: Oshinsky, *Worse Than Slavery*, 85–89; William F. Holmes, *The White Chief: James Kimble Vardaman* (Baton Rouge: Louisiana State University Press, 1970), 22–42.

000 "little, mean, coon-flavored miscegenationist": Blackmon, *Slavery by Another Name*, 167; Holmes, *The White Chief*, 98–99.

000 In his gubernatorial campaign, Vardaman promised: Oshinsky, *Worse than Slavery*, 89; Albert D. Kirwan, *Revolt of the Rednecks* (Lexington: University of Kentucky Press, 1951), 144–61; Holmes, *The White Chief*, 81–115.

000 His campaign banner read: Oshinsky, *Worse than Slavery*, 90.

000 "If the state can make money": Kirwan, *Revolt of the Rednecks*, 172.

000 This, he believed, could be accomplished: Holmes, *The White Chief*, 150–76.

000 "more interested in the salvation of men": Kirwan, *Revolt of the Rednecks*, 172.

000 In 1905, less than a year: Oshinksy, *Worse than Slavery*, 109.

000 Within ten years, state profits: Kirwan, *Revolt of the Rednecks*, 175.

000 Martin Tabert was a twenty-two-year-old: Except where otherwise noted, the details of the Martin Talbert case, quotes, and the responses to it are based on N. Gordon Carper, "Martin Tabert, Martyr of an Era," *The Florida Historical Quarterly* 52, no. 2 (October 1973): 115–31, www.jstor.org /stable/30149028.

000 On October 19, 1924, he beat: Jerrell H. Shofner, "Postscript to the Martin Tabert Case: Peonage as Usual in the Florida Turpentine Camps," *The Florida Historical Quarterly* 60, no. 2 (October 1981): 162, www.jstor.org /stable/30146766.

000 "The Tabert boy, who was killed": Mancini, *One Dies, Get Another*, 228.

000 "James Knox died in a laundering": Mancini, *One Dies, Get Another*, 115.

CHAPTER SEVENTEEN

000 "The South today is enjoying": Alex Lichtenstein, "Good Roads and Chain Gangs in the Progressive South: 'The Negro Convict Is a Slave,'" *The Journal of Southern History* 59, no. 1 (February 1993): 86, www.jstor.org /stable/2210349.

000 When Georgia abandoned convict leasing: Lichtenstein, "Chain Gangs," 100.

000 By 1923 the state was using: US Department of Labor, Bureau of Labor Statistics, *Convict Labor in 1923*, Bulletin No. 372 (January 1925), 11–12, https://fraser.stlouisfed.org/files/docs/publications/bls/bls_0372_1925.pdf.

000 "with little or no inconvenience": Lichtenstein, "Chain Gangs," 101–02.

000 "A considerable amount of evidence": Robert E. Ireland, "Prison Reform, Road Building, and Southern Progressivism: Joseph Hyde Pratt and the Campaign for 'Good Roads and Good Men'," *The North Carolina Historical Review* 68, no. 2 (April 1991): 131, www.jstor.org/stable/23521190.

000 "bronzed, sturdy, healthy and efficient": Ireland, "Prison Reform," 137.

000 The idea of roadwork as an: Ireland, "Prison Reform."

000 "the chain gang was meant to": Sellin, *Slavery and the Penal System*, 163–76.

000 In 1908, 77 percent: Lichtenstein, "Chain Gangs," 94, 96.

000 "chained with iron neck collars, poorly": Ireland, "Prison Reform," 148.

000 "the mules at the camp were": Ireland, "Prison Reform," 149.

000 "the men sleep in a moveable": Sellin, *Slavery and the Penal System*, 167.

000 "On hot days . . . the sun streams": Frank Tannenbaum, *Darker Phases of the South* (New York: G. P. Putnam's Sons, 1924), 86. Tannenbaum cites numerous official documents describing conditions in convict road camps throughout the South indistinguishable from those witnessed by Governor Gilchrist.

000 In 1930 a man in: Theodore Brautner Wilson, *The Black Codes of the South* (Tuscaloosa: University of Alabama Press, 1965), 540.

000 Arthur Maillefert, a teenage boy: "Relate How Convict Died in 'Sweat Box'," *New York Times*, July 8, 1932; "Was Convict Maillefert Tortured to Death?" *Saint Louis (MO) Star and Times*, July 14, 1932; "State Rests Case Against Guards in 'Sweat Box' Trial," *Palm Beach (FL) Post*, October 11, 1932; "Prison Horrors Related by Convicts," *Orlando (FL) Sentinel* (October 7, 1932), 2; Wilson, Walter, "Chain Gangs and Profit," *Harper's* (April, 1933), 533.

000 "Personally, I favor the employment": Lichtenstein, "Chain Gangs ," 106.

000 "a nigger is born happy": Lichtenstein, "Chain Gangs," 109.

CHAPTER NINETEEN

000 On average, a Louisiana prison alots: Louisiana Department of Public Safety and Corrections, www.doc.la.gov/wp-content/uploads/stats/5k.pdf.

000 health care is about 33 percent: Mac Taylor, *California's Criminal Justice System: A Primer* (January2013), 50, www.lao.ca.gov/reports/2013/crim/crim inal-justice-primer/criminal-justice-primer-011713.pdf.

000 Nearly 40 percent of Winn inmates: "Governor's Executive Budget," fiscal year 2016–2017. http://www.doa.la.gov/opb/pub/fy17/fy17_executive_bud get.pdf.

000 About 6 percent have a communicable: "Governor's Executive Budget."

000 The company's Idaho prison contract: Alex Friedmann, "Apples to Fish: Public and Private Prison Cost Comparisons," *Fordham Urban Law Journal* XLII, no.2 (December 2014): 504–68.

000 The contracts of some CCA prisons: Alex Friedmann, "Prison Cost Comparisons," 524–25.

000 At least 15 doctors at Winn: Fuilier v. Pacheco et al., No. 1:08-cv-01577 (W.D. La. May 11, 2009); LeMieux v. CCA of Tennessee et al., No. 1:09-cv-01486 (W.D. La. August 24, 2009); Allen v. Pacheco et al., No. 1:08-cv-00983 (W.D. La. July 1, 2008); Alfred v. Pacheco et al., No. 1:09-cv-01470 (W.D. La. August 17, 2009); Harris v. Wilenson et al., No. 1:11-cv-00831 (W.D. La. June 2, 2011); Baker v. Cleveland et al., No.

1:13-cv-02103 (W.D. La. June 20, 2013); Hodges v. Keith et al., No. 1:14-cv-00993 (W.D. La. May 14, 2014); Scott v. Corrections Corporation of America et al., No. 1:14-cv-00956 (W.D. La. May 7, 2014); McCann v. Winn Correctional Center et al., No. 1:09-cv-02232 (W.D. La. December 28, 2009); Singleton v. Stalder et al., No. 1:05-cv-01540 (W.D. La. August 18, 2015); Broussard v. Public Safety and Corr. et al., No. 1:02-cv-01570 (W.D. La. July 25, 2002); Hanna v. Corrections Corp. Am. et al., No. 1:02-cv-02653 (W.D. La. December 24, 2002); Merritt v. Creats et al., No. 1:1996-cv-02304 (W.D. La. January 10, 1996); Jackson et al v. Winn Corr Ctr et al., No. 1:98-cv-00636 (W.D. La. April 1, 1998); Williams v. Moore et al., No. 1:96-cv-02177 (W.D. La. September 13, 1996); Orange v. Corrections Corp Am et al., No. 1:95-cv-01447 (W.D. La. August 14, 1995); Frazier v. Keith et al., No. 1:13-cv-03110 (W.D. La. November 18, 2013); Jackson v. Hubert et al, No. 1:00-cv-02389 (W.D. La. October 23, 2000); Valdez v. Corrections Corp Am et al., No. 1:99-cv-01680 (W.D. La. September 14, 1999).

000 **One, Aris Cox, was hired:** Louisiana State Board of Medical Examiners, *In the Matter of Aris W. Cox, M.D.*, No. 92-I-026-X (May 21, 1992), http://apps.lsbme.la.gov/disciplinary/DocViewer.aspx?decision=true&fID=69961.

000 **While Mark Singleton was at Winn:** Louisiana State Board of Medical Examiners, *In the Matter of Mark Singleton, D.O.*, No. 13-I-689 (June 25, 2014), http://apps.lsbme.la.gov/disciplinary/DocViewer.aspx?decision=true&fID=115490.

000 **Winn hired Stephen Kuplesky after his:** Louisiana State Board of Medical Examiners, *In the Matter of Stephen Kuplesky, M.D.*, No. 06-I-008 (June 15, 2006), http://apps.lsbme.la.gov/disciplinary/DocViewer.aspx?decision=true&fID=46384.

000 **Robert Cleveland was working at:** Louisiana Board of Medical Examiners, *In the Matter of Robert Lyle Cleveland, M.D.*, No. 09-I-256 (December 4, 2009), http://apps.lsbme.la.gov/disciplinary/DocViewer.aspx?decision=true&fID=46397.

000 **He was later disciplined for prescribing:** Louisiana Board of Medical Examiners, *In the Matter of Robert Lyle Cleveland, M.D.*, No. 09-I-256 (December 4, 2009), http://apps.lsbme.la.gov/disciplinary/DocViewer.aspx?decision=true&fID=46397.

000 **In 2010 the company and Immigration:** Woods v. Myers, No. 3:07-cv-01078-DMS-PCL (S.D. Cal. 2010).

000 **In a rare case that made:** Degan v. Prison Realty Trust Inc., No. 99-2878 (E.D. Tenn. January 30, 2003).

000 **CCA has also been the subject:** Countess Clemons v. Corrections Corporation of America et al., No. 1:11-cv-00339 (E.D. Tenn. November 17, 2011).

000 **CCA settled another case for $250,000:** Meredith Manning v. Corrections Corporation of America , No. 05C-2608 (E.D. Tenn. December 2014); David Reutter, "Prison Obtains Confidential CCA Litigation Records in Tennessee," *Prison Legal News*, March 2016, www.prisonlegalnews.org /news/2016/feb/29/pln-obtains-confidential-cca-litigation-records -tennessee/.

000 **When I made public-records requests:** Data collected by *Prison Legal News* on more than 1,200 state and federal suits against CCA shows that 15 percent of them were related to medical care. (This sample is not a complete list of complaints against the company; in 2010 alone, CCA faced more than 600 pending cases. Between 1998 and 2008, the company settled another 600 cases.)

000 **mutilation of the sexually abused:** Larry K. Brown et al., "Self-Cutting and Sexual Risk among Adolescents in Intensive Psychiatric Treatment, *Psychiatric Services* 56, no. 2 (February 2005): 216–18, https://ps.psychiatryonline .org/doi/pdf/10.1176/appi.ps.56.2.216?code=ps-site.

000 **More than one-third of gay:** Allen J. Beck and Candace Johnson, *Sexual Victimization Reported by Former State Prisoners, 2008*, US Department of Justice, Bureau of Justice Statistics, May 2012, www.bjs.gov/content/pub /pdf/svrfsp08.pdf; Valerie Jenness et al., *Violence in California Correctional Facilities: An Empirical Examination of Sexual Assault*, Center for Evidence-Based Corrections (Irvine: University of California, 2007), 3, http://uci corrections.seweb.uci.edu/files/2013/06/PREA_Presentation _PREA_Report_UCI_Jenness_et_al.pdf.

000 **When I looked at the files:** Mitchell v. CCA of Tennessee Inc. et al., No. 1:04-cv-01031-DDD-JDK (USDC W.D. La.).

000 **Nearly half of all allegations:** Allen J. Beck and Ramona R. Rantala, *Sexual Victimization Reported by Adult Correctional Authorities, 2009–11*, US De-

partment of Justice, Bureau of Justice Statistics, January 2014, www.bjs
.gov/content/pub/pdf/svraca0911.pdf.

CHAPTER TWENTY

000 **When Arkansas governor Winthrop Rockefeller:** Except where otherwise
noted, details from Arkansas are derived from Tom Murton and Joe Hyams,
Accomplices to the Crime: The Arkansas Prison Scandal (London: Michael Joseph, 1969).

000 000 **On the sixteen thousand-acre Cummins plantation:** "The Arkansas
State Penitentiary," summary of 1967 Tucker farm investigation, M10A-25,
Arkansas State Library archives, Little Rock, Arkansas.

000 **The farms brought an average:** "Prisons: Hell in Arkansas," *Time*, February
9, 1968, http://content.time.com/time/magazine/article/0,9171,844402,00
.html.

000 **"To make these profits, the prisoners":** Arkansas State Police Criminal Investigations Division, "Tucker Prison Farm Investigation," file number
916-166-66, 1966.

000 **"They received insufficient food and clothing":** "The Arkansas State Penitentiary."

000 **One was a device invented by:** "Tucker Prison Farm Investigation," 10–11.

000 **"$8,000 per year, a new car":** "Tucker Prison Farm Investigation," 8–9.

000 **Rank men were typically forty to:** "Tucker Prison Farm Investigation," 5.

000 **Alabama, Mississippi, and Louisiana used them:** Oshinsky, *Worse than Slavery*, 140–48, 194–96; Carleton, *Politics and Punishment*, 116, 140–43; Perkinson, *Texas Tough*, 242–46; Tannenbaum, 102–03; Gates v. Collier, 501
F.2d 1291 (5th Cir. 1974), https://openjurist.org/501/f2d/1291/gates-v-collier.

000 **From 1928 to 1940, there were:** B. L. Krebs, "Prisoners Flogged 10,000
Times during Machine Rule," *Times-Picayune* (New Orleans, LA), May 11,
1941.

000 **He sold the plasma:** Murton and Hyams, *Accomplices to the Crime*, 111; "Board
Asked to Renew Prison Plasma Program and Share in the Profits," *Arkansas
Gazette*, May 4, 1967; "State Administration of Blood 'Business' Sought at
Cummins," *Arkansas* Gazettet, February 25, 1967; "Blood 'Concession' at

Penal Farm Eyed," *Arkansas Democrat*, February 25, 1967; Douglas Starr, *Blood: An Epic History of Medicine and Commerce* (New York: Perennial, 2002) 207–30; Walter Rugaber, "Prison Drug and Plasma Project Leaves Fatal Trail," *New York Times*, July 29, 1969; "'NBC Reports' Special About Human Medical Experiments, *Mobile (AL) Register*, May 26, 1973.

000 **A number of the drug companies:** The companies included Wyeth Laboratories Division of American Home Products Corporation; Lederle Laboratories Division of American Cyanamid Company; Bristol-Myers Company E. R. Squibb & Sons Division of Squibb Beech-Nut Inc.; Merck, Sharp & Dohme Division of Merck & Co.; and the Upjohn Company.

000 **Under Murton, Tucker produced thirty-seven:** "Murton's Policies on Farming Hit; Governor Blamed," *Arkansas Gazette*, May 30, 1968.

000 **in May 1971, he called Hutto:** "Governor Calls, Texan Takes Job as Prison Chief," *Arkansas Gazette*, May 16, 1971.

CHAPTER TWENTY-ONE

000 **CCA later hired Hardy Rauch:** Selman and Leighton, *Punishment for Sale*, 97.

000 **In 2017 Mississippi prison commissioner:** Albert Samaha, "The Prison Reform Blues," *BuzzFeed*, December 5, 2014, www.buzzfeed.com/albert-samaha/the-rise-and-fall-of-mississippis-top-prison-reformer# .yqDPLPym4K; Jimmie E. Gates, "Chris Epps Sentenced to Almost 20 Years," *Clarion Ledger* (Jackson, MS), May 24, 2017, www.clarionledger.com /story/news/2017/05/24/chris-epps-sentencing/341916001/.

000 **Auditors noted that "offenders feel Winn":** American Correctional Association, *Commission of Accreditation for Corrections Standards Compliance Reaccreditation Audit: Corrections Corporation of America Winn Correctional Center*, May 21–23, 2012, obtained by the author.

000 **In fact, CCA's average score:** CoreCivic Inc, *10-K Annual Report* (FY 2016).

000 **A guard was beaten to death:** Matt Clarke, "CCA Guard Killed during Riot Was on Prisoners' 'Hit List,'" *Prison Legal News*, June 6, 2014, www.pri sonlegalnews.org/news/2014/jun/6/cca-guard-killed-during-riot -was-prisoners-hit-list/; Janosch Delcker, "Fatal Corrections," *The Inter-*

cept, December 17, 2016, https://theintercept.com/2016/12/17/inside-the
-deadly-mississippi-riot-that-pushed-the-justice-department
-to-rein-in-private-prisons/.

000 **The ACA audit during that time:** ACA Adam's County, November 18–20,
2013, audit obtained by author.

CHAPTER TWENTY-TWO

000 **One of his first initiatives:** "Personnel a Problem, Hutto Says," *Arkansas
Democrat*, June 6, 1971; "He Will Live at Cummins, Hutto Says," *Arkansas
Gazette*, June 4, 1971.

000 **The superintendent used it:** Murton and Hyams, *Accomplices to the Crime*, 173.

000 **In August 1972, some thirty-five hundred:** Bill Lancaster, "Prison Rodeo
Draws the Public; Sellout Expected," *Arkansas Gazette*, August 26, 1972;
Bill Husted, "Inmate Rodeo Success," *Arkansas Gazette*, August 27, 1972.

000 **"Our objective here is to return":** Lancaster, "Prison Rodeo."

000 **Hutto's mandate was to implement:** "New Prisons Head Meets Press; Wants
to Wait Before Speaking Out," *Arkansas Gazette*, May 21, 1971.

000 **"A good prison is very profitable":** "A 'Hard Look' at Trusty Use," *Arkansas
Gazette*, May 21, 1971.

000 **"manual, inefficient, marginal operation":** Leland DuVall, "Cummins Starts
to Stress 'Farm' in Its Operations," *Arkansas Gazette*, March 5, 1973.

000 **During Hutto's first year in Arkansas:** Doug Smith, "1971 Farm Income at
State Prisons Is $1,793,449.49," *Arkansas Gazette*, January 6, 1971; DuVall,
"Cummins Starts to Stress 'Farm' in Its Operations."

000 **Nearly half of the high-level positions:** "Nine Texans in Top Jobs at Prisons." *Arkansas Democrat*, February 6, 1974.

000 **In a federal hearing on prison:** Leslie Mitchell, "Inmates Testify on Prison,"
Arkansas Democrat, November 16, 1971; Mike Tremble, "Cummins Uses
Cold 'Quiet Cells,' Inmates Say," *Arkansas Gazette*, November 17, 1971.

000 **Inmates also testified that failure to:** Mitchell, "Inmates Testify on Prison";
Tremble, "Cummins Uses Cold 'Quiet Cells.'"

000 **"They get you up in the":** Mike Tremble, "Confined 6 Days for 'Peace Sign,'
Inmate Says," *Arkansas Gazette*, November 18. 1971.

000 Other inmates testified that, as punishment: Tremble, "Cummins Uses Cold 'Quiet Cells'"; "Prisoner Says Religious Rights Were Violated," *Arkansas Democrat*, November 17, 1971.

000 Governor Dale Bumpers was satisfied: "Bumpers Defends Hutto," *Arkansas Democrat*, November 19, 1971.

000 a seventeen-year-old boy died: "Day in Arkansas 'Hell' Fatal for Youthful First Offender," *Oregonian*, December 19, 1971.

000 The governor and the press frequently: Leslie Mitchell, "Henley Overruled; Changes Ordered in Prison System," *Arkansas* Gazette, October 12, 1974.

000 The judge called conditions under Hutto: Mitchell, "Henley Overruled."

000 After the ruling, about two hundred inmates: "Show of Force Sends Prisoners Back to Work," *Arkansas Gazette*, October 15, 1974.

000 The year of the appeals court ruling: Arkansas Department of Correction, *Annual Report 1973–1974*, 40.

000 After Hutto, Cummins would forever operate: Arkansas Department of Corrections reports indicate that farm operations began showing a loss in 1978. See Arkansas DOC: *Annual Report March 1, 1968 to September 30, 1970; Annual Progress Report 1971–1972; Annual Report 1977; Annual Report 1978;* 1979 *Annual Report;* and 1980 *Annual Report.*

000 Lawsuits changed how prison plantations: Perhaps the most far-reaching case was the class-action case Ruiz vs. Estelle et al., 516 F.2d 480 (5th Cir. S.D. Tex. 1975), which found the entire Texas prison system to be cruel and unusual.

000 In the decade after Hutto left: US Department of Justice, Bureau of Justice Statistics, *State and Federal Prisoners, 1925–85*, October 1986, www.bjs.gov /content/pub/pdf/sfp2585.pdf; US Department of Justice, Bureau of Justice Statistics, *Prisoners in 1986*, May 1987, www.bjs.gov/content/pub/pdf/ p86.pdf.

000 It would continue to skyrocket until: US Department of Justice, Bureau of Justice Statistics, *Prisoners in 2009*, October 27, 2011, www.bjs.gov/content /pub/pdf/p09.pdf.

000 Rather than make a profit:, Tracey Kyckelhahn, *Justice Expenditure and Employment Extracts, 2012*, US Department of Justice, Bureau of Justice Statistics, February 26, 2015, www.bjs.gov/index.cfm?ty=pbdetail&iid= 5239.

CHAPTER TWENTY-THREE

000 In an Ohio prison: Gergory Geisler, *Correctional Institution Inspection Committee Report on the Inspection and Evaluation of the Lake Erie Correctional Institution* (conducted in January 2013), http://big.assets.huffingtonpost.com/lakeeriereport.pdf.

000 When CCA asked the state to: Commissioner for the Kentucky Department of Corrections LaDonna H. Thompson, to the vice president of customer contracts for the Corrections Corporation of America, CCA Correspondence Dated May 21, 2009, Renewal Per Diem Adjustment for Otter Creek Correctional Center (OCCC) ; Approval to House 20 Additional Hawaiian Inmates," July 24, 2009, www.privateci.org/private_pics/KY%20DOC%20letter%20to%20CCA.pdf; R. G. Dunlop, "Behind the Bars: Secretary Carla Meade's Suicide Raised Questions," *Courier-Journal* (Louisville, *KY*), July 5, 2010, www.privateci.org/private_pics/Meade%20suicide.htm.

000 A federal government study found: US Department of Justice, Office of the Inspector General, *Review of the Federal Bureau of Prisons' Monitoring of Contract Prisons* (August 2016), 18, https://oig.justice.gov/reports/2016/e1606.pdf. A 2001 Department of Justice study, and the last to compare public and private *state* prisons, found exactly the same result. James Austin and Garry Coventry, *Emerging Issues on Privatized Prisons*, US Department of Justice, Bureau of Justice Assistance, February 2001, www.ncjrs.gov/pdffiles1/bja/181249.pdf.

000 During the first four months: Louisiana Department of Corrections, public records request, information from calendar year 2010 to April 30, 2015, requested by author on March 2, 2015.

EPILOGUE

000 As a result, LaSalle cut medical services: Julia O'Donoghue, "Amid Budget Cuts, Louisiana Keeps Prison Costs Down in Ways Other States Don't," *Times-Picayune*, September 27, 2016, http://www.nola.com/politics/index.ssf/2016/09/louisiana_prison_costs.html; Julia O'Donoghue, "Louisiana Renews Private Prison Contracts, as Federal Government Cuts Them," *Times-Picayune*, August 26, 2016, http://www.nola.com/politics/index.ssf/2016/08/louisiana_private_prisons.html.

000 CCA hired Hillenby, a PR firm: CCA's connection to Hillenby came to light through an email sent by CoreCivic spokesperson Jonathan Burns to Hillenby CEO Katie Lilley. (CoreCivic is CCA's new name.) Burns copied Texas Public Radio reporter Aaron Schrank on the email, presumably unintentionally. Schrank forwarded the email to me. The email suggests that Hillenby has been assisting CoreCivic in developing its public response to my reporting.

000 the company sent around a memo: CCA, "Get the Facts on *Mother Jones*," https://ccamericastorage.blob.core.windows.net/media/Default/documents/Misc/Mother-Jones/Mother%20Jones%20One%20Pager.pdf.

000 A week later the DOJ inspector: US Department of Justice, Office of the Inspector General, *Review of the Federal Bureau of Prisons' Monitoring of Contract Prisons*, August 2016, https://oig.justice.gov/reports/2016/e1606.pdf; Deputy Attorney General Sally Q. Yates, memorandum to the acting director of the Federal Bureau of Prisons, August 18, 2016, "Reducing Our Use of Private Prisons," www.justice.gov/archives/opa/file/886311/download.

000 A week after that, the federal government: Deputy Attorney General Sally Q. Yates, memorandum to the acting director of the Federal Bureau of Prisons, "Phasing Out Our Use of Private Prisons," August 18, 2016, www.justice.gov/archives/opa/blog/phasing-out-our-use-private-prisons.

000 Weeks later CCA announced: Jamie McGee, "CCA to Cut Staff Amid Restructuring," *Tennessean*, September 27, 2016, www.tennessean.com/story/money/2016/09/27/cca-stock-dives-after-clintons-prison-comments-debate/91162542/.

000 During the last decade, the portion: Lauren-Brooke Eisen, *Inside Private Prisons: An American Dilemma in the Age of Mass Incarceration* (New York: Columbia University Press, 2018), 139; Homeland Security Advisory Council, *Report of the Subcommittee on Privatized Immigration Detention Facilities*, December 1, 2016, www.dhs.gov/sites/default/files/publications/DHS%20HSAC%20PIDF%20Final%20Report.pdf.

000 Nine of the ten largest: Eisen, *Inside Private Prisons*, 143.

000 ICE contracts make up 28 percent: CoreCivic Inc., SEC Filing *Form 10-K Annual Report* (FY 2016).

000 In 2014 the federal government granted: Chico Harlan, "Inside the Administration's $1 Billion Deal to Detain Central American Asylum Seekers,"

Washington Post, August 14, 2016, www.washingtonpost.com/business
/economy/inside-the-administrations-1-billion-deal-to-detain-central
-american-asylum-seekers/2016/08/14/e47f1960-5819-11e6-9aee
-8075993d73a2_story.html?utm_term=.36ddf0266c61; Eisen, Inside Private *Prisons*, 137–43.

000 **ICE placed more than 350,000:** US Department of Homeland Security,
Office of Immigration Statistics, *Annual Flow Report: DHS Immigration
Enforcement: 2016*, December 2016, www.dhs.gov/sites/default/files/publi
cations/DHS%20Immigration%20Enforcement%202016.pdf.

000 **a DOJ audit:** US Department of Justice, Office of the Inspector General,
*Audit of the United States Marshals Service Contract No. DJJODT7C0002
with CoreCivic Inc. to Operate the Leavenworth Detention Center Levenworth
Kansas*, April 2017, https://oig.justice.gov/reports/2017/a1722.pdf#page=1.

000 **Bridgestone's use of child labor:** Jonathan Stempel, "Firestone Wins Liberian Child Labor Case in US," *Reuters*, July 13, 2011, www.reuters.com
/article/ozatp-firestone-childlabor-20110713-idAFJOE76C02L20110713;
James Warren, "Well-Known Judge Stuns in Ruling on Child Labor," *New
York Times*, July 14, 2011, www.nytimes.com/2011/07/15/us/15cncwarren
.html.

SELECT BIBLIOGRAPHY

Alexander, Michelle. *The New Jim Crow: Mass Incarceration in the Age of Color-blindness.* New York: The New Press, 2010.

Applebaum, Anne. *Gulag: A History.* New York: Doubleday, 2003.

Armes, Ethel. *The Story of Coal and Iron in Alabama.* New York: Arno Press, 1973.

Austin, James, and Gary Coventry. *Emerging Issues on Privatized Prisons.* US Department of Justice, Bureau of Justice Assistance. February 2001. www.ncjrs.gov/pdffiles1/bja/181249.pdf.

Ayers, Edward L. *Vengeance and Justice: Crime and Punishment in the Nineteenth-Century American South.* New York: Oxford University Press, 1984.

Baptist, Edward E. *The Half Has Never Been Told: Slavery and the Making of American Capitalism.* New York: Basic Books, 2014.

Barnes, Harry Elmer. "Historical Origin of the Prison System in America." *Journal of Criminal Law and Criminology* 12, no. 1 (May 1921 to February 1922): 35–60. http://lawsdocbox.com/Politics/68475122-Historial-origin-of-the-prison-system-in-america.html.

Bauer, Shane, Joshua Fattal, and Sarah Shourd. *A Sliver of Light: Three Americans Imprisoned in Iran.* New York: Houghton Mifflin Harcourt, 2014.

Beck, Allen J., and Candace Johnson. *Sexual Victimization Reported by Former State Prisoners, 2008.* US Department of Justice, Bureau of Justice Statistics, May 2012. www.bjs.gov/content/pub/pdf/svrfsp08.pdf.

Beck, Allen J., and Ramona R. Rantala. *Sexual Victimization Reported by Adult Correctional Authorities, 2009–11.* US Department of Justice, Bureau of Justice Statistics, January 2014. www.bjs.gov/content/pub/pdf/svraca0911.pdf.

Blackmon, Douglas A. *Slavery by Another Name: The Re-Enslavement of Black Americans from the Civil War to World War II.* New York: Doubleday Books, 2008.

Blumenthal, Sidney. *A Self-Made Man: The Political Life of Abraham Lincoln, Vol. I, 1809–1849.* New York: Simon & Schuster, 2017.

Bly, Nellie. *Ten Days in a Mad-House.* Rockville, MD: Wildside Press, 2012.

Butler, Benjamin F., and Jessie Marshall. *Private and Official Correspondence of Gen. Benjamin F. Butler during the Period of the Civil War, Volume II.* Norwood, MA: Plimpton Press, 1917.

Brown, Harry Bates, *Cotton: History, Species, Varieties, Morphology, Breeding, Culture, Diseases, Marketing, and Uses.* New York: McGraw-Hill, 1927.

Cable, George Washington. *The Silent South.* Montclair, NJ: Patterson Smith, 1969.

Carleton, Mark T. *Politics and Punishment: A History of the Louisiana State Penal System.* Baton Rouge: Louisiana State University Press, 1971.

Carper, N. Gordon. "Martin Tabert, Martyr of an Era." *The Florida Historical Quarterly* 52, no. 2 (October 1973): 115–31.

Carter, Susan B., Scott Sigmund Gartner, Michael R. Haines, Alan L. Olmstead, Richard Sutch, and Gavin Wright, eds. *Historical Statistics of the United States: Earliest Times to the Present.* New York: Cambridge University Press, 2006.

Christianson, Scott. *With Liberty for Some: 500 Years of Imprisonment in America.* Boston: Northeastern University Press, 1998.

Cohen, Lucy M. *Chinese in the Post-Civil War South: A People without a History.* Baton Rouge: Louisiana State University Press, 1984.

Conover, Ted. *Newjack: Guarding Sing Sing.* New York: Vintage Books, 2001.

Crouch, Ben M., and James W. Marquart. *An Appeal to Justice: Litigated Reform of Texas Prisons.* Austin: University of Texas Press, 1989.

Daniel, Pete. "The Tennessee Convict War." *Tennessee Historical Quarterly* 34, no. 3 (Fall 1975): 273–92. www.jstor.org/stable/i40097530.

De Beaumont, Gustave, and Alexis de Tocqueville. *On the Penitentiary System in the United States and Its Application in France*. Trans. Francis Lieber. Philadelphia: Carey, Lea & Blanchard, 1833.

Denhof, Michael D., and Catarina G. Spinaris. *Depression, PTSD, and Comorbidity in United States Corrections Professionals: Prevalence and Impact on Health and Functioning*. Florence, CO: Desert Waters Correctional Outreach, 2013. http://desertwaters.com/wp-content/uploads/2013/09/Comorbidity_Study _09-03-131.pdf.

DePuy, LeRoy B. "The Walnut Street Prison: Pennsylvania's First Penitentiary." *Pennsylvania History: A Journal of Mid-Atlantic Studies* 18, no. 2 (April 1951): 130–44. www.jstor.org/stable/27769197.

Derbes, Brett J. "Prison Productions: Textiles and Other Military Supplies from State Penitentiaries in the Trans-Mississippi Theater during the American Civil War." Master's thesis, University of North Texas, 2011. digital.library .unt.edu/ark:/67531/metadc84198.

Derbes, Brett J. "Secret Horrors: Enslaved Women and Children in the Louisiana State Penitentiary, 1833–1862." *The Journal of African American History* 98, no. 2 (Spring 2013): 277–90. doi:10.5323/jafriamerhist.98.2.0277.

Ehrenreich, Barbara. *Nickel and Dimed: On (Not) Getting By in America*. New York: Picador, 2011.

Eisen, Lauren-Brooke. *Inside Private Prisons: An American Dilemma in the Age of Mass Incarceration*. New York: Columbia University Press, 2018.

Ekirch, A. Roger. *Bound for America*. Oxford: Clarendon Press, 1987.

Fogel, Robert W. *Without Consent or Contract: The Rise and Fall of American Slavery*. New York: W. W. Norton, 1989.

Fogel, Robert W., and Stanley L. Engerman. "Explaining the Relative Efficiency of Slave Agriculture in the Antebellum South." In *Without Consent or Contract: The Rise and Fall of American Slavery, Markets and Production: Technical Papers, Volume I*, edited by Robert W. Fogel and Stanley L. Engerman. New York: W. W. Norton, 1992, 241–65.

Foreman, James Jr. *Locking Up Our Own: Crime and Punishment in Black America*. New York: Farrar, Straus and Giroux, 2017.

Foreman, Paul B., and Julien R. Tatum. "A Short History of Mississippi's State Penal Systems." *Mississippi Law Journal*, 10 (April 1938): 255–77.

Friedmann, Alex. "Apples to Fish: Public and Private Prison Cost Comparisons." *Fordham Urban Law Journal* XLII, no.2 (December 2014): 504–68.

Goree, Thomas J. "Some Features of Prison Control in the South." In *Proceedings of the Annual Congress of the National Prison Association of the United States, Held at Austin, Texas, December 2–6, 1897.* Pittsburg: Shaw Brothers, 1898, 131–37. https://archive.org/stream/proceedingsofa1897ameruoft#page /n7/mode/2up.

Gottschalk, Marie. *Caught: The Prison State and the Lockdown of American Politics.* Princeton, NJ: Princeton University Press, 2016.

Gottschalk, Marie. *The Prison and the Gallows: The Politics of Mass Incarceration in America.* Cambridge, UK: Cambridge University Press, 2006.

Green, Fletcher Melvin. "Some Aspects of the Convict Lease System in the Southern States." In *Essays in Southern History*, edited by Fletcher Melvin Green. Westport, CT: Greenwood Press, 1976.

Griffin, John Howard. *Black Like Me.* New York: New American Library, 2003.

Harris, Carl Vernon. *Political Power in Birmingham: 1871–1921.* Knoxville: University of Tennessee Press, 1977.

Hart, Hastings H. "Prison Conditions in the South." In *Proceedings of the National Prison Association.* 1919.

Hayes, Chris. *A Colony in a Nation.* New York: W. W. Norton, 2017.

Hermann, Christina Pruett. "Specters of Freedom: Forced Labor, Social Struggle, and the Louisiana State Penitentiary System, 1835–1935." PhD diss., Michigan State University, 2015.

Hines, David Theo. *The Life and Adventures of Dr. David T. Hines: A Narrative of Thrilling Interest and Most Stirring Scenes of His Eventful Life.* Charleston, SC: J. B. Nixon, 1852.

Holmes, William F. *The White Chief.* Baton Rouge: Louisiana State University Press, 1970.

In the Public Interest. *Criminal: How Lockup Quotas and "Low-Crime Taxes" Guarantee Profits for Private Prison Corporations.* September 19, 2013. www .inthepublicinterest.org/criminal-how-lockup-quotas-and-low-crime-taxes -guarantee-profits-for-private-prison-corporations.

Ireland, Robert E. "Prison Reform, Road Building, and Southern Progressivism: Joseph Hyde Pratt and the Campaign for 'Good Roads and Good Men'," *The North Carolina Historical Review* 68, no. 2 (April 1991): 125–57. www.jstor.org/stable/23521190.

Isenberg, Nancy. *White Trash: The 400-Year Untold History of Class in America.* New York: Viking, 2016.

Jach, Theresa R. "Reform versus Reality in the Texas Era Prisons." *The Journal of the Gilded Age and Progressive Era* 4, no. 1 (January 2005): 53–67.

Jackson, Bruce. *Inside the Wire: Photographs from Texas and Arkansas Prisons.* Austin: University of Texas Press, 2013.

Jackson, Bruce. *Wake Up Dead Man.* Cambridge: Harvard University Press, 1972.

Kirwan, Albert. *Revolt of the Rednecks.* Lexington: University of Kentucky Press, 1951.

Kroeger, Brooke. *Undercover Reporting: The Truth about Deception.* Evanston, IL: Northwestern University Press, 2012.

Ledbetter Jr., Calvin R. "The Long Struggle to End Convict Leasing in Arkansas." *The Arkansas Historical Quarterly* 52, no. 1 (Spring 1993): 1–27.

Lee, W. D. "The Lease System of Alabama." In *Proceedings of the Annual Congress of the National Prison Association of the United States Held at Cincinnati, September 25–30, 1890.* Pittsburgh: Shaw Brothers,1891, 104–23. https://archive.org/stream/proceedingsofa1890ameruoft#page/104/mode/2up/search/Lee.

Lewis, Ronald. *Black Coal Miners in America.* Lexington: The University Press of Kentucky, 1987.

Lichtenstein, Alex. "Good Roads and Chain Gangs in the Progressive South: The Negro Convict Is a Slave." *The Journal of Southern History* 59, no. 1 (February 1993): 85–110. www.jstor.org/stable/2210349.

Litwack, Leon F. *Been in the Storm So Long: The Aftermath of Slavery.* New York: Knopf, 1981.

Logan, Frenise A. *The Negro in North Carolina 1876–1894.* Chapel Hill: University of North Carolina Press, 1964.

Lundahl, Brad W., Chelsea Kunz, Cyndi Brownell, Norma Harris, and Russ Van Vleet. "Prison Privatization: A Meta-analysis of Cost and Quality of

Confinement Indicators." *Research on Social Work Practice* 19, no. 4 (April 8, 2009): 383–94. doi.org/10.1177/1049731509331946.

Mancini, Matthew J. *One Dies, Get Another*. Columbia: University of South Carolina Press, 1996.

McLennan, Rebecca M. *The Crisis of Imprisonment: Protest, Politics, and the Making of the American Penal State, 1776–1941*. Cambridge, UK: Cambridge University Press, 2008.

Melossi, Dario, and Massimo Pavarini. *The Prison and the Factory: Origins of the Penitentiary System*. Totowa, NJ: Barnes & Noble Books, 1981.

Murakawa, Naomi. *The First Civil Right: How Liberals Built Prison America*. Oxford, UK: Oxford University Press, 2014.

Moen, Jon R. "Changes in the Productivity of Southern Agriculture between 1860 and 1880." In *Without Consent or Contract: The Rise and Fall of American Slavery, Markets and Production: Technical Papers, Volume I*, edited by Robert W. Fogel and Stanley L. Engerman. New York: W.W. Norton, 1992.

Murton, Tom, and Joe Hyams. *Accomplices to the Crime: The Arkansas Prison Scandal*. London: Michael Joseph, 1969.

Myers, Martha. "Inequality and the Punishment of Minor Offenders in the Early 20th Century." *Law & Society Review* 27, no. 2 (1993): 313–44.

Novak, Daniel. *The Wheel of Servitude: Black Forced Labor After Slavery*. Lexington: University Press of Kentucky, 1978.

Oshinsky, David M. *Worse than Slavery: Parchman Farm and the Ordeal of Jim Crow Justice*. New York: Free Press Paperbacks, 1996.

Perkinson, Robert. *Texas Tough: The Rise of America's Prison Empire*. New York: Picador, 2010.

Pfaff, John F. *Locked in: The True Causes of Mass Incarceration and How to Achieve Real Reform*. New York: Basic Books, 2017.

Powell, J. C. *American Siberia*. Chicago: H. J. Smith & Co, 1891.

Roberts, Alasdair. *America's First Great Depression: Economic Crisis and Political Disorder after the Panic of 1837*. Ithaca, NY: Cornell University Press, 2012.

Sample, Albert Race. *Racehoss: Big Emma's Boy*. Fort Worth, TX: Eakin Press, 1984.

Sellin, Thorsten. *Slavery and the Penal System*. New York: Elsevier Scientific, 1976.

Selman, Donna, and Paul Leighton. *Punishment for Sale: Private Prisons, Big Business, and the Incarceration Binge*. New York: Rowman & Littlefield, 2010.

Schlosser, Eric. "The Prison-Industrial Complex" *The Atlantic*, December 1998. www.theatlantic.com/magazine/archive/1998/12/the-prison-industrial -complex/304669/.

Shapiro, Karin A. *A New South Rebellion: The Battle against Convict Labor in the Tennessee Coalfields, 1871–1896.* Chapel Hill: University of North Carolina Press, 1998.

Shilstone, Cecile James. *My Plantation Days: The Memoirs of Cecile James Shilstone 1887–1979.* Memoir in possession of author.

Shirley, Neal, and Saralee Stafford, *Dixie Be Damned: 300 Years of Insurrection in the American South.* Oakland, CA: AK Press, 2015.

Shofner, Jerrell H. "Postscript to the Martin Tabert Case: Peonage as Usual in the Florida Turpentine Camps." *The Florida Historical Quarterly* 60, no. 2 (October 1981): 161–73. www.jstor.org/stable/30146766.

Sims, P. D. "The Lease System in Tennessee and Other Southern States." In *Proceedings of the Annual Congress of the National Prison Association of the United States.* Chicago: Knight, Leonard & Co Printers, 1893. https://archive.org /details/proceedingsofa1893ameruoft.

Sinclair, Harold. *The Port of New Orleans.* The Seaport Series. Garden City, NY: Doubleday, Doran & Company, 1942.

Starr, Douglas. *Blood: An Epic History of Medicine and Commerce.* New York: Perennial, 2002.

State of Louisiana. *Acts Passed at the First Session of the Seventeenth Legislature of the State of Louisiana.* New Orleans: Magne & Weisse, State Printers, 1845.

Tanielian, Terri, and Lisa H. Jaycox, eds. *Invisible Wounds of War: Psychological and Cognitive Injuries, Their Consequences, and Services to Assist Recovery.* Santa Monica: Rand Corporation, 2008. www.rand.org/pubs/monographs/MG720.html.

Tannenbaum, Frank. *Darker Phases of the South.* New York: G. P. Putnam's Sons, 1924.

Tarbell, Ida M. *The Life of Elbert H. Gary: The Story of Steel.* New York: D. Appleton & Company, 1925.

Teeters, Negley K. *The Cradle of the Penitentiary.* Philadelphia: Temple University Press, 1955.

Third Biennial Report of the Inspectors of Convicts, from October 1, 1888 to September 30, 1890. Montgomery: Brown Printing, 1890.

Twain, Mark. *Life on the Mississippi.* Leipzig, Germany: Tauchnitz, 1883.

US Department of Justice, Office of the Inspector General. *Review of the Federal Bureau of Prisons' Monitoring of Contract Prisons.* August 2016. https://oig.justice.gov/reports/2016/e1606.pdf.

US Department of Labor, Bureau of Labor Statistics. *Convict Labor in 1923.* Bulletin No. 372, January 1925.

US General Services Administration. *Hard Labor: History and Archaeology at the Old Louisiana State Penitentiary, Baton Rouge, Louisiana.* Fort Worth, TX: The Administration, 1991.

Walker, Donald R. *Penology for Profit: A History of the Texas Prison System, 1867–1912.* College Station, TX: Texas A&M University Press, 1988.

Walmsley, Roy. *World Prison Population List.* University of Essex, International Centre for Prison Studies. 2013. www.apcca.org/uploads/10th_Edition_2013.pdf.

Walter, Wilson. "Chain Gangs and Profit." *Harper's,* April 1933.

Ward, Robert David, and William Warren Rogers. *Convicts, Coal, and the Banner Mine Tragedy.* Tuscaloosa: University of Alabama Press, 1987.

Wharton, Vernon Lane. *The Negro in Mississippi 1865–1890.* New York: Harper Torchbooks, 1947.

Wheatcroft, S. G. "More Light on the Scale of Repression and Excess Mortality in the Soviet Union in the 1930s." *Soviet Studies* 42, no. 2 (April 1990): 355–67. www.jstor.org/stable/152086.

Wilson, Theodore Brantner. *The Black Codes of the South.* Tuscaloosa: University of Alabama Press, 1965.

Winters, John D. *The Civil War in Louisiana.* Baton Rouge: Louisiana State University Press, 1963.

Woodward, C. Vann. *Origins of the New South, 1877–1913.* Baton Rouge: Louisiana State University Press, 1951.

Wright, Carroll Davidson. *Second Annual Report of the Commissioner of Labor, 1886, Convict Labor.* Washington, DC: Government Printing Office, 1887.

Zimbardo, Philip G. *The Lucifer Effect: Understanding How Good People Turn Evil.* New York: Random House Trade Paperbacks, 2008.

Zimmerman, Jane. "The Penal Reform Movement in the South during the Progressive Era, 1890–1917." *The Journal of Southern History* 17, no. 4 (November 1951): 462–92. www.jstor.org/stable/2954512.